75 Scrambles in
OREGON

best nontechnical ascents

75 Scrambles in
OREGON

best nontechnical ascents

BARBARA I. BOND

THE MOUNTAINEERS BOOKS

DEDICATION

For Taliah and Evan—the next generation of scramblers.

THE MOUNTAINEERS BOOKS
is the nonprofit publishing arm of The Mountaineers, an organization founded in 1906 and dedicated to the exploration, preservation, and enjoyment of outdoor and wilderness areas.

1001 SW Klickitat Way, Suite 201, Seattle, WA 98134

First edition, 2005

Distributed in the United Kingdom by Cordee, www.cordee.co.uk
Manufactured in the United States of America

Acquiring Editor: Christine U. Hosler
Project Editor: Mary Metz
Copy Editor: Julie Van Pelt
Cover and Book Design: The Mountaineers Books
Layout: Jennifer Shontz
Cartographer: Jennifer Shontz

Unless otherwise noted, all photographs are by the author.

Cover photograph: *Scramblers ascending Little Brother in the Three Sisters Wilderness. Mounts Washington, Three Fingered Jack, and Jefferson are in the background.*

Frontispiece: *Across the John Day River rises the basalt-capped Sheep Rock.*

Maps shown in this book were produced using National Geographic's *TOPO!* software. For more information, go to *www.nationalgeographic.com/topo*.

Library of Congress Cataloging-in-Publication Data

Bond, Barbara I., 1957-
     75 Scrambles in Oregon : best non-technical ascents / Barbara I. Bond.—
1st ed.
          p.   cm.
     Includes bibliographical references and index.
     ISBN 0-89886-550-6
     1. Alpine scrambling—Oregon—Guidebooks. 2. Oregon—Guidebooks. I.
Title: Seventy-five scrambles in Oregon. II. Title.
     GV199.42.O7B66 2004
     796.52'2'09795—dc22

                                                            2004030510

Contents

KEY TO MAP SYMBOLS

– – ~ – –	trail	❶ ❷	GPS waypoint
···········	user trail or cross-country	▲	campground or backcountry campsite
– – ~ – –	intersecting trail	帯	picnic area
– · – ~ – ·	wilderness boundary	○	town
≡(90)≡	interstate highway	■	building
–(2)–	U.S. route	•	point of interest
≡(530)≡	state route	🔭	lookout
≡(5302)≡	Forest Service road	▲	peak
≡≡≡≡	paved road	～～～	river or stream
====	unimproved road	▱	lake
_ _[561]_ _	trail, trail number		

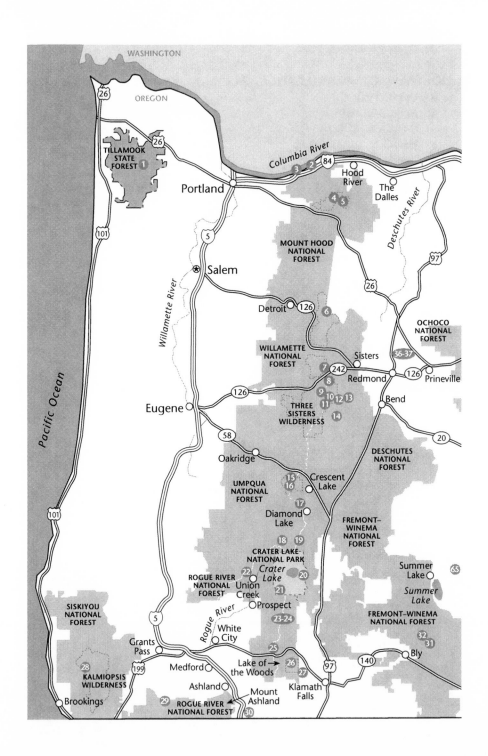

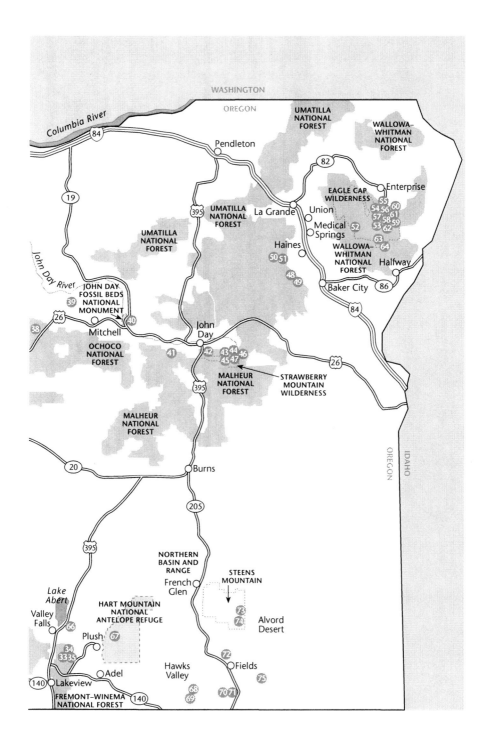

Scramble	Elevation (feet)	Strenuousness	Technical Difficulty	Best Season	Distance Round-trip (miles)	Highlights
1 Elk and Kings Mountain	2788, 3226	Difficult	Class 3	May to October	9.5	Temperate rain forest, views of the Wilson River and the coast
2 Munra Point	1740	Moderate	Class 3	April to November	4.4	Short but difficult ascent to rocky outcrops, wildflowers, and views
3 Rock of Ages	3010	Moderate	Class 2+	April to December	9.1	Steep backcountry ridge ascent with old-growth trees along the way
4 Mount Hood, Barrett Spur	7863	Moderate	Class 2+	July to October	8.8	Trail along Hood's north side, glacier views
5 Mount Hood, Cooper Spur	8875	Moderate	Class 2+	July to October	5.6	Trail along Hood's east side, views of the Hood River valley and Columbia River
6 Goat Peak	7159	Difficult	Class 3	July to October	16.2	Popular wilderness with high meadows, dense forest, alpine lakes, and mountain views
7 Belknap Crater	6872	Moderate	Class 2+	July to October	6	Short and strenuous, views of crater
8 Little Brother	7810	Moderate	Class 2+	July to October	11	Dense forest, Obsidian Cliffs, views of volcanoes and North Sister
9 Middle Sister	10,047	Difficult	Class 3	July to October	16.4	Dense forest to alpine zone, views of North Sister
10 South Sister	10,358	Moderate	Class 2+	July to October	12.4	Varied, scenic route with top-notch views
11 The Wife	7054	Moderate	Class 3	July to October	8.8	Views of The Husband and South Sister from the summit
12 Broken Top	9175	Moderate	Class 3	July to October	12	Climb up loose talus to view of insides of a volcano
13 Tam McArthur Rim and Broken Hand	8290	Moderate	Class 3	July to mid-October	9.6	Fault scarp climb, views of Three Creek Lake and Broken Top
14 Mount Bachelor	9065	Easy	Class 2+	June	4.4	Ski resort in winter, views of Three Sisters and Broken Top
15 Mount Yoran	7100	Moderate	Class 3+	June to November	8.0	Densely forested, alpine flowers in early season

Scramble	Elevation (feet)	Strenuousness	Technical Difficulty	Best Season	Distance Round-trip (miles)	Highlights
16 Diamond Peak	8744	Moderate	Class 2+	July to October	10	Pleasant trail with dramatic views
17 Cowhorn Mountain	7664	Moderate	Class 2+	July to October	9.2	Mixed conifer forest, whitebark pines
18 Mount Bailey	8368	Moderate	Class 2+	June to October	10	Mount Thielsen and Diamond Lake views, wildflowers
19 Mount Thielsen	9182	Moderate	Class 3+, some Class 4	July to October	8.8	Climb on steep talus to small, dramatic summit
20 Mount Scott	8929	Easy	Class 2	July to October	5	Trail hike along eastern side of Crater Lake
21 Union Peak	7698	Moderate	Class 3	July to mid-October	9	Approach along the Pacific Crest Trail to eroded summit
22 Abbott Butte and Elephant Head	6131, 5871	Moderate	Class 2+	July to October	9.4	Little-known area with spring wildflowers, hemlock, and fir trees
23 Venus, Jupiter, and Lucifer	7315, 7415, 7474	Moderate	Class 2+	July to October	9.8	Three-peak traverse in unique wilderness
24 Devils Peak	7582	Moderate	Class 2+	July to October	11.7	Views of lake basin from eroded volcanic remnant
25 Mount McLoughlin	9495	Moderate	Class 2+	June to October	11	Young volcano with views of its northern and eastern exposures
26 Whiteface Peak	7652, 7684, 7703	Moderate	Class 2+	July to October	13.4	Moderate peaks offering lesser-known views
27 Aspen Butte	8208	Moderate	Class 2+	July to October	13	Scenic approach hike leading through a mixed-conifer forest and wildflowers
28 Mislatnah Peak	3124, 3720, 4150	Difficult	Class 2+	April to November	13.8	Hike among tan oak and madrone to view the *Kalmiopsis leachiana*, an ancient flower
29 Grayback Mountain	7055	Easy	Class 2+	June to October	4.5	Rich forest with old-growth trees; wildflowers in early summer
30 Pilot Rock	5908	Easy	Class 3+	June to November	2	Steep climb up a Native American landmark

Scramble	Elevation (feet)	Strenuousness	Technical Difficulty	Best Season	Distance Round-trip (miles)	Highlights
31 The Dome	7380	Moderate	Class 3	Late June to November	7	Wildflowers, ponderosa pines, unique rock formations
32 Gearhart Mountain	8370	Moderate	Class 2+	Late July to November	11.8	Less frequented area with old-growth pines; abundant wildlife habitat
33 Twelvemile Peak	8144	Easy	Class 2+	May to October	3.6	Pine and fir forests, high desert country with sensitive plant species
34 Crook Peak	7834	Moderate	Class 2+	May to October	8.2	Huge ponderosa pines, abundant wildflowers in spring
35 Drake Peak	8407	Moderate	Class 2+	May to October	7	Pine and fir forest leading to ridge past the highest lookout in Oregon
36 The Monument	3241	Moderate	Class 3+	August to November	2–3	Views of vivid rock formations and the Crooked River
37 Marsupial Crags	4230	Moderate	Class 3+	April to November	4.6	Quiet climb amid once-prominent Smith Rock climbing area
38 Twin Pillars	5500	Moderate	Class 3	April to November	10.8	Popular landmark climb among 200-foot-high volcanic remnants
39 Sutton Mountain	4694	Moderate	Class 2	May and June	4.8	Dramatic climb, views of basalt columns, wildflowers
40 Windy Point	4578	Moderate	Class 2+	April to November	11.3	Stunning views of John Day Fossil Beds, variety of unusual flowers
41 Fields Peak and Moon Mountain	7362, 7043	Moderate	Class 2+	June to November	10	Varied peaks surrounded by mixed conifers
42 Canyon Mountain	7999	Very difficult	Class 2+	July to November	17.6	Lovely, rugged hike featuring creek crossings, wildflowers, and rare views
43 Strawberry Mountain	9038	Moderate	Class 2+	July to November	10.2	Raw and colorful geographic features, home to abundant wildlife
44 Slide Mountain	8544	Moderate	Class 2+	July to November	10.4	Volcanic traces, glacial cirques, dense forests
45 Indian Spring Butte	8529	Easy	Class 2+	July to November	4.5	Short scramble amongst high volcanic remnants

Scramble	Elevation (feet)	Strenuousness	Technical Difficulty	Best Season	Distance Round-trip (miles)	Highlights
46 Graham Mountain	8570	Moderate	Class 2+	July to October	9.3	Hike through beautiful basin leading to scenic views
47 Peak 8511	8511	Moderate	Class 2+	July to October	8.8	Waterfalls, woodpeckers, elk, grouse, wildflowers
48 Rock Creek Butte	9106	Moderate	Class 2+	July to November	9.7	Rocky climb up highest peak in the Elkhorn Mountains
49 Elkhorn Peak	8931	Moderate	Class 2+	July to October	9	Remote mountains; rich wildlife population includes mountain goats and elk
50 Gunsight Mountain	8342	Moderate	Class 3	July to October	3	Short, steep scramble to twin summit
51 Van Patten Butte	8729	Moderate	Class 2+	July to October	5.4	Craggy butte near lake
52 China Cap	8656	Moderate	Class 3	July to November	9.3	Dense conifer forest, elk, deer
53 Eagle Cap	9595	Difficult	Class 3	July to November	17	Namesake mountain of Eagle Cap Wilderness
54 Sacajawea Peak	9838	Difficult	Class 3	July to November	13	Distinctive peak with dramatic views and a rich habitat
55 Chief Joseph Mountain	9616	Difficult	Class 3	July to October	13.4	Miles of isolated ridges and glacial valleys
56 Hurwal Divide	9776	Difficult	Class 2+	July to October	10.8	Unbeatable views of Chief Joseph; bird habitat
57 Matterhorn	9832	Difficult	Class 2+	July to November	16.8	Beautiful climb up this limestone and marble mountain, dramatic geographic features
58 Petes Point	9675	Difficult	Class 3	July to November	17	Secluded hike among wildflowers, mountain bluebirds, whitebark pines, stunning views
59 Aneroid Mountain	9702	Difficult	Class 3	July to November	17	Varied views, wildflowers, solitude
60 East Peak	9447	Easy	Class 2+	July to October	4.3	Long ridge leading to views

Scramble	Elevation (feet)	Strenuousness	Technical Difficulty	Best Season	Distance Round-trip (miles)	Highlights
61 Peak 9495	9495	Moderate	Class 2+	July to October	6.1	Scramble from Mount Howard
62 Sentinel Peak	9401	Very difficult	Class 3	July to November	20.4	Quiet trail, wonderful views
63 Krag Peak	9048	Difficult	Class 3	July to November	14.4	Steep, precarious climb up talus and boulders leading to majestic views
64 Cornucopia Peak	8643	Moderate	Class 2+	July to October	9.6	Gray granite slopes among open wilderness
65 Diablo Peak	6147	Moderate	Class 2+	May to November	9.8	Varied scramble covering sand dunes and volcanic ridges
66 Abert Rim	6370	Moderate	Class 3	May to November	8.8	Unique rimrock scramble amongst wildflowers, sagebrush, and juniper
67 Warner Peak	8017	Moderate	Class 2+	June to October	10	Less-visited area with occasional eagles, sheep, and mule deer
68 Hawks Mountain	7234	Easy	Class 2	May to October	4	Quiet hike in isolated grasslands
69 Lone Mountain	6675, 6903	Moderate	Class 2+	May to October	4.8	Quiet area with unusual rock formations, springs, grasses, and flowers
70 West Pueblo Ridge	8420	Moderate	Class 3	June to November	10.1	Remote area with great views
71 Pueblo Mountain	8632	Moderate	Class 2+	June to November	8.6	Uninterrupted, undeveloped area with mountain mahogany and quaking aspen
72 Alvord Peak	7132	Easy	Class 2+	June to November	4.8	Remote, barren scramble with horned lizards
73 Steens Mountain	9733	Very difficult	Class 3	July to November	24	Classic, challenging climb offering unique views
74 Peak 7698	7698	Moderate	Class 2+	July to November	6.6	Sage, juniper, aspen, unique views of Steens Mountain and Alvord Desert
75 Flagstaff Butte	6029	Easy	Class 3	May to November	2.5	Unique views of river, sagebrush, and grasslands

Acknowledgments

Completion of this book would not have been possible without the contributions of many people. Thank you.

Kate Evans and Judy Jewell generously invited me to join this project. Mazamas supported me by providing me underwriting, use of quiet office space, use of their extensive outdoor library and map collection, and access to their members and staff who generously shared their knowledge of Oregon mountains.

Fred Barstad and Andy Kerr were kind enough to spend time with me and share their understanding of the Wallowas and Northern Basin and Range. Their helpful suggestions gave me greater insight into those wonderful areas.

The many dedicated and enthusiastic employees and volunteers of the various management agencies kindly reviewed my draft chapters, corrected my errors, and made thoughtful suggestions. I was impressed with their knowledge and interest.

Art Walker, D.C., kept me upright—thanks, Art. Tom, Brad, and the staff at Halsey kept my VW in tiptop shape, allowing me to travel more than 16,000 miles without a hitch.

To the editors and staff at The Mountaineers Books, thank you. I appreciate your patience, enthusiasm, and support during this process.

Cathy Martin, Pete Sandrock, and Leslie Moten patiently read and re-read the text. Thank you for your time, suggestions, and good sense of humor!

Several adventurous folks patiently accompanied me on more than a couple of scrambles. They put up with bad weather, routefinding challenges, and ever-changing plans. To my super scrambler, Pete Sandrock—a heartfelt thank you! From the Wallowa Mountains to the remote Kalmiopsis Wilderness, Pete was a great partner on and off trail.

Stacy Allison, David Burdick, Steve Burton, Dieter Cohrs, Chris Kabel, John Godino, Derick Moten, Jr., Gerry Itkin, Ken Osher, Jeff Litwak, Ian Malkasian, John McGilvra , and Nancy Miller kept me company on scrambles around the state.

Dieter Cohrs did a tremendous job with the maps—thanks.

Many years ago Ron Crutchfield took me on my first backpacking trip to Yosemite. Thanks, Ron, for showing me the beauty of the backcountry.

Finally, I thank my family. My partner, Cathy Martin, was an enthusiastic supporter of this project from start to finish. My children, Taliah and Evan, endured my long absences and endless discussions of various peaks—and still came out to do a scramble of their own.

A wonderful old whitebark pine on Cowhorn Peak

Preface

Oregon has so many options for outdoor recreation that we are in danger of becoming a cliché. There is a guidebook for every pursuit imaginable and Oregonians love getting outside.

Mountaineers and hikers flock to the Cascades and to the rich national forests throughout the state. The Columbia River Gorge, famous for its high winds, attracts windsurfers and kiteboarders. White-water kayakers run the wild and scenic rivers of central and southern Oregon. Rock climbers, bicyclists, and skiers populate central Oregon's high desert outdoor playground.

When I was approached to write this book, I wondered if we really needed another guidebook. But, as I learned more about the concept and began the research, I realized it was perfect: a guidebook for nontechnical climbing (called "scrambling") covering peaks in every ecoregion of the state. It sounded like a working vacation.

As I embarked on the scrambles, I discovered that getting to the trailhead in remote mountain ranges is not straightforward at all. Detours scraped into ridges; washboarded and rutted roads ended abruptly; and jeep roads were so out of grade my van threatened to flip every time I hit a rut. I never quite knew what I would find. I began carrying a tow rope, and fortunately I only needed it once!

Even my months of preparation had not prepared me for the stunning natural beauty I would encounter. At Steens Mountain a full moon illuminated the towering western juniper as coyotes howled a serenade. The darkness and quiet were almost palpable. In the Wallowa Mountains I was struck by the number of high peaks surrounded by deep glacial valleys and high, sharp ridges. The awe-inspiring scenery was matched by the wilderness solitude—I was almost always alone on Wallowa summits.

Yet not all scrambles are so remote. Scrambling in more accessible and popular locations has its rewards, too. It may be a nice change, after primitive camping or backpacking, to visit a campground with running water.

This book covers a range of scrambles that should appeal to many types of scramblers. Some scrambles are short, located in unique places that deserve your attention. These are a good introduction to scrambling for less-intrepid hikers or perhaps families hiking with older children.

Some scrambles are for the adventurous and hardy—mile after mile of harsh terrain, difficult climbing, and endless sky once you reach that summit. Those scrambles demand patience. Those scrambles reward you with a surprise view of a family of mountain goats nimbly crossing a nearly vertical cliff face, or a herd of pronghorn antelope racing away across the sage-covered plain.

I hope this book will inspire you to explore new places around Oregon—some wild and some not so wild. Use it, too, for visiting familiar places with a fresh perspective. We are stewards of a rich heritage of natural wonder. By visiting these places, we can enjoy them and work for their preservation for the future.

Crossing Hurricane Creek in late summer

Introduction

Scrambling is the bridge between trail hiking and rock climbing. It involves hiking and/or climbing over rough or rocky terrain, but does not require technical climbing gear. Scrambling is mostly off trail travel requiring agility and a good sense of balance. You will often have to use your hands as you ascend or descend on nearly vertical rock.

Some scrambling will require you to have a keen sense of adventure. There may be travel on narrow ridges or blocky cliff faces with considerable drop-offs (exposure) on one or more sides. Good physical fitness and backcountry skills are essential for scrambling. This includes navigation using a map and compass, altimeter, and Global Positioning System (GPS) receivers.

The Yosemite Decimal System has been used for many years to describe and rate mountaineering and rock climbing routes on a scale of 1 through 5. Class 1 is trail hiking or walking on a maintained path. Technical rock climbing begins at class 5.

Scrambling will usually consist of class 2, 3, and sometimes 4. Class 2 is off trail travel that may be uneven, rocky, and requires navigation and routefinding skills. Class 3 is over steeper terrain and requires the use of your hands for balance and safety. Class 4 has all of the previous characteristics and may have substantial enough exposure that some people will use a rope for additional safety. Most of the scrambles in this book are class 2 and 3.

OREGON SCRAMBLING

Oregon scrambling is for any outdoor person looking for challenges beyond the constraints of maintained trails. It is for peak baggers looking for mountain summits off the beaten path. It is for adventurers seeking to explore Oregon's wild places and experience its diverse landscapes, ecoregions, and remote communities.

Oregon is a big state and may be divided up into nine specific areas with similar environmental characteristics—ecoregions. The scrambles in this guidebook take place in six different ecoregions.

The Coast Range typically has low-elevation peaks and a wet, temperate climate heavily influenced by the Pacific Ocean. This range is home to some of the richest forests of Douglas fir in Oregon and historically has been heavily logged.

The Cascades are a dominating physical presence that influence much of the state's weather patterns and landscape. The west side tends to have weather subject to marine influences. The old Cascades, west of the high Cascades, represent volcanic remnants and highly eroded peaks. The high Cascades contain younger composite and shield volcanoes and are home to Oregon's highest peaks, including Mount Hood, Mount Jefferson, and the Three Sisters group.

An example of what sharp-eyed scramblers may find on Northern Basin and Range scrambles

The Eastern Cascades consist of lower-elevation peaks with dense forests. They form a transition zone as you head eastward. Drier than their westside counterparts, these peaks receive less snow and as a result have a very different look and feel. The forest composition in this ecoregion shifts to dry eastside species such as western larch, lodgepole pine, western juniper, and mountain mahogany.

Southern Oregon's Klamath Mountains contain the uniquely positioned Siskiyou Mountains. The Siskiyous are one of the most biologically diverse ecosystems in Oregon. The Siskiyous form a bridge between the wet Coast Range and the Cascades. Due to their location and elevation, the Siskiyous provide the habitat for an unusually high number of flowers, plants, trees, insects, and animals species. Made up of moderate-elevation peaks, the Siskiyous have only seven peaks above 7000 feet. This range also contains an assortment of unique geological features.

The Blue Mountains of eastern Oregon are a discontinuous jumble of broken-up mountain ranges. From the Ochocos near Prineville to the Elkhorns west of Baker City, these ranges represent folded, uplifted peaks further shaped by glacial ice.

At the east end of the Blue Mountains, and just before Hells Canyon, are the Wallowa Mountains. The Wallowas are distinct, more similar to the Rockies than any other mountains in Oregon. The Wallowas contain eighteen peaks over 9000 feet in elevation and many glacial valleys, lakes, tarns, and high ridges. Limber pine, normally a Rocky Mountain species, is found within Oregon only in the Wallowas.

The isolated Northern Basin and Range occupies Oregon's southeastern quadrant. This vast landmass has few residents yet contains some of Oregon's most distinctive and unusual mountains. Surrounded by high lava plains and sagebrush steppe, these mountains feel remote and offer adventurous scramblers a unique outdoor experience. Many of the Northern Basin and Range mountains are fault-block mountains, huge uplifts oriented along a north-south axis. Of these, Steens Mountain and Hart Mountain are the most well-known.

These wonderfully diverse mountains offer Oregon scramblers a variety of mountain character and unique natural beauty.

CONDITIONING FOR SCRAMBLING

Scrambling is a strenuous activity and often requires you to travel for miles over rough ground for 8 to 12 hours. You must be fit enough to be able to safely navigate the routes and still enjoy yourself!

Conditioning for scrambling is similar to that for other mountain activities. A high level of aerobic fitness will allow you to enjoy the longer scrambles. Running, trail running, and mountain or road biking regularly are all good choices for aerobic conditioning. Scrambling-specific strength training can also be helpful. Hike, run, or walk up stairs or hike over hilly terrain wearing a heavier-than-usual backpack.

Endurance training will also help to prepare you for scrambling. Endurance may be built over time by hiking, running, biking, or any other activity that allows you to be out for several hours at time, over a longer distance, and at a moderate pace. Finally, good balance and core strength will add to your comfort and safety on narrow ridges, ledges, and up blocky rocks. Working out with an exercise ball, wobble board, or at a local indoor rock-climbing gym will all improve your core strength and balance.

The best training for scrambling is to scramble. Being outdoors on a scramble route uses all your physical skills—strength, aerobic ability, endurance, and agility. Find some routes nearby that you can incorporate into your training routine.

In your area there are probably hiking routes that you can also incorporate into your training regimen. Using a regular, steep hiking route as a training tool can enhance your fitness and be a good gauge of your preparedness. Additionally, training outdoors on trails will help you develop a sense of pacing. Scrambling, since it takes all day, is not a sprint activity. Pace yourself so you can maintain a steady rate of travel—regardless of whether you are ascending, descending, or on level ground. Energy conservation will also be important at times during your scrambles. Using techniques such as the rest step, where you pause to shift your weight, can be the difference between a successful ascent and a struggle.

TRIP PLANNING

Skills needed for scrambling go beyond those necessary for hiking on maintained trails. Since most scrambling is done off trail, you will need a wide range of outdoor skills to reach your destination efficiently and safely.

Trip planning covers a broad range of tasks you will need to accomplish before you hit the road, including how to get to the trailhead, knowing where to camp, understanding access issues, and knowing where water sources are located.

Using a state atlas or state map is a good way to get an overview. Pick up a copy of the Oregon Department of Transportation's Official State Map, which shows major cities, towns, landmarks, rest stops, highways, roads, and other points of interest. It is free and widely available, and it is updated every couple of years.

Next, check with the land-management agency for the area you are planning to visit ahead of time. The Forest Service (FS), National Park Service, Bureau of Land Management (BLM), and Oregon State Parks all provide useful information, including that on permits, closures, restrictions, and regulations. See Appendix B for contact information. Self-issue permits are often available at trailheads for travel in the state's designated wilderness areas.

Forest Service and/or BLM maps are often essential for getting to the trailhead. To reach trailheads or parking spots you will have to travel over highways, primary roads, and perhaps a combination of dirt or gravel secondary roads. Some are not maintained. Many of these secondary roads are not clearly labeled. An atlas or state map combined with the FS and BLM maps will get you to the trailhead. These are invaluable when trying to navigate unfamiliar roads with little or no markings. DeLorme publishes the popular *Oregon Atlas and Gazetteer*, which provides detailed information tailored for outdoor recreation. Other state atlases are available from other publishers. You can never have too many road maps.

For the actual route planning you will need a topographic map. The United States Geological Survey (USGS) publishes the popular 7.5-minute series of maps, which cover the whole state of Oregon. The map scale is 1:24,000; and the contours and elevations are listed in feet. These topographic maps are accurate representations of the natural features you will encounter. They are your best choice for both planning and use in the field.

In recent years map software has become increasingly available. These programs, available from several sources, allow you more flexibility when planning. National Geographic Topo! State Series is an example of this innovation in mapping. The World Wide Web also has sites, such as Topozone, where you can obtain topographic map data.

The summary at the start of each scramble in this book lists the name of the map or maps you need; each scramble also provides you with a route map for general information. Never go into the field without the appropriate topographic map.

NAVIGATION AND ROUTEFINDING

Good navigation skills are essential for scrambling. Scramblers frequently travel off established trail systems or in areas with no trails at all. This type of backcountry travel will require the use of navigational tools: a topographic map, compass, altimeter, and/or GPS receiver.

Map and Compass

Most outdoor enthusiasts have used a map and compass. You may use a basic compass, or one with more advanced features. Useful features include adjustable declination, sighting mirror, and an inclinometer. You should understand how to use your compass to take a bearing, and to orient your map.

Altimeter

An altimeter, which measures your elevation using barometric pressure, is another important tool when traveling in the mountains. Calibrate your altimeter daily at a known elevation such as your campsite or the trailhead, and then use it to track your progress. Knowing your elevation will help you locate yourself on the map, or help solve route-finding puzzles. Your altimeter can also tell you when the weather is changing. By using a combination of map, compass, and altimeter you will be able to follow the route you intend and find your way if you become lost or disoriented. For further reading on map and compass skills see Appendix C.

GPS

GPS receivers are being used more and more in the outdoors. A GPS receiver may provide you with a variety of useful information applicable to off trail travel. The most basic receiver records coordinates that, when combined with a topographic map, allow you to find your location on the map. More sophisticated receivers may have a barometric altimeter, electronic compass, and the ability to load base maps into their substantial memory. A GPS receiver that is WAAS-enabled and has differential GPS will record more accurate coordinates for backcountry users.

Typical USGS benchmark found atop many mountain summits

To use your GPS receiver for scrambling, you should understand some basic concepts about its use. Make sure your GPS unit is set to the correct datum for the maps you are using; maps list the datum in the legend. The coordinates in this book all use the NAD27 datum. If your receiver has a compass it should be set to true north.

You may choose how to display the coordinates, which show your location as a waypoint. Most GPS receivers will at least offer you a choice of latitude/longitude or Universal Transverse Mercator (UTM). In this book, all the waypoints are in the UTM system.

UTM coordinates are easy to use with USGS topographic maps, the most common maps used in the backcountry. UTM coordinates for a location will provide you with the zone, easting, and northing. USGS maps have UTM coordinate tick marks along the margins; each tick represents 1000 meters. The zone is listed in the map legend. It is relatively easy to estimate your location on the map by taking a GPS reading and matching the coordinates to the map. For maps without UTM grid marks you may purchase a grid from a map or outdoor store that sells maps. For more information on how to use a GPS see Lawrence Letham's excellent book *GPS Made Easy*.

For backcountry navigation a GPS receiver is a good way to check the route, find your location in situations with limited visibility, or help get you reoriented if you are off route. GPS receivers have a "go to" feature. You can use this feature to retrace your steps to a known location where you recorded a waypoint, which may be useful when you suddenly realize you have wandered off the route.

There are circumstances in the mountains that inhibit the receiver's ability to lock onto enough satellites for an accurate waypoint. When traveling in heavily forested areas, canyons or gorges, or in changing weather with heavy cloud cover, you may not be able to acquire an accurate waypoint. Make sure you understand the specific limitations of your brand of receiver and have it set to the proper specifications before relying on it in the backcountry. Remember to always carry an extra set of batteries for your GPS receiver.

Routefinding

Routefinding is a skill you develop in the field. It is here that you put it all together—your navigation, observation, and planning skills combined with judgment. Routefinding is when you can take the route you planned with the map and transfer it to the actual physical challenge of following it under variable conditions. You must judge how quickly you can travel and be flexible enough to plan for alternate routes if you run into hazards or other difficulties.

Routefinding difficulties in the mountains may include finding your way along narrow, rocky ridges; navigating through thick brush; or staying on route in varying visibility. You can often travel by compass bearing to stay on route and use your topographic map to determine what features will be easiest and most direct to reach your destination.

The unique rocks of The Palisades are a scrambler's delight.

Combined with a topographic map, compass, and altimeter you may also use the GPS receiver effectively to reach or return to a specific location. But remember that the visual clues you get about the route from topography, and the ability to translate that information to your map, will always be your strongest navigational tool.

WHAT TO TAKE ALONG
Clothing
Proper clothing is important for any outdoor activity and for scrambling will offer you protection from the elements, comfort, and freedom of movement. Wear synthetic or wool clothing; do not wear cotton into the backcountry, as it loses its insulating ability when wet and is slow to dry.

Dressing in layers allows you to regulate your body temperature and be flexible under changing conditions. Long underwear made of polypropylene, wool, or other synthetic material can be a good first layer. Long-sleeved shirts and long pants will protect you from the sun, insects, and brush. An insulating layer of fleece will keep you warm even when damp or wet, and is light-weight. High-quality wool, or wool-blend, socks and thin synthetic sock liners will protect your feet from blisters.

Wind and/or rain protection is essential in the mountains. Waterproof, breathable pants and hooded jackets are available in lightweight, packable styles. A brim hat for sun protection and a warm hat and gloves for changing weather all will make your scrambles more fun and safe. Eye protection is also necessary in the mountains, particularly as you spend time above timberline in the glare of the sun. If you are doing a lot of travel on snow, your glasses should have side shields. Your glasses should offer 100 percent protection from ultraviolet light.

Sunscreen is a necessity for scrambling. Apply a high-quality sunscreen often, and don't forget your lips, nose, and under your chin. The alpine sun is unforgiving.

Equipment

Scrambling uses much of the same equipment as hiking or mountaineering. Carry a backpack large enough to hold your food, water, clothing, and maps. Remember to check your list of Ten Essentials (see Appendix A). In some cases you will want to carry an ice ax, crampons, or helmet. Sturdy hiking boots are best suited for the scree and talus slopes you will encounter. Gaiters will help keep the rocks out of your shoes. In the summer or in the desert, light-colored, short gaiters may work best. For snow travel choose full-length water-proof gaiters.

Some scrambles will be easier with trekking poles. These sectional poles, designed to aid hikers in traveling over rough terrain, also are useful for relieving joint strain when descending. Trekking poles can come in handy when fording creeks or streams, traversing across steep slopes, or when tired. You may also use them as a splint or to help stabilize an emergency shelter.

Nutrition

Scrambling is a high-energy activity. When planning a trip you must consider your nutritional needs. Know your body. Eat foods that are both nutritious and appealing to you when you are out in the field. Make sure you have

A typical gate on public lands, Steens Mountain, Wilderness Study Area (WSA)

enough calories for the day, and consume a good blend of protein, carbohy-drates, and fat.

Carbohydrates can give you the quick energy you need to sustain a short push through a difficult section of a scramble. Energy gels are easy to digest when you are working hard, and they give you quick results. Some scramblers carry dried fruit, trail mix, or candy bars. Whatever you choose, make sure it is something you will eat.

The type of proteins and fats you eat are a matter of taste. Nuts, jerky, and protein bars are all good sources of protein and fat, as are a variety of snack bars. Find a product that suits your taste and calorie needs.

Hydration

Alpine air is dry and just the act of breathing will quickly dehydrate you. Pay attention to staying well hydrated. Waiting until you are thirsty means you are already on your way to becoming dehydrated. A good rule of thumb is to occasionally check the color of your urine. Pale yellow color is a good indica-tion you are meeting your fluid needs. Being well hydrated can mean the difference between a successful summit and an epic nightmare.

Water is still the best choice under nearly all circumstances. Make drinking it easy to do while on the move. Carry water bottles in a convenient, easy-to-reach location; don't put them in your pack where you cannot reach them. Using a hydration reservoir in your pack facilitates frequent drinking. Drink 4 to 6 ounces at intervals, rather than taking tiny sips more frequently.

If possible, carry adequate water for your day. On multiday trips you must be able to treat the water you obtain from any natural source. Although the water may look clean and clear, you should always treat your water in the backcountry. Lightweight water filters are popular. You may also boil your water or treat it chemically.

It is possible to become overhydrated. Consuming too much water and not replacing your sodium, chloride, and potassium can upset the balance of electrolytes in your system. Severe hyponatremia (low salt content in the body) is dangerous and can cause dizziness and confusion. Snacks with salt and potassium are a good way to take care of your electrolyte needs. You may want to supplement your water with an electrolyte solution or other sports formula containing electrolytes and carbohydrates. Be sure to test these drinks on training trips before relying on them out in the mountains.

SCRAMBLING SAFETY
Altitude

The medical definition of high altitude is an elevation above 8000 feet. For the most part scrambling in Oregon will not put you at risk for altitude-related illnesses. However, since more than half of the Oregon scramble sum-mits are above 8000 feet, you should be aware of the symptoms of acute mountain sickness (AMS).

When scrambling at high altitude AMS may occur at any time regardless

On some remote peaks almost anything can house a summit register.

of fitness level, experience, or general health. Although being well hydrated seems to help, it is not truly prevention. AMS seems to strike everyone who plays in the mountains at one time or another.

The symptoms of AMS are nausea, vomiting, dizziness, fatigue, or loss of appetite. You may also have a headache when above 8000 feet. There is only one treatment—descending to an altitude where the symptoms dissipate. Until you prove differently, any sickness at high altitude is altitude related. Descending immediately is the only safe course of action.

Time and Planning

Scrambling in the backcountry requires more in-depth planning than trail hiking. Travel off trail over rough, overgrown, hilly terrain is slow. Always consider how long it may take your party to reach the destination; and also consider what time you will turn around in order to reach your starting point safely.

Be realistic when estimating time and speed. Extreme bushwhacking may slow your pace to 1 mile per hour, or less in some cases. Try to travel on ridges, near dense trees, or in creek drainages to minimize thrashing through heavy brush. Sometimes it is easier to go around obstacles than work your way over or through them.

A good rate of ascent is about 1000 feet per hour, but your party may not be able to sustain that pace. Downhill usually is faster; however, when descending an uneven, slippery talus slope your pace will likely be the same as your ascent. Be ready to be flexible and adjust your plans when necessary.

Even though you should always be prepared to be out longer than anticipated, some situations will not lend themselves to safe nighttime cross-country travel. In some such cases it may be safer to bivouac for the night.

Accidents

Accidents sometimes occur in the outdoors. Be sure a member of your party has had first aid and CPR training. Some organizations offer training specifically aimed at mountaineering or backpacking, and this type of activity-specific first aid will better prepare you for mountain hazards or accidents.

When faced with an accident, be prepared to calmly assess the situation and then decide on a plan of action. Remember the basics: check the airway, stop the bleeding, and check for circulation (heartbeat, pulse). If necessary, administer CPR.

If the accident is associated with a natural occurrence such as a rockslide, you may need to move the victim to a safe location. If a life-threatening or other serious accident occurs you may need either to call for help (when possible) or send a party member out for help. Keep the victim warm, dry, fed, and hydrated, unless the injuries contraindicate food and water.

Staying Found

If you get lost try not to panic. When you do a lot of backcountry travel you are likely to be lost or disoriented once in a while. This is when your topographic map, compass, altimeter, and/or GPS receiver come into play. As soon as you realize you are lost, and if you are in a safe location, stop. Look around and determine your location with your map, compass, and altimeter. Take a GPS reading, and if you get a good signal you may also use that information to find yourself on the map.

If you have limited visibility, wait until the weather clears, particularly if you are attempting ridge travel or other travel with cliffs or any exposure. Once you figure out where you are, use the map to pick a line to get you back on route. Resume travel, keeping track of your elevation and direction of travel, until you are back on route. Use your compass and altimeter frequently when traveling in dense forests, featureless plains, or other areas where it is easy to wander off route.

THE ENVIRONMENT
Weather

Mountain weather can be extremely variable and hazards exist, even in summer and particularly above timberline. Check with the National Weather Service or land managers for the area you plan to visit.

Mountains create their own microclimate. Even in the summer there may be sudden electric storms, rain, high winds, or hail. One way to monitor the weather is using your altimeter. When the barometric pressure begins to fall suddenly, causing an elevation increase on your altimeter, the weather is usually destabilizing. If the pressure drops precipitously, causing an elevation increase of more than 60 to 80 feet over 3 hours, it is time to descend and/or seek shelter.

Watch the sky when you are scrambling above timberline in changing conditions. Thunderclouds may be easy to track and avoid. A large, lens-shaped cloud (called a "lenticular") may build up over or around mountain peaks. The presence of lenticulars usually indicates a weather change within 24 to 48 hours.

Static electricity builds up in the dry mountain air when a storm is moving in. This is another good sign to retreat below timberline. When your hair starts standing on end, or if your metal equipment starts humming or sparking, get rid of metal objects and seek lower ground. If you have no shelter, use your sit pad or backpack as an insulating layer between you and the ground.

Oregon has several types of weather depending upon location. West of the Cascade Crest gets the most rain and snow. Most areas in the state are dry in July, August, and September. Eastside mountains have a more continental climate with very cold winters and extremely short summers. All mountains are prone to summer thunderstorms. Southern Oregon mountains will be warmer in the summer but still are prone to sudden storms in early season when the weather is still unsettled. Understanding a little bit about the weather patterns in the area you are visiting will make your scrambles more enjoyable.

Heat and Cold

Temperature variations are also part of the mountain environment. Hypothermia may be a factor when it is cold, or wet and windy. You will be most susceptible in such conditions, especially when dehydrated and hungry. By carrying extra clothing and using it, you can prevent hypothermia.

A hypothermic party member puts the entire group at risk. Make sure all members of your group are familiar with the symptoms of hypothermia. The inability to get warm, shivering, stumbling, change in mood, or slurred speech may indicate the condition's onset. To treat hypothermia, add clothing and/or shelter, eat, drink, and keep moving if possible.

Exposure to the sun on a long day above timberline is another part of the alpine environment. Heat-related illnesses such as heat cramps, heat exhaustion, and heat stroke may be avoided by taking some precautions. A hat with a brim, sunglasses, sunscreen, and adequate water consumption will all contribute to your well-being. If you are in the desert during the summer, use care when you travel during the heat of day.

Snow Travel

Many scrambles will require you to cross snowslopes or snowfields. When alpine scrambling, you may be on a snow-covered route the entire day. Travel on steep, hard snow may require the use of crampons and an ice ax. Crampons will provide the traction and stability you need on hard snow, and an ice ax may be used to stop a fall or as a walking stick.

In the spring, be aware of avalanche danger. Generally, slopes between 30 and 60 degrees may be avalanche prone, with the greatest number of slides occurring between 35 and 45 degrees. Be sure you understand the conditions for the route you are attempting and know how to use all your equipment properly.

On some peaks, snow cornices may form. Be aware of the hazards of traveling across snowslopes under varying conditions and plan your route accordingly.

Rock

Oregon mountains, with some exceptions, are known for having broken, loose rock. When traveling up talus slopes, be aware that even huge blocks may be unstable and could slide unexpectedly. On steep or vertical sections, maintain a safe distance between party members. Never scramble directly below another person, or party, on loose rock or steep, rocky slopes. They may dislodge rock that could cause significant injury to anyone below.

If you do knock some rock loose, call out "Rock!" loudly downslope as a warning. When you hear this call, do not turn toward the person shouting. Rather, get behind any available protection or cover your head, neck, and back with your arms or backpack and turn your back toward the falling object. Helmets are recommended on any scramble with significant rockfall.

Water Crossings

Stream or creek crossings may present a significant obstacle in spring and early summer. Snowmelt feeds mountain streams with cold, fast-moving water. In very early season it may be necessary to look for fallen logs or shallow areas to cross. Cross the water one person at a time, using trekking poles for stability. You may also carry plastic bags to put over your stocking feet to keep them dry. Well-fitted waterproof gaiters combined with waterproof boots will also keep your feet dry. Sandals are always an option in warmer weather.

The cold rushing waters of Oneonta Creek

Wildlife

Be aware of the wildlife in the area you are visiting. You are sharing the land they call home. Many of Oregon's national forests, wilderness areas, and other wild areas are home to black bear, deer, cougar, elk, bobcat, and a variety of smaller mammals. Eastern Oregon is home to snakes, including rattlesnakes. Most animals will stay away from noisy human interlopers, and animal attacks in Oregon are rare.

Cougars. In areas reporting cougar encounters, avoid solo travel. If you do meet up with a cougar, do not run away. Running only triggers the cougar's instinct to chase and hunt. Stay put; use your pack, trekking poles, or ice ax to make your physical profile larger. Avoid direct eye contact with a cougar. According to the Portland Audubon Society there has never been a cougar death in Oregon.

Snakes. You may encounter snakes in the mountains, particularly on the east side of the state. The only poisonous snake in Oregon is the rattlesnake. Rattlesnakes live in the dry, rocky areas of the John Day highlands and mountains of eastern Oregon. Do not put your hands or feet where you cannot see them when you are in rattlesnake country. If you come across a snake, it is most likely trying to get away from you. A rattlesnake will warn you with a loud, startling rattle. A rattler can strike from a distance about half its body length.

If a snake bites you—or a member of your party—stay calm. Get the victim away from the snake and make a plan. A small percentage of rattlesnake bites are not venomous. Some signs of a venomous bite are a severe burning at the bite location and swelling within 5 minutes, which continues. Suction is only useful if it is done quickly, within a few minutes of sustaining the bite. Do not attempt to extract venom with your mouth. Use a commercially available extractor and follow the instructions. Antivenin is the best treatment for rattlesnake bites that are venomous. If the victim is able to walk to the trailhead, do so slowly. Take the victim to the nearest medical facility for treatment.

Insects. Insects are a necessary part of the natural world. In alpine basins and glacial cirques, snowmelt creates many stagnant pools in which mosquitoes flourish. Judicious use of insect repellent may offer you some protection from this nuisance. Wasps or other stinging insects may also be present in summer and fall in some areas. Spring hiking in the forest will expose you to ticks. Long-sleeved shirts and long pants in light colors can make it easier for you to identify ticks.

If you have any sensitivity to stings or bites, carry the necessary treatment and tell members of your party where you keep your medication.

SCRAMBLING RESPONSIBLY

Scrambling, like mountaineering or rock climbing, will often take you into areas with no trails and a sensitive environment. Responsible backcountry travel requires you to take care when going off trail. Please obey signed restrictions that may include closures for nesting birds or habitat restoration from overuse or fire damage. Obtain necessary permits in advance. Always respect private property. As scramblers, you are caretakers of some of Oregon's most wild places. As such, you must be committed to taking care of them.

Camping. Use established camping spots in the backcountry. When there are none available, camp on a durable surface such as duff, sand, or bare dirt. Leave your site as natural as you found it.

Sanitation. Dispose of all your waste properly. "Pack it in and pack it out" is something all outdoor lovers have heard before and it is a good principle to follow strictly. Use good sanitation practices. Deposit solid human waste at least 200 feet from water. Dig a cat hole in the soil with your hiking pole or boot. Deposit your waste into the hole, which should be at least 6 inches deep, and cover it with dirt and organic material. Leave the spot looking as natural as the surroundings. Pack out toilet paper and feminine hygiene products. When traveling on snow, check with land managers and use established waste-disposal systems (e.g., blue bags, kitty litter, poop tubes).

Cross-country travel. When scrambling in remote areas, avoid establishing trails. If trails exist, or when abandoned roads or jeep track are visible, use them as much as possible. Whenever possible, travel on durable surfaces such as rock, snow, sand, and dry grasses. Spread out instead of traveling in a single line. If you find yourself in a fragile location, travel single file and try to step in each other's footprints to minimize your impact. Do not create rock cairns or alter stacked rocks on mountain summits or routes.

Leave No Trace

Leave No Trace (LNT) is an educational program that coordinates with managing agencies to promote stewardship of our public lands (see Appendix B for the LNT website). Understanding, following, and promoting the LNT outdoor skills and ethics will ensure that our wild lands are available for generations to come. The LNT principles are:
- Plan ahead and prepare.
- Travel and camp on durable surfaces.
- Dispose of waste properly.
- Leave what you find.
- Minimize campfire impacts.
- Respect wildlife.
- Be considerate of other visitors.
- And for rock climbing (and scrambling), minimize climbing impacts.

Conservation. Conservation in Oregon is a key responsibility of anyone who uses the outdoors for recreation. Traveling around the state and scrambling in different regions will allow you to become a knowledgeable advocate for preservation of our public lands.

Learn more about the different ecoregions you are visiting. When you are scrambling in a particular ecoregion, practice techniques appropriate to that type of terrain and ecology. When you have the chance, express your views in public forums, to land managers, or by getting involved with a local conservation organization.

HOW TO USE THIS BOOK

Scrambles in this guidebook are grouped into mountain regions. Each scramble begins with summary information and provides specifics so you can choose the appropriate trip for the time you have available and your level of fitness, navigational skill, and scrambling ability.

The **elevation** listed is based upon either of two systems. If the elevation is listed on a USGS topographic map, then it was accurately measured in the field. That is the preferred elevation for peaks, when available. If there is no elevation published, then the elevation was estimated using the USGS quad contour lines.

Difficulty is defined using a letter (S and T) and number (1 through 5). An "S" describes how strenuous a scramble will be; a "T" describes technical difficulty or technique. The numbers 1 through 5 rate the route from easy (1) to difficult (5). How strenuous a route is depends upon the amount of off trail travel, elevation gain, terrain, and mileage. A 5-mile scramble through overgrown brush, which climbs 1500 feet in the first mile, may be rated S3. A 10-mile scramble mostly using a maintained trail, with a short section of off trail travel, will be only an S2. A typical pace will ascend approximately 1000 feet an hour.

Technical difficulty or technique describes the type of scrambling each route will require. Many scramblers are familiar with the standard scale for rock climbing. Technical rock climbing begins at class 5. Scrambling is the middle ground between class 1 (trail hiking) and class 5 (rock climbing). Class 2 is scrambling and includes off trail travel over rough ground, using your hands occasionally. Class 3 is scrambling using your hands often over steep rock, loose rock, or with exposure. You may encounter a short section of class 4 in this book, where you might want to carry and use a rope; no belay is necessary, but some scramblers will be more comfortable using a rope as a hand line for extra security.

T1 or 2 likely has mostly class 2 travel with little or only occasional use of the hands. T3 or 4 has mostly class 3 travel, which will require the use of hands more often and likely will have increasing amounts of exposure or loose rock. T5 will define routes with more class 3 scrambling, with longer periods of exposure, loose rock, steeper slopes, or a short section of class 4 travel. A fall from a T5 scramble will result in serious injury. Some scramblers will want to use a rope as a hand line for safety on T5 routes.

Your experience, comfort level, and current conditions all contribute to your subjective experience of a particular rating. A scrambler who is a rock climber may be more comfortable on a T4 route than a hiker without any previous outings on steep or vertical terrain.

Elevation gain includes all the elevation gained during the scramble. For most scrambles, the elevation gain is the difference between the elevation

Unique stacked rock of a Wallowa Mountains summit cairn

at the trailhead and at the summit. However, for some scrambles there are many ascents and descents on the way to the summit. Because of all the ups (and downs) en route, these scrambles have more total elevation gain than a comparison of the trailhead and summit elevations would suggest. The elevation gain listed for each scramble is approximate.

Round trip distance is calculated from the trailhead and back.

Trip time is the estimate of the amount of time required to complete the round trip. This includes short breaks and a short time on the summit. This is in hours for day trips, or days for backpacks.

Time to summit refers to the approximate amount of time to reach the destination, and includes short breaks. All time estimates are provided as a guideline only. Different parties will move at widely varying paces, and times will vary accordingly.

Best time of year refers to the months in which the scramble route is in the best shape. This may be early spring for routes that melt out quickly, are lower elevation, or are snow routes. Some routes may be done all year. However, due to the high level of snow and associated dangers (such as avalanche), the optimal time for most scrambles is from April to November. A few lower-elevation scrambles may be safely done in winter as long as there has been no recent rain or snow on the route.

Maps. All the scramble routes include the name of the appropriate USGS 7.5-minute series topographic map. Occasionally other topographic maps are available, such as Geo-Graphics and Green Trails, but they are not listed. These maps often have contour lines that do not give you enough information for scrambling, but may provide you with a good overview of the area. For scrambles in special areas such as the Kalmiopsis and Wild Rogue Wildernesses, specific maps are available from the managing national forest. These Forest Service wilderness maps have contour intervals ranging from 20 to 80 feet and may provide you with useful information about some routes, trailheads, roads, camping, and other services.

Contact information provides the name of the managing agency for each scramble. Addresses, phone numbers, and websites are given in Appendix B.

Special considerations refer to any other information necessary for a scramble. This includes equipment that is nonstandard, such as an ice ax, crampons, or a helmet. This line also includes useful information on regulations, closures, or seasonal hazards.

Following this scramble summary, the **waypoint route** is intended to be a guideline for each scramble. Many of the waypoints were acquired in the field, then checked for accuracy using topographic map software. Some of the waypoints were taken directly from the map software. The waypoints are a powerful tool in your navigational system of map, compass, altimeter, and GPS unit.

Each scramble is then briefly introduced. Trailhead directions are given from the nearest town or city that appears on Oregon's Official State Map. And, finally, a specific route description guides you through the scramble.

Although it is difficult to accurately convey information about the natural world through language, the author has made every attempt to provide useful and accurate descriptions. Please be aware that conditions change due to extreme weather, wildfires, and overuse. Check with the managing agency on current conditions.

A NOTE ABOUT SAFETY

Safety is an important concern in all outdoor activities. No guidebook can alert you to every hazard or anticipate the limitations of every reader. Therefore, the descriptions of roads, trails, routes, and natural features in this book are not representations that a particular place or excursion will be safe for your party. When you follow any of the routes described in this book, you assume responsibility for your own safety. Under normal conditions, such excursions require the usual attention to traffic, road and trail conditions, weather, terrain, the capabilities of your party, and other factors. Keeping informed on current conditions and exercising common sense are the keys to a safe, enjoyable outing.

— *The Mountaineers Books*

THE COAST RANGE

1 ELK AND KINGS MOUNTAINS

Elevations: 2788 feet, 3226 feet

Difficulty: S4/T3

Round trip: 9.5 miles

Elevation gain: 4352 feet

Trip time: 6–8 hours

Time to summit: 3 hours to Elk Mountain, 5 hours to Kings Mountain

Best time of year: May to October; accessible year-round

Maps: USGS Cochran, Jordan Creek, Rogers Peak, Woods Point

Contact: Oregon Department of Forestry, Tillamook State Forest, Forest Grove District

Special considerations: In winter, only experienced scramblers should attempt this route. Carry and be proficient with an ice ax. Deep snowdrifts may linger until spring on north or shady slopes.

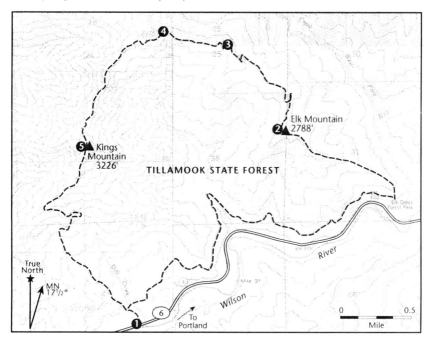

37

WAYPOINT ROUTE
1. Kings Mountain Trailhead: 680 feet (10T 460628mE 5049200mN)
2. Elk Mountain: 5.0 miles, 2788 feet (10T 462292mE 5051327mN)
3. Rock cairn/old road: 5.6 miles, 3000 feet (10T 461545mE 5052270mN)
4. Kings Mountain summit sign: 6.1 miles, 3025 feet (10T 460808mE 5052421mN)
5. Kings Mountain: 7.4 miles, 3226 feet (10T 460029mE 505115mN)

The Tillamook State Forest is a thriving example of a major reforestation project. The forest was formerly known as the Tillamook Burn, since a cycle of four fires from 1933 to 1951 destroyed much of the old-growth forest. The restored forest is a temperate rain forest and contains Douglas fir, rare and fragile wildflowers, flowing creeks and streams, and miles of trails for recreational use. The scramble up to Elk Mountain is athletic and will reward you with views of the Wilson River and surrounding forestlands. From Kings Mountain you can see to the coast on a clear day.

Trailhead directions: From Portland take U.S. Route 26 west and turn left onto State Route 6. Drive 13 miles to the Kings Mountain parking area on the right. There is parking for more than a dozen cars and a large sign at the trailhead with a map, hike information, and regulations. No bathrooms or water are available.

Route description: Begin on the Kings Mountain Trail, which goes 0.1 mile to the sign marking the junction with the Wilson River Trail. Turn right onto the Wilson River Trail, a beautiful path through a rich second-growth forest. The trail follows the river, contouring through a drainage. After the second footbridge the trail climbs a few switchbacks to the Elk Mountain Trail, at about 3.5 miles. Turn left onto the trail. Most scramblers will prefer to ascend the Elk Mountain Trail. The reverse, clockwise route has steep, slippery descents and is not recommended. Indeed, the ascent is steep, but the route is easier when done counterclockwise.

The trail climbs sharply up on a rocky, dusty trail passing through 1500 feet. After a brief descent of less than 100 feet, the trail continues and climbs steeply. Scramble and hike up the trail to a bench at about 2500 feet; continue up and down until 2550 feet, and ascend the trail to the Elk Mountain summit at 5 miles. There are great views all around in clear weather. Look west to the summit of Kings Mountain. The trail continues alongside the back of the rocky ridge you can see to the right of the Kings summit.

Continue on the trail, which drops down steeply as it heads away from the summit. Scramble down and across a rocky ridge, through the forest, then ascend a series of short switchbacks. The trail now joins an old road through the forest for a while, passing a large cairn at 5.6 miles. Continue past the cairn to a wide flat section, good for a lunch spot with views.

At 6.1 miles come to the sign "Kings Mountain summit 1.3 miles," and turn left. In about 0.5 mile there is a tricky descent—scramble down, traverse west along the ridge, always continuing on the main, well-used trail. Keep

Scramblers check out the summit register on Kings Mountain.

descending through what may be overgrown brush in late summer. This section of the route has steep drop-offs on the right, which may be hidden by the brush. Eventually the trail begins climbing short, steep switchbacks and comes around to a false summit.

Continue to the Kings Mountain summit at 7.4 miles, where there is a sign and register. Enjoy the views of the Cascades and west to the ocean on a clear day. The descent starts steeply and the elevation quickly falls to 1500 feet as you scramble down a dirt trail through the forest. Then the grade becomes more moderate. This part of the trail passes by historical remnants of the forest's logging past. Note the huge stumps and sections of log throughout the forest. Finally you will pass a sign marking the Wilson River intersection; continue 0.1 mile to the parking area.

2 MUNRA POINT

Elevation: 1740 feet

Difficulty: S2/T3

Round trip: 4.4 miles

Elevation gain: 1982 feet

Trip time: 4 hours

Time to summit: 2 hours

Best time of year: April to November; accessible beginning in March

Map: USGS Multnomah Falls

Contact: Columbia River Gorge National Scenic Area

WAYPOINT ROUTE
1. Wahclella Falls Trailhead: 75 feet (10T 581540mE 5053413mN)
2. Trail junction: 1.3 miles, 152 feet (10T 579855mE 5052508mN)
3. Ridge: 1.7 miles, 855 feet (10T 580395mE 5052481mN)
4. Exposed rocky section: 1.8 miles, 1222 feet (10T 580575mE 5052471mN)
5. Final ridge: 2.0 miles, 1522 feet (10t 580858mE 5052416mN)
6. Munra Point: 2.2 miles, 1740 feet (10T 581055mE 5052433mN)

The Columbia River Gorge is the lowest pathway through the Oregon Cascades. As such, it allows remarkable access to a wide range of hiking, climbing, and scrambling opportunities. The gorge is full of undulating ridges, vertical cliff faces, and high plateaus. These are all built on Columbia River basalts, multiple layers of rich dark basalt. Munra Point is the remote horn, which sits at the north end of a long ridge between Moffett and Tanner Creeks. If you follow the long ridge south, you reach the protected Bull Run Watershed, which supplies Portland with its drinking water. Scramblers will enjoy this short but difficult scramble up a series of rocky, exposed basalt outcrops leading to a uniquely shaped viewpoint. In spring there are abundant wildflowers blooming throughout the forest and on the upper slopes.

Trailhead directions: From Portland drive east on Interstate 84. Take exit 40 and turn right for the Wahclella Falls Trailhead. No services are available at this trailhead. A Northwest Forest Pass is required.

Route description: Walk north out of the parking lot, across the bridge, and turn left onto Gorge Trail 400. The trail begins climbing right away on

Scrambling above the chimney en route to Munra Point, Columbia River in the background

some short switchbacks through dense forest. Old-growth Douglas fir can be seen along this trail, and you may also see western hemlock and true firs. This part of the gorge is known for its waterfalls, creeks, and all the beautiful

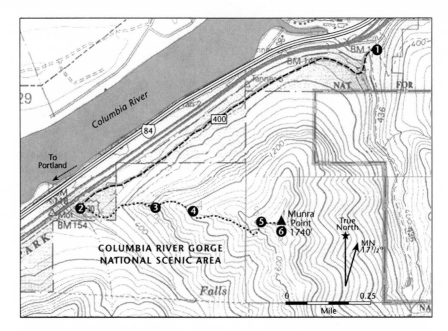

wildflowers that grow in these moist environments. Trillium springs up early, as do fawn lilies, fairy slipper, and lupine.

The trail goes south for a short distance before turning northward, then dropping down to parallel the interstate for about the next mile. Although not remote, this still is a pretty section of Trail 400, which climbs gently to about 300 feet before dropping down to meet the user trail to Munra Point at 1.3 miles.

This route enters the forest and begins to climb quickly, up short, steep switchbacks through scrubby oak trees. You will reach the first rocky outcrop at around 700 feet; scramble up and continue ascending along the left side of the ridge crest.

There will be another rocky scramble up steep rock ahead. Enjoy the fun and continue eastward, now on the right of the ridge crest. Keep ascending steeply on the rocky, sometimes exposed trail. You will next come upon a short, nearly vertical section of rock at about 1.8 miles. Scramble up the rock by using the ledges and knobs. Then continue across a rocky exposed spine, and head back into the forest to continue climbing.

You will ascend to the final ridge at about 2 miles after another short, nearly vertical section, which is wide. Scramble up this third-class section carefully. Do not dislodge any rock. You will pop out and continue ascending across the ridge.

Cross the ridge eastward to the obvious knob that is the high spot on Munra Point. After enjoying the view of the Columbia River and Mount Adams, drop back down to the trail below the point and walk out to the northern-most point. Here, too, you will enjoy the views of the Columbia River nearly 1800 feet below. Return the way you came.

Scrambler below Munra Point

3 ROCK OF AGES

Elevation: 3010 feet

Difficulty: S3/T2

Round trip: 9.1 miles

Elevation gain: 4179 feet

Trip time: 6 hours

Time to summit: 3 hours

Best time of year: April to December

Map: USGS Multnomah Falls

Contact: Columbia River Gorge National Scenic Area

Special considerations: Not recommended when rainy or snowy. No foot-bridge over Oneonta Creek; the creek may be very difficult to ford after heavy rain or during spring snowmelt.

WAYPOINT ROUTE
1. Horsetail Falls Trailhead: 57 feet (10T 572950mE 5048819mN)
2. Unmaintained trail junction: 0.3 mile, 422 feet (10T 572790mE 5048609mN)
3. Midpoint on ridge: 1.3 miles, 1860 feet (10T 573843mE 5048238mN)
4. Junction Horsetail Creek Trail: 2.5 miles, 3010 feet (10T 575650mE 5047684mN)
5. Cross Oneonta Creek: 5.6 miles, 1439 feet (10T 573370mE 5046116mN)

The Columbia River Gorge National Scenic Area is one of Oregon's outdoor playgrounds. While there are many hikes, scrambles, and rock climbs, most are well traveled. Rock of Ages is a scramble up a very steep ridge, which will take you away from the crowded gorge mainstream and into the backcountry. This route travels through areas where early gorge hikers and even climbers traveled when the area was developing as a recreation spot in the mid-twentieth century. This scramble is quite steep in spots, which adds to the challenge as you ascend to the plateau. Enjoy the old-growth trees along the upper plateau before you reach the trail junction.

Trailhead directions: From Portland drive east on Interstate 84. Get off at exit 35. Turn south on the old highway and park at the lot for Horsetail Falls. The trail is on the south side of the street, adjacent to the falls picnic area.

Route description: Horsetail Falls Trail 438 begins climbing right away, ascending eastward away from the falls. The trail climbs on switchbacks, passing Gorge Trail 400 in less than 0.2 mile. Continue up toward Upper Horsetail Falls. The forest here is thick with Douglas fir, ferns, and colorful wildflowers in spring and early summer.

As you round a corner to the falls, on the left above the trail begins a ridge with a trail. There is an old wooden sign on a tree, which says "trail not maintained." Turn left onto this trail, at about 0.3 mile, and begin scrambling.

The trail, which goes southeast along Rock of Ages ridge, is steep, rocky, and loose in places. That said, if you go to the trouble of hauling yourself up this steep scramble you will thoroughly enjoy the upper plateau of cool green forest and utter silence. The trail begins steeply, and then switches back as it continues. You will pass by two huge old fir trees then scramble up a very steep section to a barely visible junction with another huge fir on the right side. Bear left here, and then continue back and forth while climbing up a rocky steep section of trail. At the next fork keep left, then stay right at the next two forks. All this back and forth is actually just getting you up the path to a viewpoint.

Continue to climb on the trail. In some places the rocks are very loose and you will have to pick your way around eroded sections. Avoid dislodging rocks whenever possible. Keep ascending and at about 1.2 miles you will ascend along a rocky spine with great views west along the river.

You will pass the ridge midpoint at about 1.3 miles, and the trail will continue steeply for another 0.5 mile before it starts to go through spots that

A rocky spine along the Rock of Ages route, with the Columbia River in the background

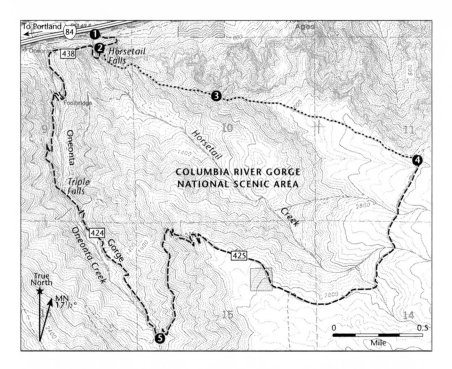

seem almost flat. After the steep scrambling, almost anything will seem flattish.

Ascending past 2600 feet, the steepness decreases as you pass through the upper plateau area on the way to the Horsetail Creek Trail. This upper plateau, composed of Columbia River basalt like the rest of the ridge, is a lush green vision after the sometimes-barren rocky ridge. Enjoy the plentiful vine maples, firs, and cedars scattered throughout the forest.

Continue along southeast until you reach the Horsetail Creek Trail junction at 2.5 miles. For impressive views down some extremely steep sections, walk north to the edge of the plateau while making your way to the trail. Once you pass 2800 feet, almost any point along the northern edge of the plateau has nearly vertical drop-offs to the drainage below.

The Horsetail Creek Trail is just the beginning of the hike back. You will now pass some of the most beautiful creeks in the gorge. Wild mushrooms and abundant wildflowers are all along the trail as you make your way back down to the falls.

The trail descends gradually for the first 2 miles, passing the Bell Creek Trail leading south. Then you will descend steep switchbacks for more than 2000 feet. Continue hiking southward along this still-descending section of trail, heading for the crossing at Oneonta Creek at 5.6 miles.

The creek may be a tough ford if the water is high. There are a number of large logs that partially cross the creek, and there are also plenty of large rocks in the water. Cross safely, then resume hiking out on the trail. There are some camping spots on the west side of the creek.

Ascending away from the creek, you will reach another trail junction marked with an old sign. Turn right onto the Oneonta Trail 424, which will lead north along the creek. Finally, after passing and enjoying the lovely Triple Falls, turn right onto the Horsetail Falls Trail 438. Here you will cross the footbridge over the Oneonta Gorge and return to your car.

MOUNT HOOD, BARRETT SPUR

Elevation: 7863 feet	
Difficulty: S3/T2	
Round trip: 8.8 miles	
Elevation gain: 3435 feet	
Trip time: 5–6 hours	
Time to summit: 3 hours	
Best time of year: July to October	
Map: USGS Mount Hood North	
Contact: Mount Hood National Forest, Zigzag Ranger District	
Special considerations: Considerable snow possible until late July	

WAYPOINT ROUTE
1. Vista Ridge Trailhead: 4493 feet (10T 599409mE 5032716mN)
2. Leave trail: 2.9 miles, 5854 feet (10T 600676mE 5029082mN)
3. On user trail: 3.3 miles, 6480 feet (10T 601002mE 5028512mN)
4. Top of moraine: 3.7 miles, 6931 feet (10T 601336mE 5028111mN)
5. First high point: 4.25 miles, 7872 feet (10T 601867mE 5027382mN)
6. Barrett Spur: 4.4 miles, 7863 feet (10T 601915mE 5027163mN)

Mount Hood is Oregon's highest mountain and enjoys widespread popularity as a hiking, climbing, and tourist destination. Mount Hood is an active volcano, evidenced by the stench of sulfur from vents near the summit. Prominent ridges divide the mountain's northern slopes. Vista Ridge orients almost exactly on a north-south axis and provides hikers with excellent access to alpine meadows and close-up views of the north-side glaciers. Vista Ridge also provides the approach hike to the Barrett Spur scramble. Barrett Spur juts out against Hood's heavily glaciered north side. Surrounded by the Ladd and Coe Glaciers, Barrett Spur offers an impressive look at the rugged upper reaches of this familiar mountain.

Trailhead directions: From Portland drive east on U.S. Route 26. At Zigzag turn left and head north on East Lolo Pass Road, continuing after it turns into Forest Road 18. Wind around on FR 18 until you reach the junction with FR 16. Turn right onto FR 16 and drive almost 5 miles to the junction with FR 1650. Take FR 1650 until it ends in a small parking area. The trail begins at

Scrambling up the talus to the first high point of Barrett Spur, the Hood River Valley in the background

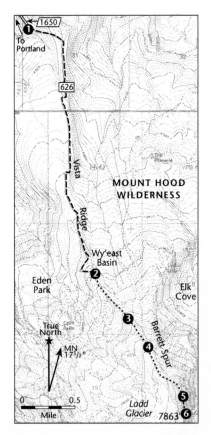

the trailhead sign at the north end of the parking area. A Northwest Forest Pass is required.

Route description: Vista Ridge Trail 626 does not actually begin until you have hiked through the forest a short while on the overgrown remnant of FR 1650. In early summer there are wildflowers along the old roadbed. After about 0.2 mile you will reach the trailhead proper, complete with trail register, signs, maps, and other forest information. Turn right onto Trail 626.

The Vista Ridge Trail follows the ridge southward through the forest on the way to Wy'east Basin. As you climb enjoy the thick subalpine forest, which includes mountain hemlock. In summer you will appreciate the shade of the thick canopy of trees; there is no shade once you emerge from the forest.

At around 2.5 miles, the trail passes by Wy'east Basin to reach a trail junction. Here you may go to either Elk Cove or Eden Park. Continue left, toward Elk Cove, on the trail for a short distance.

Look south and savor the views of Mount Hood looming in front of you. Note also that there will be a ridgeline to the south, which leads up to Barrett Spur.

Walk off the trail at about 2.9 miles and gain the ridge. Follow south-southeast along the ridgeline, going around pines when necessary and occasionally glimpsing a user trail. This area is heavily visited and there may be a variety of trails in late season.

Continue south-southeast, using the user trail if you want at 3.3 miles, and ascend to the top of the moraine. Continue working your way southeast now, on the crest of the moraine/ridge at 3.7 miles, and you will reach a large bench just north of the ascent to the first point on Barrett Spur.

Dump your pack here if you want. Scramble up the steep, loose slope to the first high point of Barrett Spur's narrow upper section at 4.25 miles. After the first high point, if you choose to continue, scramble south and ascend the loose slope of rocks and cinders to the spur's highest point at 7863 feet and 4.4 miles. Of course the view from here is all Mount Hood, the summit just visible above the upper reaches of the Coe Glacier. In late season you may hear occasional rock- or icefall as the snow and ice melt in the afternoon heat.

MOUNT HOOD, COOPER SPUR

Elevation: 8875 feet

Difficulty: S3/T2

Round trip: 5.6 miles

Elevation gain: 3000 feet

Trip time: 5 hours

Time to summit: 2–3 hours

Best time of year: July to October

Map: USGS Mount Hood North

Contact: Mount Hood National Forest, Hood River Ranger District

WAYPOINT ROUTE
1. Cloud Cap Saddle: 5863 feet (10T 605355mE 5028341mN)
2. Cooper Spur Trail: 1.1 miles, 6643 feet (10T 605063mE 5026950mN)
3. Leave trail: 1.4 miles, 6689 feet (10T 604741mE 5026804mN)
4. Rock shelters: 2.4 miles, 8370 feet (10T 603744mE 5025448mN)
5. Cooper Spur endpoint: 2.8 miles, 8875 feet (10T 603324mE 5025253mN)

The Mount Hood National Forest has many recreation opportunities despite being one of the most overlogged forests in Oregon. Climbers flock to the Portland-area mountain, making it one of the most popular mountain-climbing peaks in the country. Scrambling up the east side of Mount Hood is one way

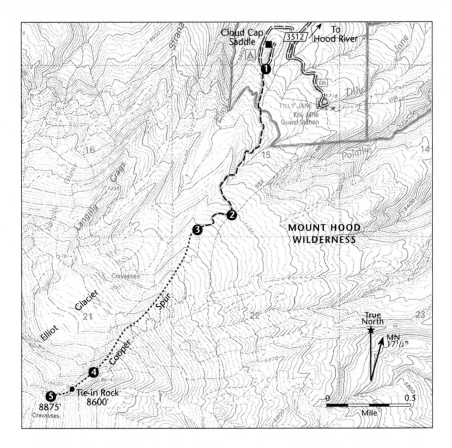

to get relatively close to the summit without climbing the mountain completely. On the eastern side you have views of the Hood River valley and Columbia River. The forest thins as you climb higher; Douglas fir and hemlock give way to subalpine fir and whitebark pine and well-known displays of alpine wildflowers. Early climbers on Mount Hood used the Cooper Spur route frequently to reach the summit. Scramblers can expect challenging slopes, dramatic glacier views, and a close look at the crumbling eastern upper mountain of Mount Hood.

Trailhead directions: From Hood River drive south on State Route 35 toward Mount Hood. At about 24 miles, turn right onto Cooper Spur Road. Turn left on the Cooper Spur access road (in front of the Cooper Spur Inn) and drive about 2 miles, turning right at the prominent sign to Tilly Jane and Cloud Cap on Forest Road 3512. It becomes rough and after about 9 miles you reach the Cloud Cap Saddle and campground. There is a main parking area between a wilderness information booth and water spigot. There is some parking along the road also. Walk south-southwest between the booth and water spigot to the trailhead for Timberline Trail 600. A Northwest Forest Pass is required.

The route on Cooper Spur has wonderful views of Mount Hood's steep upper mountain.

Route description: Ascend about 30 yards, passing the wilderness boundary, to a self-registration and information sign. For about the next mile the trail climbs, sometimes steeply, to a junction with the Tilly Jane and the Cooper Spur Trails. Along the way enjoy the beautiful mountain hemlock, whitebark pine, lupine, asters, and other alpine wildflowers.

Turn right onto the Cooper Spur Trail at 1.1 miles and ascend to the stone shelter at 1.4 miles. Leave the main trail and walk on the user trail to the right of the shelter and toward the rocky ridge that parallels the lateral moraine of the Eliot Glacier. Follow the sometimes faint user trail, or just head north across the bench to the edge of the ridge and then continue climbing toward Tie-in Rock, up on the spur. From this point the trail follows the ridgeline up to the spur, winding around rocks and boulders. Use it or rock-hop on a path of your own choosing. The routefinding is straightforward. Watch out in early season or if the ground is wet—the edge can be very crumbly and soft with a tendency to slide.

Enjoy the views of the Eliot Glacier, which has huge crevasses in late season. You may see teams of climbers down on the glacier practicing crevasse rescue or fine-tuning their ice-climbing technique.

As you continue scrambling, occasionally the Cooper Spur Trail will cross your path. At about 8300 feet you will reach the bench where Tie-in Rock is perched, and where the early mountain climbers roped up for safety as they climbed up the mountain. There are several rock shelters here, at 2.4 miles. Continue about another 0.4 mile to the glacier's edge. There is another rock shelter here and a rock with a plaque. Enjoy the views of the glaciers and summit. On a clear day Mounts Rainier, Adams, and St. Helens are dramatic to the north. Return as you came or on the Cooper Spur Trail.

GOAT PEAK

Elevation: 7159 feet

Difficulty: S4/T3

Round trip: 16.2 miles

Elevation gain: 4745 feet

Trip time: 10 hours

Time to summit: 6–7 hours

Best time of year: July to October

Map: USGS Mount Jefferson

Contact: Willamette National Forest, Detroit Ranger Station

Special considerations: The Pamelia Lake area has restricted access due to overuse; contact the ranger station to obtain an entry permit. The final 20 feet to the summit of Goat Peak are exposed and not recommended.

WAYPOINT ROUTE

1. Woodpecker Ridge Trailhead: 4430 feet (10T 588309mE 4947899mN)
2. Milk Creek: 3.0 miles, 4365 feet (10T 591497mE 4946188mN)
3. Leave trail: 6.6 miles, 5842 feet (10T 593634mE 4943474mN)
4. Above talus slope: 7.6 miles, 6774 feet (10T 594895mE 4944287mN)
5. Goat Peak high point: 8.1 miles, 7139 feet (10T 595364mE 4943812mN)

The Willamette National Forest is home to some of central Oregon's most scenic wilderness. The Mount Jefferson Wilderness is a popular destination due to the combination of beautiful high meadows, dense forest, alpine lakes, and distinctive mountains. Just south of Oregon's second-highest peak is little-known Goat Peak. The scramble to a notch right below Goat Peak's summit is full of alpine beauty. The rock is solid, and the views are spectacular. Scramblers who prefer a more vertical experience will enjoy this ascent.

Trailhead directions: From Detroit drive east on State Route 22 about 12 miles to Forest Road 040. Turn left onto the gravel forest road and drive about 5.5 miles to the well-marked trailhead. There are no services, but parking is plentiful along the road. The trailhead information sign and wilderness self-register are on the east side of the road. A Northwest Forest Pass is required.

Route description: Woodpecker Ridge Trail 3442 climbs right from the trailhead through dense westside forest. The surroundings are quite beautiful

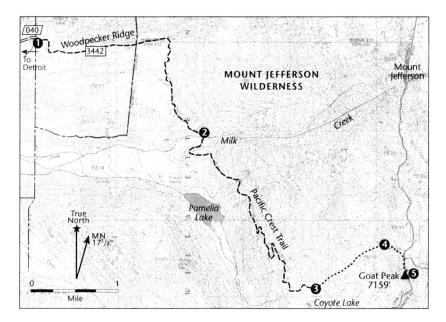

as you ascend past huckleberry bushes, rhododendrons, and bear grass.

You will quickly arrive at the ridge crest around 5000 feet. Continue eastward through the forest to the clearly marked junction with the Pacific Crest Trail at 1.7 miles and turn south onto the PCT.

The PCT descends to cross Milk Creek where you may see a beautiful display of flowers, including pink monkeyflower. The hike down to the creek crossing is quiet as you pass through the thick trees. Cross Milk Creek at 3 miles, using a fallen log or by rock hopping. This is a good source of cold water from Mount Jefferson's high western glaciers, but only drink the water if you treat it with chemical purification tablets or use a water filter.

Ascend after leaving the creek drainage, soon passing the clearly marked trail junction to Pamelia Lake. Keep left to stay on the PCT. Note the fireweed and lilies along the trail. The forest seems drier along this section of the PCT as you continue southward toward Coyote and Shale Lakes.

At about 6.6 miles, leave the trail just before Coyote Lake at about 5800 feet. Scramble northeast through the forest to 6100 feet. Now you will begin ascending through a series of talus spurs, which are remnants from Mount Jefferson's southern glaciers. These moraines extend off Jefferson's southern flanks, fanning out as they get farther from the mountain.

By continuing to scramble northeast you will eventually ascend to a broad bench directly south of Jefferson and north of Goat Peak. Along the way you will pass flower-filled meadows with Indian paintbrush, penstemon, lupine, and pink mountain heather. These are only a few of the flowers blooming in the alpine meadows in early summer.

Once you reach 6800 feet or so, and are up above a talus slope, begin to

turn southerly to continue ascending to the bench. The trees will still be thick in some places, but work around them as best you can.

The flatter area is around 6900 feet and there may be a tarn in a slight bowl to the east as you turn south. Continue south toward Goat Peak's north side. As you get closer it becomes clearer that there are two prominent gullies that lead up to the upper mountain's blocky rock.

Head up the westernmost gully to a notch in the rock on the upper mountain. Ascend on loose scree and talus to get up onto the rock, then turn east toward the summit. There is some loose rock among the mostly solid rock; use care when climbing with a large party.

Scramble up and over some blocks, then traverse left around a vertical section on a ledge that leads up through a notch to point above the other gully. Continue to the small platform in a notch right below the summit. The final 20 feet or so to the top include dropping down off the platform and traversing up and across an exposed ramp. The views from the notch are incredible and the traverse is not recommended.

Mount Jefferson dominates the northern skyline. To the south, on a clear day, you will see the Mount Washington and Three Sisters high Cascade peaks.

To descend, use the gully on the right that is nearly in front of the notch. This gully is filled with scree and loose rock; stay on the more solid rock to keep from slipping. Continue back down to the bench and return the way you came.

Mount Jefferson dominates the view from Milk Creek.

7 BELKNAP CRATER

Elevation: 6872 feet

Difficulty: S2/T2

Round trip: 6 miles

Elevation gain: 1620 feet

Trip time: 5 hours

Time to summit: 3 hours

Best time of year: July to October

Map: USGS Mount Washington

Contact: Willamette National Forest, McKenzie Ranger District

WAYPOINT ROUTE
1. PCT Trailhead: 5223 feet (10T 595084mE 4901238mN)
2. Turn left on user trail: 2.3 miles, 6099 feet (10T 593339mE 4903974mN)
3. Northwest turn to ridge: 2.5 miles, 6104 feet (10T 592986mE 4903988mN)
4. End of ridge: 2.8 miles, 6379 feet (10T 592680mE 4904179mN)
5. Belknap Crater: 3.0 miles, 6872 feet (10T 592466mE 4903967mN)

The Mount Washington Wilderness is an austerely beautiful place. The landscape is one of dark and forbidding lava punctuated by the contrasting green of whitebark pines and mountain hemlock and the red cinders of the various cones and peaks. Belknap Crater is one of the youngest volcanoes in the area and was largely responsible for the formidable lava flows in the area 1400 years ago. The young shield volcano is a gently sloping broad peak, which retains its shape due to the lack of any recent glacial activity. A scramble up the northeast slope is short, and steep, and provides a good introduction for those less-experienced scramblers, including older children. The summit of Belknap Crater reveals a distinctive, steep-sided crater, which may be viewed from all angles if you so choose.

Trailhead directions: From Sisters drive west on State Route 126. Follow the signs for SR 242 (Note: Traffic was rerouted in summer 2004 from Sisters to Route 242). Drive west on SR 242, passing the Dee Wright Observatory (with vault toilets) and then McKenzie Pass. Shortly after the pass there is a turnoff on the right for the PCT trailhead. There is parking for several cars.

The trailhead and self-register are at the end of the parking area. A Northwest Forest Pass is required.

Route description: The approach to Belknap Crater begins on the PCT heading northward through the forest. Enjoy your time in the forest; in a short distance you will be on rough, dry lava with no shade in sight. In the early summer you may see wildflowers scattered about, such as lupine and penstemon. The trail crosses the wilderness boundary almost immediately.

After passing through the forest the trail enters the lava flow for a short distance. The trail then contours around the remaining edge of a patch of trees before entering the huge lava flow for the rest of the approach. Hiking along the dark irregular shapes is tough and requires constant attention to the uneven surface. No matter, the lava provides a quick geology lesson and is dissected by features such as lava tubes and channels.

The trail gradually makes its way up to the junction with the trail to Little Belknap Crater to the east. Like its bigger neighbor, Little Belknap was a major contributor to the extensive lava flows in the vicinity. Little Belknap has a small rounded summit cone whose red cinders stand out against the surroundings.

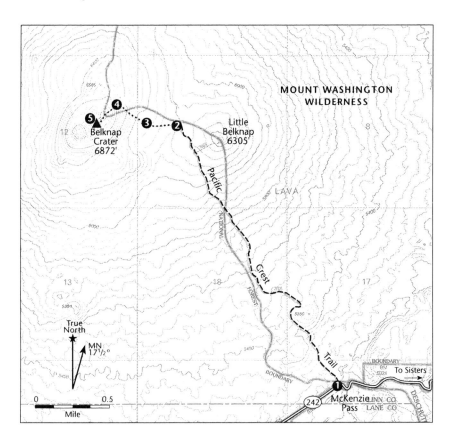

Kids can scramble, too—happy scramblers atop Belknap Crater, Mount Washington in the background.

Continue northward a short distance and turn left at 2.3 miles onto an obvious user trail leading toward Belknap Crater. It may be marked with a rock cairn. This unofficial trail will lead across a plain covered with ash and cinders, surprisingly rich plant life, and a smattering of scrubby trees. The few trees will provide you with an opportunity to take a break in the shade before the steep scramble to the summit.

After about 0.3 mile begin angling northwest toward the skyline ridge. Gain the ridge and turn left to ascend the final 0.3 mile to the edge of the broad summit. The scramble up the ridge is on a loose slope of cinders and ash. Try to keep on rocky areas and to avoid stepping on plant life.

At the edge of the summit continue toward the main summit less than 0.1 mile away. The summit is directly south of Mount Washington and provides you with an up-close look at the steep, eroded, and colorful volcanic plug.

Once on the summit walk down toward the huge crater rim. If you have time, circumnavigate the crater by walking down to the right and circling counterclockwise. The crater has a rocky headwall to the south and is a colorful reminder of this mountain's origin. The views south are imposing, as North Sister stands out starkly against the horizon.

To descend easily you may hike easterly to drop down the steep slope of ash and cinders, which is crisscrossed by a couple of user trails. This is a fun descent and return. Once you reach the trail you can follow it back through the plain to the PCT.

𝄞 LITTLE BROTHER

Elevation: 7810 feet	
Difficulty: S3/T2	
Round trip: 11 miles	
Elevation gain: 3165 feet	
Trip time: 6–7 hours	
Time to summit: 4 hours	
Best time of year: July to October	
Map: USGS North Sister	
Contact: Willamette National Forest, McKenzie Ranger Station	

Special considerations: The Obsidian Trail has restricted access; contact the ranger station to obtain the required entry permit.

WAYPOINT ROUTE
1. Obsidian Trailhead: 4774 feet (10T 590244mE 4895038mN)
2. Glacier Way Trail 4336: 3.4 miles, 5867 feet (10T 593637mE 4892702mN)
3. PCT junction: 4.0 miles, 6399 feet (10T 594507mE 4892245mN)
4. Scramble off trail: 4.3 miles, 6354 feet (10T 594558mE 4892628mN)
5. Little Brother: 5.5 miles, 7810 feet (10T 596233mE 4892296mN)

North Sister is the oldest, most eroded peak of the Three Sisters. On the northwest side of the mountain is Little Brother, a remnant peak that is little known yet provides an amazing view of the North Sister from its 7810-foot summit. The approach to the scramble up the west ridge winds through the dense forest of the Three Sisters Wilderness and past several outstanding geological features including the distinct Obsidian Cliffs. This scramble is fun and offers great views of some very different volcanoes and cinder cones in this well-known wilderness.

   Trailhead directions: From Sisters drive west on State Route 126. Follow the signs for SR 242 (Note: Traffic was rerouted in summer 2004 from Sisters to SR 242). Drive west on SR 242, passing the Dee Wright Observatory, then the McKenzie Pass. About 6.5 miles after the observatory turn left onto Forest Road 250. There is also a sign for the trailhead. Park in one of the pullouts along the road and walk to the end of the road to the well-marked trailhead. There are a trailhead sign, self-register, and vault toilets. A Northwest Forest Pass is required.

   Route description: Obsidian Trail 3552 is a popular gateway into the west side of the Three Sisters Wilderness for backpackers, climbers, and hikers. The trail begins climbing gently through the dense forest of mixed conifers, which includes Douglas fir and western hemlock.

   The terrain changes sharply though as the trail climbs through a substantial

Scrambling up the final pitch to the summit of Little Brother

lava flow east of the trailhead. This lava flow extends for miles in either direction. The ascent up the west edge of the flow is a sudden reminder of this area's rich volcanic past and the lava flow is a startling contrast to the forest you just left behind. A few mountain hemlocks and whitebark pines punctuate the dark lava with their bright green limbs, and an occasional penstemon or lupine blooms in small pockets.

The Obsidian Cliffs come into view as you crest the flow and begin heading to the junction with Glacier Way Trail 4336 at 3.4 miles, just past White Branch Creek. Continue ahead at the junction and sign for Minnie Scott Springs. The Glacier Way Trail crosses through meadows alive with pink heather and wildflowers in early summer.

You will reach the junction with the Pacific Crest Trail in a little more than 0.5 mile. The PCT travels through the wilderness just off the crest and allows easy access to many high peaks. Turn left onto the PCT for a short distance. You will quickly cover the 0.2 mile northward to a point west of Little Brother where you will scramble off the trail through the forest to gain the west ridge.

Scramble eastward through the thinning trees and begin ascending, scrambling up the rocky ridge and around a short cliff face. Once you gain the ridge the route follows the ridge crest eastward to the upper mountain. This route takes you into constantly shifting terrain as you pass through rough bands of jagged lava and benches covered with ash, pumice, and glittering obsidian.

Ascend to the bottom of a steepish slope leading to the upper mountain's cliffy outcrops. Cross below the huge rock outcrop and ascend the loose slope, turning slightly southward just below the summit. Scramble up the gullies to gain the summit.

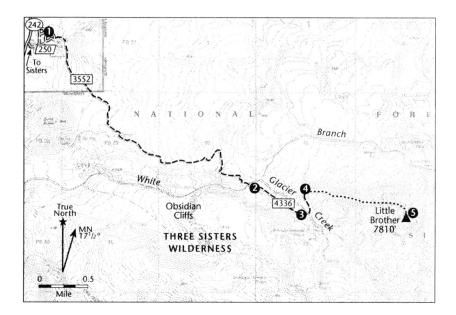

Enjoy the unique views southeast to the North Sister. The Collier Cone, just to the north, is a wonderful illustration of a colorful cinder cone. Continuing north are more extensive lava flows as you look farther to Mount Washington, Three-Fingered Jack, and Mount Jefferson in the distance.

Descend as you came, or use the scree slope of the western bowl to quickly reach the forest east of the PCT. Continue west to the PCT, turn left, and you will reach the Glacier Way Trail junction in about 0.1 mile. Follow the trails in reverse to reach the trailhead.

MIDDLE SISTER

Elevation: 10,047 feet

Difficulty: S5/T3

Round trip: 16.4 miles

Elevation gain: 4757 feet

Trip time: 12 hours

Time to summit: 6 hours

Best time of year: July to September; accessible to October

Map: USGS North Sister

Contact: Deschutes National Forest, Sisters Ranger District

Special considerations: In early season you may need crampons and ice ax. Self-issue permits are available at trailheads for entrance into the Three Sisters Wilderness.

WAYPOINT ROUTE

1. Pole Creek Trailhead: 5290 feet (10T 603960mE 4893289mN)
2. Northeast of Camp Lake: 5.9 miles, 6938 feet (10T 599383mE 4887363mN)
3. North turn: 7.0 miles, 7683 feet (10T 598160mE 4887538mN)
4. Begin traverse: 7.3 miles, 8282 feet (10T 597973mE 4887936mN)
5. Middle Sister: 8.3 miles, 10,047 feet (10T 597340mE 4888882mN)

Middle Sister is the smallest of the Three Sisters in central Oregon's high Cascades. Although not as old as her two-pinnacled sister to the north, nor as tall as South Sister, Middle Sister nevertheless is a formidable scramble in a beautiful alpine environment. From high atop Middle Sister's broken summit you can see directly across North Sister's highly eroded summit and imagine the strength of the glaciers that carved off the top of that mountain. The approach to the Middle Sister scramble will take you through the dense eastside forest near Pole Creek to the barren alpine zone of Middle Sister's south flank.

Trailhead directions: From Sisters drive west on State Route 126. Bear left at the junction with SR 242 and drive west. Turn left at the sign for Pole Creek onto Forest Road 15. Drive about 7.0 miles on FR 15 then bear left on FR 1524 for another 3.5 miles. Continue on FR 1524 to the Pole Creek Trailhead.

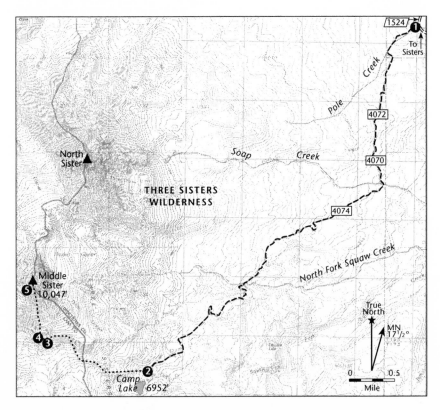

Middle Sister from the summit of Little Brother

There are vault toilets at the trailhead. A Northwest Forest Pass is required.

Route description: Pole Creek Trail 4072 follows the creek southwest then turns south as it takes you through the mixed conifer forest of the Three Sisters Wilderness Area's east side. After ascending the first 1.4 miles you will pass the first of several trail junctions. At 1.4 miles, continue 0.5 mile south on Green Lakes Trail 4070. The trail then drops down a short distance and crosses Soap Creek. Just after crossing it, the trail turns westward and becomes Camp Lake Trail 4074. The trail heads southwest, making a steep ascent after crossing the North Fork Squaw Creek at 4.4 miles. Continue gently climbing until you reach almost 7000 feet and are about 0.1 mile northeast of the trail's end at Camp Lake.

As the trail makes a slight turn southwest at 5.9 miles (waypoint 2), walk off the trail west for about 0.5 mile. As you scramble west you will ascend to close to 7400 feet and turn northwest for a short distance to work your way up a rocky section. In a very short distance, nearing 7600 feet, traverse west again for about 0.3 mile to pass below some steep rocks.

Turn northward around 7700 feet (waypoint 3) and bear north along the easternmost ridge. Climb this ridge for 0.3 mile, and then begin an ascending traverse at about 8250 feet (waypoint 4) that will take you directly to the south ridge. Follow the south ridge to the summit. As you make your way, there will likely be a climbers trail in late summer or fall. Just note where you are on the mountain so you can make a safe descent.

The up-close look at North Sister from the Middle Sister summit

The summit of Middle Sister is broad and covered with broken rock. The views across the saddle to North Sister give you an up-close look at the effects of glacial ice. The red and black of North Sister stand out against the blue sky of summer. Enjoy the views down the steep east face of Middle Sister, down to the Hayden Glacier—a popular mountaineering ascent. Turn around and note the looming silhouette of South Sister. On a clear day you can trace the spine of the Cascade chain north to Mount Hood.

Descend the way you came.

10 SOUTH SISTER

Elevation: 10,358 feet

Difficulty: S3/T3

Round trip: 12.4 miles

Elevation gain: 4987 feet

Trip time: 7–9 hours

Time to summit: 4–6 hours

Best time of year: July to October

Map: USGS South Sister

Contact: Deschutes National Forest, Bend–Fort Rock Ranger District

Special considerations: In early season you may need crampons and ice ax. Some areas in the Three Sisters Wilderness may be closed for restoration; please respect all closures. The South Climb Trail is periodically rerouted to control erosion. Call ahead for current trail information.

WAYPOINT ROUTE

1. Devils Lake Campground and Trailhead: 5447 feet (10T 598990mE 4876338mN)
2. Moraine Lake Trail junction: 1.6 miles, 6698 feet (10T 598571mE 44878583mN)
3. "Closed Trail" sign: 3.0 miles, 7008 feet (10T 598713mE 4880679mN)
4. South Sister: 5.3 miles, 10,358 feet (10T 598588mE 4883911mN)

Few visitors to central Oregon's Three Sisters Wilderness can forget their first view of South Sister. Majestically rising 10,358 feet above the surrounding forest, South Sister is a fine example of a high Cascade volcano; it is younger than its volcanic siblings, and it is still active. In recent years geologists began tracking earthquakes and other activity on the peak's west side.

South Sister is a worthwhile endeavor for scramblers in spite of its popularity in peak season. There is a little bit of everything along this route as you make the abrupt transition from dense forest to open plain, to a steep scramble up red cinders alongside broken and dramatic lava flows. The upper mountain is particularly scenic with the Lewis Glacier receding to the west to reveal its shattered blue ice. The summit crater is huge and contains Oregon's highest pool of water. Views are unsurpassed in central Oregon.

Oregon's highest pool of water is in the summit crater of South Sister.

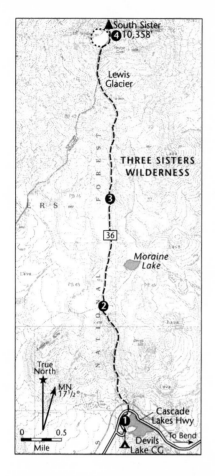

Trailhead directions: From Bend drive west on the Cascade Lakes Highway (Century Drive) 6.5 miles past Mount Bachelor resort to the Devils Lake Campground on the south side of the road. You may park in the outer lot. Walk through the campground to get on the trail. A Northwest Forest Pass is required.

Route description: From the parking lot walk south and then curve back north, crossing a creek and the Cascade Lakes Highway. The clearly marked trailhead sign reading "South Climb Trail 36" and the self-register are in the woods just past the highway. Ascend a dry, dusty trail through the mixed conifer forest. The trail climbs steeply in places, eventually emerging on a gently ascending trail along a plateau. You will pass the junction to the Wickiup Plains Trail (left) and the Moraine Lake Trail (at 1.6 miles). Continue north on the trail.

After about a mile, the trail begins a long ascent along a fantastic lava flow on the right, to the bottom of the south crater. Along the way you will pass through several mixed stands of majestic mountain hemlock and whitebark pine. You will pass a "Closed Trail" sign for the Moraine Canyon area restoration. Continue along the trail north as it climbs rather steeply to a viewpoint that looks northwest at the Lewis Glacier. Continue along the ridge, passing several rock shelters. The trail again climbs in earnest to the summit rim. At the rim, notice several rock shelters (probably with people huddled in them). Turn right and follow the contour of the rim to the summit, right in front of Middle and North Sister.

After you tire of the summit views and crowds, scramble 0.5 mile around the rest of the summit crater by continuing counterclockwise. From the summit, you will descend slightly, ascend once again to another high point, and scramble down a steep ramp and then across a rock band, which is on the north side of the summit rim. Ascend the other side rim to reach the point where you crested the rim on the south side.

Views of the other Three Sisters peaks and Broken Top can be spectacular on a clear day. Note also the smaller summit of The Wife to the west across the plain.

From the summit rim of South Sister, scramblers have a wonderful view of Middle and North Sister

Descend the way you came, scrambling down carefully on the loose cinders and scree. Please use care and stay on the path—the whole upper mountain is heavily eroded from overuse.

11 THE WIFE

Elevation: 7054 feet

Difficulty: S2/T3

Round trip: 8.8 miles

Elevation gain: 1600 feet

Trip time: 5–7 hours

Time to summit: 3 hours

Best time of year: July to October

Map: USGS South Sister

Contact: Deschutes National Forest, Bend–Fort Rock Ranger District

WAYPOINT ROUTE

1. Elk–Devils Lake Trailhead: 5480 feet (10T 598951mE 4876159mN)
2. Northwest turn: 2.2 miles, 6100 feet (10T 596973mE 4877773mN)
3. PCT crossing: 3.3 miles, 6200 feet (10T 595503mE 4878435mN)
4. South ridge: 4.1 miles, 6538 feet (10T 594328mE 4878825mN)
5. Summit ridge: 4.3 miles, 7000 feet (10T 594206mE 4879176mN)
6. The Wife: 4.4 miles, 7054 feet (10T 594287mE 4879215mN)

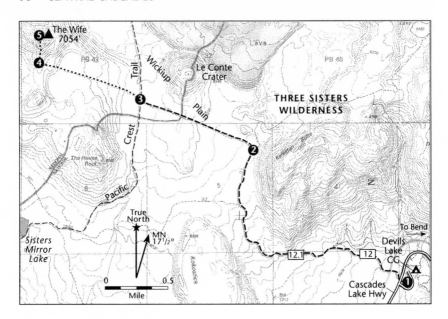

The Three Sisters Wilderness is famous for its namesake peaks but also contains many other mountains. The Wife is part of the Three Sisters group and is on the west side of the Three Sisters across the Wickiup Plain. This small, rugged peak is a wonderful scramble with remarkable views of the surrounding peaks. Scramblers on the summit may look across Separation Creek Meadow to the north and see the crumbly summit of The Husband, another little-known peak in the wilderness.

Trailhead directions: From Bend drive west on the Cascade Lakes Highway (Century Drive) 6.5 miles past Mount Bachelor Resort to the Devils Lake Campground on the south side of the road. You may park in the outer parking lot. The trailhead is northwest from the first lot; walk into the lot for the campground and turn left to the sign and register. A Northwest Forest Pass is required.

Route description: The approach to The Wife begins on a section of pack trail. Elk–Devils Lake Trail 12 is dusty and dry as it ascends gently to a trail junction in about 0.9 mile. The forest is a rich mix of conifers including Douglas fir, mountain hemlock, and western white pine. Bear right at the junction, heading toward the Pacific Crest Trail and Sisters Mirror Lake on Wickiup Plains Trail 12.1. Although animals are scarce due to the popularity of the trails, deer, elk, pika, or black bear may roam the area. Different bird species abound, including birds of prey.

Continue northward on the Wickiup Plains Trail as it passes a trail to Sister Mirror Lake at around 1.8 miles. In another 0.4 mile, turn northwest at the junction with the Moraine Lake Trail and head toward the PCT across the Wickiup Plain. The Wickiup Plain is a vast open area covered with bunch grass, which thrives in the ashy soil. While crossing the plain notice the Le

The Wife from across the Wickiup Plain

Conte Crater on the right. Evidence of volcanism is all around on this scramble approach.

The trail ends at 3.3 miles, but continue past the PCT junction northwest to and up through a small but visible drainage. In a short distance you will enter the trees and scramble through them, while maintaining a northwest heading toward the sandy plain ahead.

Cross the sandy plain and turn west to reach the south ridge. Ascend to the south ridge at 4.1 miles. Climb the steep slope northerly until you reach the summit ridge at 4.3 miles and a nice viewpoint. Turn right slightly (northeast) to ascend about 50 yards to the false summit, and scramble up some rocks to a chute. Traverse the upper part of the chute just below the ridge top and ascend to the summit. The summit is small and has cliffs on the east side.

The views are impressive down the vertical east face of The Wife. Surrounding peaks include the Middle and South Sisters. To the north is the North Sister remnant called The Husband, and in the distance are Mounts Washington and Jefferson. Mount Bachelor and Broken Top round out the views east.

12 BROKEN TOP

Elevation: 9175 feet

Difficulty: S3/T3

Round trip: 12 miles

Elevation gain: 3450 feet

Trip time: 8 hours

Time to summit: 5–6 hours

Best time of year: July to October

Map: USGS Broken Top

Contact: Deschutes National Forest, Bend–Fort Rock Ranger District

Special considerations: In early season you may need crampons and ice ax.

WAYPOINT ROUTE
1. Green Lakes Trailhead: 5400 feet (10T 601416mE 4875930mN)
2. Green Lakes area: 4.2 miles, 6541 feet (10T 601711mE 4881413mN)
3. Turn northeast onto climbers trail: 4.3 miles, 6546 feet (10T 601970mE 4881616mN)
4. Meadow crossing: 4.6 miles, 6800 feet (10T 602388mE 4881816mN)
5. Ridge junction: 5.2 miles, 7792 feet (10T 603405mE 4882136mN)
6. Viewpoint: 5.95 miles, 8916 feet (10T 604152mE 4881755mN)

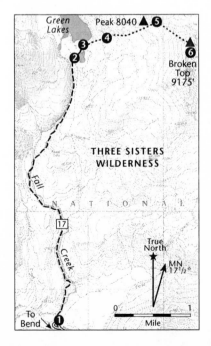

Broken Top is a highly dissected composite volcano and an older member of the Three Sisters group. The scramble to the viewpoint near the summit will give you a keen view of the exposed insides of a Cascade volcano. Glacial ice and erosion have carved away three sides of Broken Top, leaving a colorful remnant with crumbly basaltic lava and impressive rocky ridges. There are two major glaciers atop Broken Top; you will look down on the Bend Glacier as you make your final ascent. The scramble up the southwest ridge is athletic and will require balance and agility to avoid dislodging the loose talus while ascending.

Trailhead directions: From Bend drive west on the Cascade Lakes Highway (Century Drive) past Mount Bachelor.

At the Green Lakes Trailhead, turn north into the parking lot. Vault toilets are available. There is a Forest Service information booth staffed by rangers during the summer months. The trail begins at the sign marked Green Lakes Trail 17. A Northwest Forest Pass is required.

Route description: Follow Green Lakes Trail 17 across the creek and along a gently ascending route through the dense pine forest and past numerous waterfalls. Enjoy the wildflowers that include lupine, paintbrush, pink monkeyflower, and yellow composites. After climbing, the trail continues along Fall Creek and alongside a huge glacial moraine made of glistening gray obsidian from South Sister. At 2 miles you will pass the junction with the Moraine Lake Trail.

The Green Lakes Trail continues northward for 2.5 more miles to the

The shattered rock of Broken Top

Green Lakes area at 4.2 miles. Green Lakes is a beautiful, if overused, basin bounded by South Sister and Broken Top. From Green Lakes, continue on the right trail alongside the north side of the smaller lake. Continue along until waypoint 3 at 4.3 miles, turn right, and ascend on a sometimes-faint climbers trail that will cross a meadow at 4.6 miles and lead to the southwest ridge and a small saddle between Peak 8040 and Broken Top. The trail turns sharply left as it crests the small rise into the forest, which is easy to miss. Follow the trail, which climbs steeply through the forest and across grassy hills leading to the saddle and the ridge junction at 5.2 miles.

Once you gain the saddle turn right and spend the next mile or so scrambling carefully along the ridge crest, skirting steep drop-offs and lousy sections by dropping down on the right. The climbers path meanders on both sides of the ridge crest. Use your own judgment to choose which side to ascend. If you stay on the right side you reduce your exposure to some steep drop-offs.

As you gain in elevation, enjoy the views across to the north and the northeast. Behind you to the west, South Sister looms above. Approaching the summit you will pass a gendarme on the left, but continue toward the main summit. You will then work your way left and traverse over to the base of the summit block on loose, red pumice that threatens to give way with every step.

At the base of the summit block at 5.95 miles, about 200 feet below the summit, pause to enjoy the views and call it a day. There is a little room for further scrambling and exploration around the base of the summit.

13 TAM MCARTHUR RIM AND BROKEN HAND

Elevation: 8376 feet	
Difficulty: S2/T3	
Round trip: 9.6 miles	
Elevation gain: 1850 feet	
Trip time: 6 hours	
Time to summit: 3 hours	
Best time of year: July to mid-October	
Map: USGS North Sister	
Contact: Deschutes National Forest, Sisters Ranger District	

Special considerations: Self-issue permits are available at trailheads for entrance into the Three Sisters Wilderness.

WAYPOINT ROUTE
1. Tam McArthur Rim Trailhead: 6560 feet (10T 610244mE 4883777mN)
2. Viewpoint: 2.7 miles, 7732 feet (10T 608670mE 4882879mN)
3. Trail's end: 4.3 miles, 8000 feet (10T 606355mE 4882004mN)
4. Broken Hand viewpoint: 4.8 miles, 8290 feet (10T 605799mE 4881802mN)

The Three Sisters Wilderness is one of Oregon's most popular wilderness destinations. Flanked by the Willamette and Deschutes National Forests, the

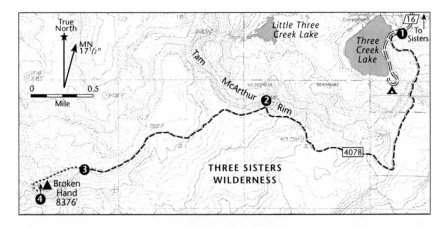

The hike across Tam McArthur Rim features stunning views of Broken Top.

wilderness highlights dense forests, volcanoes, pumice plains and lava flows, and dramatic peaks heavily eroded by glaciation. The Three Sisters group is an impressive collection of high Cascade peaks with enough variety for scramblers and alpinists alike. Tam McArthur Rim is a fault scarp with a vertical face dramatically framing Three Creek Lake. This scramble has incredible views of Broken Top across the rim plateau as you approach Broken Hand.

Trailhead directions: From Sisters drive south on South Elm Street, which turns into Deschutes County Road 16 and then becomes Forest Road 16. Drive about 16 miles following signs for Three Creek Lake. The trailhead is at 1.8 miles on the left after the pavement ends. The gravel road is not bad, but it does have some rough, rocky sections. Please register at the trailhead. There may be a portable toilet near the trailhead. The campground, about 0.5 mile down the road, has a small store and vault toilets but no running water. A Northwest Forest Pass is required.

Route description: Tam McArthur Rim Trail 4078 takes right off and climbs steeply through lodgepole pine, mountain hemlock, whitebark pine, and fir forest. It is dusty, rocky, and has a lot of exposed roots for the first mile. After going south for another 0.5 mile or so, the trail turns west. The wilderness boundary is about a mile from the trailhead.

The trail continues to climb through thinning forest as it winds up on the plateau of Tam McArthur Rim where it passes through stands of whitebark pine and mountain hemlock. Notice that some of the pines are bent at a 45-degree angle—their flexible limbs allow them to survive the harsh winds and heavy snowfall of this alpine environment.

As you approach 2.5 miles, take the right-hand fork to reach the rim viewpoint at 2.7 miles. The highlight is the view of Three Creek Lake below with 500-foot cliffs all around. Return to the trail and continue west toward Broken Top and Broken Hand. Pass through several sandy bowls, and then climb past a large snowfield on the right, heading for a red cinder mound with an obvious trail. This takes you up onto a ridge that leads to Broken Hand.

Hike and scramble through rocky sections past the high point of Tam McArthur Rim, and emerge onto a saddle leading to Broken Hand. As you approach Broken Hand continue west as the maintained trail ends. Scramble carefully around to either the right or the left along the base of Broken Hand. Going left leads to some wonderful views of the windswept south slopes with whitebark pines clinging to the rock. Return to the east corner and scramble around the right side of Broken Hand to get to another viewpoint at 4.8 miles.

As you traverse under nearly vertical, blocky rock with sloping ledges, it is tempting to try and scramble up various open sections. Do not give in to temptation—these routes are on terrible rock and end with hard rock climbing. Instead, continue westward along the base, carefully traversing across a steep section of red volcanic rock and then back to the blocky sections. Go to the western corner and scramble up toward a small gendarme right in front of Broken Top. This spot has just enough room for one person to stand—with great views. Do not continue up toward the summit—the rock is lousy and there is a lot of exposure. Downclimb back to the ramp you ascended and back down to the base.

Continue west toward Broken Top and go around until you are facing south and the vertical south wall of Broken Hand is to your left. Relax and enjoy the view of Broken Top's highly eroded summit and the Bend Glacier.

14 MOUNT BACHELOR

Elevation: 9065 feet

Difficulty: S2/T2

Round trip: 4.4 miles

Elevation gain: 2713 feet

Trip time: 5–6 hours

Time to summit: 3–4 hours

Best time of year: June

Map: USGS Mount Bachelor

Contact: Deschutes National Forest, Bend–Fort Rock Ranger District

Special considerations: Route is open only after the resort closes for the season. You may need crampons and an ice ax.

WAYPOINT ROUTE

1. Dutchman Flat Sno-Park: 6352 feet (10T 607230mE 4872556mN)
2. Cirque: 1.5 miles, 7994 feet (10T 605608mE 4870845mN)
3. Mount Bachelor: 2.2 miles, 9065 feet (10T 605287mE 4870219mN)

Mount Bachelor is a central Oregon landmark with its distinctive symmetric shape and isolation from the peaks of the Three Sisters group. Known as Bachelor Butte originally, the mountain was renamed in the wake of the Mount Bachelor ski area's increasing popularity. Now known for its snow sports, Bachelor is also a good scrambling destination. Once the ski area closes the slopes are uncrowded and you can get a close look at the northside cirque and summit features without the distraction of skiers or snowboarders. The views of the Three Sisters and Broken Top are amazing as you ascend the northeast side of the mountain. On a clear day the many lakes and central Oregon Cascade peaks add to the worthy summit view.

Trailhead directions: From Bend drive west on the Cascade Lakes Highway (Century Drive) about 3 miles past the Sunriver turnoff. Turn right into the Dutchman Flat Sno-Park.

Route description: Begin the scramble by crossing the highway and walking back toward Bend about 25 feet before crossing into the forest southwest toward Bachelor. Cross the resort road and continue southwest onto the snow slopes of the ski area. It will seem a little weird at first, hiking on a ski slope, but that feeling will fade quickly as you ascend and start getting views northward of the Three Sisters peaks.

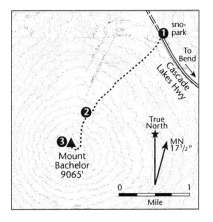

Shortly you will approach a Y junction where two ski runs meet; bear left and continue up the snow slope. You will be flanked by tall, dense stands of trees, which will gradually be replaced by scattered mixed stands of mountain hemlock and whitebark pine that add a touch of natural beauty to the stark slopes. Ascend south-southwest up to a spur of rock around 7500 feet. Keep heading south-southwest, passing more rocky spurs and a chairlift.

You will eventually cross the large snowfield that leads to the cirque (at 1.5 miles) on the north side of the summit. Cross the bowl southerly, heading for the prominent skyline ridge to the south. Ascend the snow or loose talus and scree to gain the ridge. Continue south, then west, to cross the broad mountaintop to the summit.

The summit is a place of contradiction—great views into the undeveloped Three Sisters Wilderness contrasting with the various structures of the ski area. Enjoy the view and take some time to walk around the summit to

Scramble up the snowy slopes of Mount Bachelor. The Three Sisters are in the background.

check out the geological features. There will probably be some kind of barrier around a depression in the snow called a "collapse crater." Do not venture past the barrier; the walls of the crater drop away from the rim sharply.

Cascade peaks are visible in almost all directions. Diamond Peak is to the south, and north views include Mount Washington. There is no escaping the dominance of the Three Sisters peaks, which stand out against the northwestern sky.

For a quick and fun descent, walk around the summit to a point adjacent to the chairlift. From the top of the chair it is a great glissade down the steep slope. Slide down as far as you can, then walk northeasterly back to the sno-park.

15 MOUNT YORAN

Elevation: 7100 feet	
Difficulty: S3/T4	
Round trip: 8 miles	
Elevation gain: 2033 feet	
Trip time: 6–7 hours	
Time to summit: 3 hours	
Best time of year: June to November	
Map: USGS Diamond Peak	
Contact: Willamette National Forest, Middle Fork Ranger District	
Special considerations: Many mosquitoes right after the snow melts.	

WAYPOINT ROUTE

1. Vivian Lake Trailhead: 5320 feet (10T 565295mE 4824871mN)
2. Northeast corner of Divide Lake/climbers trail: 3.7 miles, 6300 feet (10T 569814mE 4823205mN)
3. Below gendarme: 3.9 miles, 6700 feet (10T 569953mE 4823359mN)
4. Mount Yoran: 4.0 miles, 7100 feet (10T 569993mE 4823494mN)

Mount Yoran is an old eroded volcanic remnant in the Diamond Peak Wilderness just south of Waldo Lake. The peak is north of the Cascade Crest, which bisects this densely forested wilderness of true firs, mountain hemlock, and western white pine. In early season you can expect to see alpine wildflowers including lupine, Indian paintbrush, penstemon, and bear grass. Mount Yoran is a challenging scramble in a quiet and picturesque wilderness area.

   Trailhead directions: From Oakridge drive 2 miles east to Kitson Springs

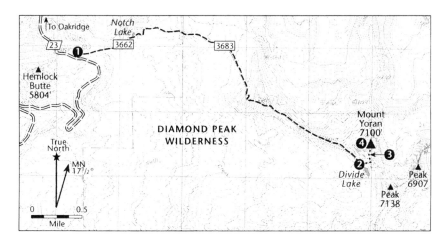

Crumbling slopes of Mount Yoran from near Divide Lake

County Road (follow sign to Hills Creek Reservoir) and turn right. At the intersection the road turns into Forest Road 23. Continue straight ahead for 14 miles to Hemlock Butte Pass. The Vivian Lake Trailhead is on the left and across from Hemlock Butte. The road is well signed and is gravel for about the last 4 miles. Parking is at the turnaround area.

Route description: Vivian Lake Trail 3662 begins at 5320 feet and enters the wilderness right after the trailhead. A short distance in from the trailhead is the self-register and information bulletin board. The trail then starts a series of short ascents, alternating with flat sections through the mixed conifer forest and bear grass.

At 0.4 mile the trail goes past Diamond Peak Tie Trail 4239. In another 0.5 mile, after passing Notch Lake, the trail meets Mount Yoran Trail 3683.

Turn right here to hike to Divide Lake. The Mount Yoran Trail goes through dense forest and meadows, climbs up a ridge, and then drops down to the lake. In 3.7 miles you reach the northeast corner of Divide Lake, where the scramble route begins. There are some nice spots around Divide Lake to take photographs of Mount Yoran.

Turn left (east) on a climbers trail toward the saddle between Yoran and Peak 7138. Scramble up the slope a short distance, then turn north on a faint climbers trail that weaves up a scree and talus slope. Head for the gendarme evident above. At 3.9 miles bear left below the prominent gendarme and proceed north up the steep chute on moderate rock (staying to either side of the chute to avoid rockfall and loose rock). Continue to an obvious notch in the ridge, where you will scramble up and over to another chute. At this notch the gendarme will be behind you and your feet will be approximately level with its top. Cross the chute by traversing, staying high and on solid rock, heading northeast to the false summit.

At the false summit continue scrambling up on the right side of the ridge, carefully proceeding to the small summit with a rock wall. The views are great of Odell Lake, the Willamette Pass Ski Area, Diamond Peak, and in the distance the Three Sisters and Cowhorn Mountain. There are dense trees in all directions.

On the descent scramble back across the ridge, then down to the chute. Traverse up high and back to the notch then cross over to the other side by using the gendarme as a checkpoint.

Additional scrambles: There are two other peaks in close proximity to Divide Lake. To scramble to the summit of Peak 7138 ascend the northwest ridge from the saddle south of Mount Yoran. Keep to the south of the ridge on the loose scree and talus, scrambling around the steeper sections of rock. You can also reach Peak 6907 from the same saddle. Head east then south from the saddle to gain the south ridge and scramble to the top. Both of these peaks are along the Cascade Crest.

16 DIAMOND PEAK

Elevation: 8744 feet

Difficulty: S3/T2

Round trip: 10 miles

Elevation gain: 3255 feet

Trip time: 8–9 hours

Time to summit: 5 hours

Best time of year: July to October

Map: USGS Diamond Peak

Contact: Willamette National Forest, Middle Fork Ranger District

Special considerations: Many mosquitoes in early season.

WAYPOINT ROUTE

1. Diamond Peak Trailhead: 5489 feet (10T 568616mE 4812767mN)
2. Rockpile Trail 3632: 1.8 miles, 5951 feet (10T 568070mE 4815056mN)
3. Scramble off trail: 3.1 miles, 6045 feet (10T 569286mE 4815770mN)
4. Rock spur: 4.1 miles, 7097 feet (10T 568875mE 4817310mN)
5. False summit: 4.7 miles, 8421 feet (10T 568928mE 4818287mN)
6. Diamond Peak: 5.0 miles, 8744 feet (10T 568835mE 4818790mN)

Diamond Peak, south of Willamette Pass, is a distinctive landmark with its broad flanks and often-snowy slopes. The Diamond Peak Wilderness is home to its namesake peak and several other eroded volcanic remnants along the Cascade Crest. Odell Lake and Crescent Lake form the north and south boundaries on the eastern side of the wilderness. Although Diamond Peak is not the oldest peak in the wilderness, it is the highest and its summit views command respect. The surrounding forest is dense with a mixture of remaining old-growth and second-growth trees. Diamond Peak is a pleasant early summer scramble with dramatic views all along the upper ridge and summit.

Trailhead directions: From Crescent Lake drive southwest on Forest Road 60 about 5 miles. The road to Summit Lake is on the west side of the road and is a very sharp right turn. Drive west on the very rough FR 6010 for about 6 miles, past Summit Lake. At the junction with FR 380, continue west on FR 380.

Looking at the ridge scramble across to the summit of Diamond Peak, from the false summit

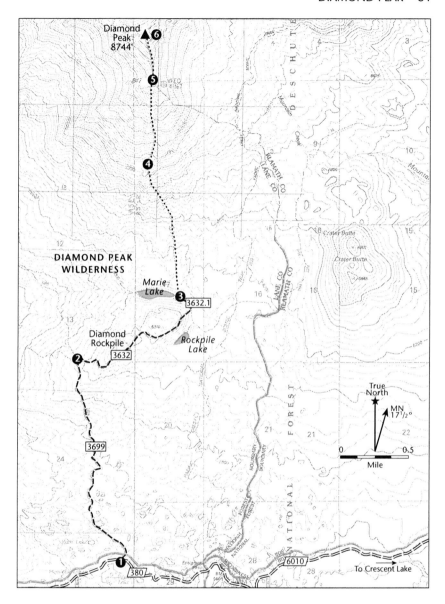

You will pass the Pacific Crest Trail Trailhead in about 0.1 mile, then Emigrant Pass. Keep driving west until you reach the trailhead in about 1 mile.

Route description: Diamond Peak Trail 3699 skirts the southwest corner of the wilderness heading northward. For the first 1.3 miles or so the trail barely climbs at all, instead winding northward among glacial tarns. The combination of snowmelt and glacial pools is the perfect breeding ground for mosquitoes—there are clouds of them in early season.

The wilderness is beautiful with its dense forest of mountain hemlock, lodgepole pine, and true fir. Seasonal wildflowers form bright spots along the way as you begin to ascend toward the junction with Rockpile Trail 3632 at 1.8 miles.

The Rockpile Trail heads easterly past Diamond Rockpile to a trail junction north of Rockpile Lake. The trail climbs rather gently before descending to the junction with Marie Lake Trail 3632.1 at 3 miles.

Turn north onto the Marie Lake Trail and head north toward Diamond Peak's south ridge. In the early summer there will likely be snow covering parts of the trail here. It does not hamper your progress though. Just head north past Marie Lake's eastern tip toward the mountain, leaving the trail at about 3.1 miles.

For the next mile you will be scrambling through the trees, heading slightly northwest toward the more open south ridge, where you will gain a prominent rock spur at 4.1 miles. Scramble up and across several spurs of rock and gain the main ridge.

Once on the ridge continue north toward the upper mountain and false summit. Soon you will leave the trees completely for the more open ridge of scree leading to the false summit. Gain the false summit at 4.7 miles, where there is a rock shelter in the corner and great views back to Summit Lake and Oregon's southern Cascades.

From the false summit begin the ridge scramble to the summit. Keep mostly to the ridge crest as you make your way north the final 0.3 mile to the summit. Keeping on the crest is more challenging than skirting the sometimes steep, blocky sections by dropping down on the gentler slope below. The red cinders are a rich contrast as you ascend the final loose slope to the rounded summit. The summit views of the Central and Southern Cascades are wonderful.

Return the way you came.

17 COWHORN MOUNTAIN

Elevation: 7664 feet

Difficulty: S2/T2

Round trip: 9.2 miles

Elevation gain: 2007 feet

Trip time: 7 hours

Time to summit: 3–4 hours

Best time of year: July to October

Map: USGS Cowhorn Mountain

Contact: Deschutes National Forest, Crescent Ranger District

Special considerations: Forest Road 60 (Windigo Pass Road) usually has deep snow until July; call the ranger district to find out when the road opens.

WAYPOINT ROUTE

1. PCT Trailhead: 5821 feet (10T 578403mE 4801878mN)
2. Leave trail at ridge junction: 3.9 miles, 7075 feet (10T 576029mE 4805014mN)
3. Rocky ridge: 4.3 miles, 7250 feet (10T 576345mE 4805402mN)
4. Cowhorn Mountain: 4.6 miles, 7664 feet (10T 576708mE 4805430mN)

Cowhorn Mountain is a highly eroded Central Cascades volcano just south of Crescent Lake in the Oregon Cascades Recreation Area (OCRA). Established in 1984, the OCRA contains 156,900 acres of land managed by the Forest Service. The OCRA is flanked on the north by the Diamond Peak Wilderness and on the south by the Mount Thielsen Wilderness, and offers visitors a range of scrambling, hiking, and climbing opportunities. The approach to Cowhorn Mountain begins in mixed conifer forest, which gives way to a short ridge scramble on fairly solid rock. Along the ridge the forest changes to subalpine trees that include whitebark pines. Cowhorn, which at one time had a summit spire, was once called Little Cowhorn to distinguish it from Big Cowhorn, but Big Cowhorn has since been renamed Mount Thielsen.

Trailhead directions: From Diamond Lake drive north on State Route 138 and turn right on Forest Road 60 (Windigo Pass Road). Follow FR 60 northeast to Windigo Pass and the parking area for the Pacific Crest Trail.

Route description: This scramble begins on the PCT and ascends steadily

The view of Diamond Peak from the summit of Cowhorn Peak

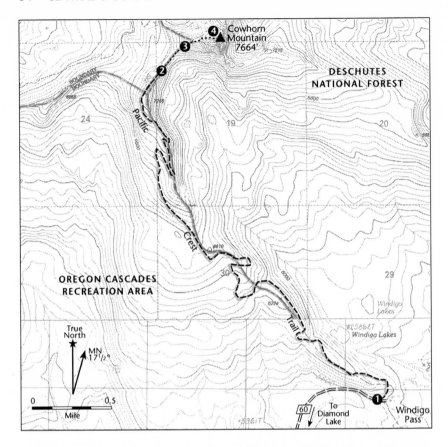

through thick, mixed-conifer forest that includes lodgepole pine and true fir. As the trail begins to head north, note that the forest is dense and feels overgrown. As you continue northward through the trees, approaching Cowhorn Mountain, the forest thins a bit and there are abundant alpine wildflowers in early season. The bright columbine and blue penstemon are a welcome contrast after the darkness of the forest.

After crossing a rocky ridge, with great views of the scramble route, you will descend slightly to the saddle and junction with the ridge, where you leave the PCT at 3.9 miles. The ridge scramble to the summit is mostly east for about the next 0.5 mile. The scramble route begins in the forest, which quickly thins out into an open rocky ridge at 4.3 miles. Continue upslope as you keep ascending and scrambling up rocks as you head to the false summit.

After enjoying the view up the summit ridge, you will cross a beautifully banded cinder saddle leading to the final scramble to the summit. The final pitch is up solid blocks with whitebark pines scattered throughout the rocks. The summit is small and the rock relatively fragile. Be aware of the steep drop-off on the east side of the summit. But do enjoy the sweeping views of Diamond Peak, the Three Sisters, Crescent Lake, and Mount Thielsen.

18 MOUNT BAILEY

Elevation: 8368 feet	
Difficulty: S3/T2	
Round trip: 10 miles	
Elevation gain: 3000 feet	
Trip time: 6 hours	
Time to summit: 3–4 hours	
Best time of year: June to October	
Map: USGS Diamond Lake	
Contact: Umpqua National Forest, Diamond Lake Ranger District	

Diamond Lake and Mount Thielsen from Mount Bailey

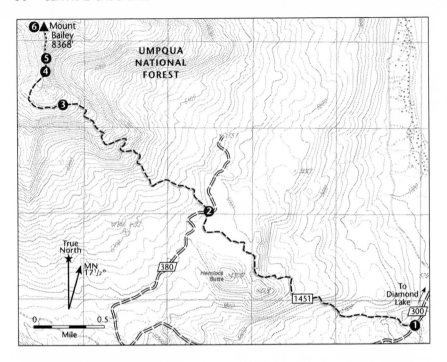

WAYPOINT ROUTE

1. Mount Bailey Trailhead: 5245 feet (10T 567956mE 4774742mN)
2. FR 380 junction: 2.1 miles, 6041 feet (10T 565471mE 4776011mN)
3. Trail turns west: 4.0 miles, 7758 feet (10T 563725mE 4777230mN)
4. False summit: 4.5 miles, 8141 feet (10T 563514mE 4777609mN)
5. Notch: 4.7 miles, 8145 feet (10T 563512mE 4777913mN)
6. Mount Bailey: 5.0 miles, 8368 feet (10T 63520mE 4778130mN)

Mount Bailey is a Cascade shield volcano west of Diamond Lake and north of Crater Lake National Park. The long summit ridge is an easy scramble on typical Cascade rock—nice to look at but lousy for hiking. Approaching the summit, scramblers will encounter striking whitebark pines, particularly along the windswept west slope. From the summit scramblers will enjoy views of Mount Thielsen and Diamond Lake to the east. Wildflowers along the route feature Indian paintbrush, lupine, and penstemon.

Trailhead directions: From Diamond Lake take Forest Road 4795 south then west to FR 300 (a dirt road) just past Silent Creek. Turn left (south) on FR 300 and proceed less than 0.3 mile to the well-marked trailhead. There is ample parking on the left. The Mount Bailey Trailhead is on the right.

Route description: Mount Bailey Trail 1451 begins by climbing through a dense subalpine forest of lodgepole pine, western white pine, and mountain hemlock. Just before 2 miles, the trail climbs more steeply. At 2.1 miles the trail is bisected by FR 380, a spur road with limited access.

Mount Bailey scrambler on the route to summit from false summit

At about 2.5 miles the trail begins to climb in earnest. As you approach 3 miles and crest a small rise, turn to look eastward at Mount Thielsen—the view is stunning. From here Mount Thielsen looks impossible to climb!

The trail continues climbing, sometimes very steeply, as it becomes more rocky and rough. Eventually you emerge from the now-scrubby pine forest onto a pumice landscape and continue contouring to the false summit. The trail swings westward at 4 miles around a huge bowl as it continues to the false summit. This part of the mountain is windswept and seems quite barren after the dense forest below.

After enjoying the views from the false summit at 4.5 miles, look north to the summit. Head down and across a pumice saddle and begin scrambling up along a rocky spine, just to the west and below the rocks. A faint climbers trail is sometimes evident. At about 8100 feet and 4.7 miles, 0.25 mile from the summit, scramble up and through a notch in the rocks and head up to the ridge above. Intersect the ridge or a climbers trail and head north to the summit along the ridge crest. From the summit take in the stunning views all around, including Mount Thielsen, and enjoy the rugged character of Mount Bailey's upper terrain.

MOUNT THIELSEN

Elevation: 9182 feet

Difficulty: S3/T5

Round trip: 8.8 miles

Elevation gain: 3820 feet

Trip time: 7–8 hours

Time to summit: 4–5 hours

Best time of year: July to October

Map: USGS Mount Thielsen

Contact: Umpqua National Forest, Diamond Lake Ranger District

Special considerations: The correct location for the Mount Thielsen Trailhead is on the Umpqua National Forest Diamond Lake Ranger District map. It is incorrect on the USGS Mount Thielsen map.

WAYPOINT ROUTE
1. Mount Thielsen Trailhead: 5400 feet (10T 571032mE 4777198mN)
2. PCT junction: 3.9 miles, 7267 feet (10T 574976mE 4777570mN)
3. Right around outcrops: 4.2 miles, 8922 feet (10T 575890mE 4777944mN)
4. Mount Thielsen: 4.4 miles, 9182 feet (10T 576007mE 4777990mN)

Mount Thielsen's summit spire is dramatic against the skyline north of Crater Lake National Park. Once called Big Cowhorn, Mount Thielsen's fractured slopes feature an unrelenting scramble up the west ridge. You will balance atop precarious piles of talus as you ascend toward the final vertical pitch to the small summit. Mount Thielsen is known as the "lightning rod of the Cascades." This overused phrase rings true when you view Thielsen's summit from a distance and when you observe the weather-beaten rock up close. Managed by the Umpqua National Forest, the Mount Thielsen Wilderness is for through-hikers, backpackers, and scramblers. Although you may approach the scramble from the south using the Pacific Crest Trail, most people will want to use the Mount Thielsen Trail on the east side of Diamond Lake.

Trailhead directions: From the junction of State Routes 230 and 138, east of Diamond Lake, drive north 1.5 miles on SR 138. The trailhead is on the right side, clearly marked, with parking for about fifteen cars. There are toilets available. A Northwest Forest Pass is required.

Route description: Mount Thielsen Trail 1456 begins climbing gently through the thick mixed-conifer forest. As you ascend, the lodgepole pine that dominates at lower elevations will give way to mountain hemlock and whitebark pine.

Mount Thielsen scramblers ascending talus slope to summit pinnacle

Looking at Mount Thielsen from the scramble start

On the left, glimpses of Mount Bailey appear through the trees. The junction with Spruce Ridge Trail 1458 is at about 1 mile. Shortly after the junction, Mount Thielsen becomes visible through the trees. The trail continues to climb, occasionally steeply, through the forest and past the Mount Thielsen Wilderness boundary. At 2 miles views of Thielsen improve, taunting you through the trees. At about 3.9 miles is the intersection with the PCT. This ridge area is well signed and has great views of Mount Bailey, Diamond Lake, and the Crater Lake peaks. There are also views north of Diamond Peak, Cowhorn, and South Sister.

As you emerge onto the ridge, continue ascending on a climbers trail that skirts the left side of the ridge. This trail winds around to the right side of the ridge, and there climbs steadily to the rocky ridge leading directly to the summit. Scramble up to 8400 feet where the steep slope becomes noticeably rougher and more difficult to navigate. Here the slope consists of broken talus and scree, and every step is a gamble. Head up to the two large rock outcrops below the summit spire. Bear slightly right, and go around the right of the larger outcrop (at 4.2 miles, 8922 feet), continuing up to the base of the summit spire. Here you can catch your breath and enjoy the views of the rugged east side of the mountain. If you continue to the summit, you can drop your pack here.

To reach the summit, scramble up the spire by picking a route you are comfortable with. Looking up from the east corner, there are many ascent routes. There are plenty of handholds, ledges, and gullies. The rock is fairly solid, but test each handhold before committing to it. Sign the summit log, enjoy the views, and downclimb carefully to the base of the spire.

SOUTHERN CASCADES

20 MOUNT SCOTT

Elevation: 8929 feet	
Difficulty: S2/T1	
Round trip: 5 miles	
Elevation gain: 1479 feet	
Trip time: 3 hours	
Time to summit: 1.5 hours	
Best time of year: July to October	
Map: USGS Crater Lake West	
Contact: Crater Lake National Park, Steel Information Center	

WAYPOINT ROUTE
1. Mount Scott Trailhead: 7683 feet (10T 579256mE 4753197mN)
2. Mount Scott: 2.5 miles, 8929 feet (10T 580393mE 4752519mN)

Crater Lake National Park contains opportunities for scrambling to the top of Mount Mazama's last remaining high peaks, remnants from this once-giant volcano. Mount Scott, a broad peak east of Crater Lake, is the highest of those peaks. When Mazama collapsed, the almost 2000-foot-deep caldera became what is now Crater Lake. This is one of the largest bodies of freshwater in the United States. Mount Scott is on the eastern side of the lake and has an active lookout atop its summit. The summit is approached from the south via a ridge trail, which allows scramblers to reach other points along the upper mountain. Although largely a trail hike, Mount Scott is a good warm-up for the more challenging peaks in the area.

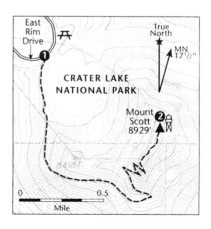

Trailhead directions: From the Crater Lake North Entrance, turn left onto East Rim Drive. At about 10.8 miles, just past the picnic spot, is the trailhead parking area on the left. Mount Scott is right in front of you, the peak with the large avalanche chute and

Along the upper mountain you have stunning views of Crater Lake and its rim peaks.

a lookout tower on top. Park and walk west to the beginning of the trail.

Route description: The Mount Scott Trail begins inconspicuously through a meadow and then gently climbs through the mixed-conifer forest. Here, at higher elevations than many Oregon forests, the main trees are mountain hemlock, Douglas fir, white pine, and whitebark pine. There are also many varieties of wildflowers in early season including Indian paintbrush, penstemon, forget-me-not, wild onion, and buttercup. The trail goes south for the first 0.7 mile while contouring around the northwest ridge. The views are already great, with Mount McLoughlin to the south and Klamath Lake to the east.

At 7900 to 8000 feet, the trail turns more eastward and begins climbing 200 feet. It then dips south again before the switchbacks begin. The trail turns north and the well-graded switchbacks lead up the southwest corner of the peak. The views are stunning—Crater Lake looks more dramatic as you ascend and there are also vistas that include the surrounding peaks.

As you near the summit the lookout comes into view. Turn the corner and ascend the last, flatter section of the rocky summit ridge. If you pause a minute you will notice, on your right, a rocky upper ridge. Scramble up onto this ridge and continue right to its high point. This viewpoint reveals the stark ridges and impressive drop-offs of the mountain's south side. Scramble around for the best views, but be careful of all the loose rock.

When through, return to the summit trail and visit the lookout area. Past the lookout you may scramble around for good views. You will be right above the wide avalanche chute, which leads down almost to the parking area.

Use the trail to descend back to the parking area.

21 UNION PEAK

Elevation: 7709 feet

Difficulty: S2/T3

Round trip: 9 miles

Elevation gain: 1780 feet

Trip time: 4 hours

Time to summit: 2–3 hours

Best time of year: July to mid-October

Map: USGS Union Peak

Contact: Crater Lake National Park, Steel Information Center

WAYPOINT ROUTE

1. PCT Trailhead: 6180 feet (10T 567062mE 4746636mN)
2. Union Peak Trail junction: 2.2 miles, 6519 feet (10T 565825mE 4743320mN)
3. Union Peak: 4.5 miles, 7709 feet (10T 563586mE 4742139mN)

Crater Lake National Park is Oregon's only national park. The centerpiece, Crater Lake, is one of the deepest lakes in the world. It is the caldera of the ancient volcano, Mount Mazama, and the peaks surrounding the lake are all that remains of the mountain. Union Peak, in the southwest corner of the park, is a volcanic remnant and was first climbed in 1862. The Pacific Crest Trail provides the well-maintained approach for this scramble. Although the scramble is on a trail, the upper section of the mountain is loose and the trail is difficult to follow. Note that the Park Service completely rerouted the Union Peak Trail, a project lasting three years that was completed in late summer 2003.

Trailhead directions: From the Crater Lake South Entrance go west on State Route 62. Approximately 1 mile past the South Entrance is a Pacific Crest Trail sign indicating a parking lot on the south (left) side of the road and trail access. The trail begins from the parking lot (there is a metal sign indicating the trails and distances).

Route description: The PCT leaves the parking area and begins gently climbing through a sometimes dense forest of lodgepole pine, mountain hemlock, and western white pine. This section of the PCT is largely level and does not ascend or descend much for the first 2 miles. The junction with the new

Looking down a rock-filled chute to the dense pine forest from the summit of Union Peak

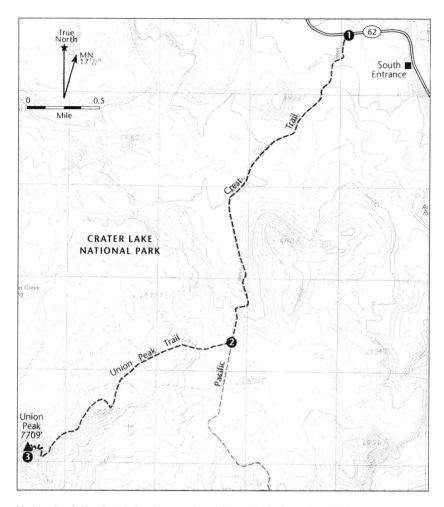

Union Peak Trail at 2.2 miles is about 0.5 mile before the old junction.

Turn right onto the Union Peak Trail. This trail meanders through the forest, ascending along a rocky ridge and passing a fine viewpoint before reaching a saddle just east of Union Peak. Continue across a boulder slope along a great trail, below the dramatic rocky cliffs of Union Peak's southeast side. The trail will pass through the boulder field and begin to switchback up a red pumice slope to reach the upper mountain. From here, although there is less than 0.5 mile remaining, you still must ascend 700 feet.

The trail climbs steeply on switchbacks that get shorter and steeper. Scramble through a rocky section and continue on the switchbacks. About 40 feet below the summit, the switchbacks peter out into a scramble trail up to the rocky summit. The summit is not that large, but the views are grand of the surrounding national park lands. Mount McLoughlin is the highlight in the southern sky. Enjoy the views and descend back to the trail.

22 ABBOTT BUTTE AND ELEPHANT HEAD

Elevations: 6131 feet, 5871 feet

Difficulty: S2/T2

Round trip: 9.4 miles

Elevation gain: 2350 feet

Trip time: 6 hours

Time to summit: 3 hours

Best time of year: July to October

Map: USGS Abbott Butte

Contact: Umpqua National Forest, Tiller Ranger District; Rogue River National Forest, Prospect Ranger District

The abandoned lookout atop Abbott Butte

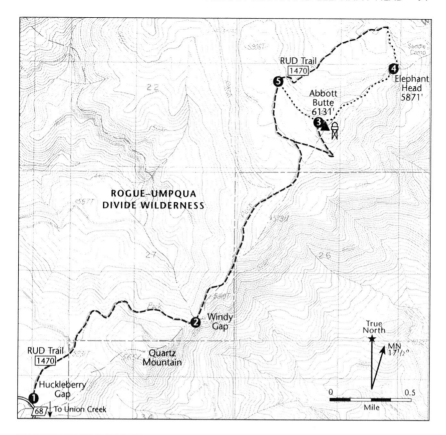

WAYPOINT ROUTE

1. Rogue–Umpqua Divide Trailhead: 5389 feet (10T 533994mE 4751697mN)
2. Windy Gap: 1.3 miles, 5142 feet (10T 535645mE 4752584mN)
3. Abbott Butte: 3.2 miles, 6131 feet (10T 536850mE 4754406mN)
4. Elephant Head: 3.9 miles, 5871 feet (10T 537487mE 4754909mN)
5. RUD Trail: 5.0 miles, 5854 feet (10T 536393mE 4754828mN)

The Rogue–Umpqua Divide Wilderness is a narrow, 33,000-acre wilderness in the western Cascades west of Crater Lake National Park. This wilderness is full of dense forest and high ridges. The western Cascades are older than the high Cascades and the mountains are more eroded and lower elevation than the young volcanoes along the Cascade crest. This wilderness scramble will provide you with a look at an unknown area with abundant spring wildflowers, dense mountain hemlock, and true fir.

   Trailhead directions: From Union Creek drive south on State Route 62. Turn right on Forest Road 68 at the sign for the Woodruff Bridge and Abbott Creek Campground. Drive westerly on FR 68 about 12 miles until you reach the parking area at Huckleberry Gap. The trailhead for the Rogue–Umpqua Divide Trail is on the east side of the road.

Route description: Rogue–Umpqua Divide (RUD) Trail 1470 winds it way through the dense forests, mountains, and ridges of the remote Rogue–Umpqua Divide Wilderness. The trail begins in the south wilderness at Huckleberry Gap. You head north through the forest, passing some basalt columns as you contour around Quartz Mountain along the way to Windy Gap.

The trail descends eastward to Windy Gap at 1.3 miles, a lovely and lonely spot just northeast of Quartz Mountain. From Windy Gap the trail climbs along the ridge northeast to Abbott Butte. The trail is mostly the RUD Trail, but it is entwined with an old CCC road that packers now use.

Continue northward to a spur that leads to Abbott Butte. You may as well take the trail to the old, abandoned lookout. Enjoy the broad summit (at 3.2 miles), but do not attempt to climb to the 1939 lookout tower. It is not safe.

Elephant Head is a vertical rocky outcrop just northeast of Abbott Butte. To reach a viewpoint at the top of the cliffs descend the trail off Abbott Butte's summit southwest for a short distance. Then, work your way around the northwest corner of the butte and continue northeast to a point above the cliffs of Elephant Head. You will first cross the northern tip of Abbott Butte, then descend to a spot right above the vertical cliffs of Elephant Head at 3.9 miles.

When you are through with the dramatic view down the north face of Elephant Head, you can take in the view of this face from the bottom. Retrace your steps to the northwest corner of Abbott Butte. Turn northwest for about 0.4 mile to reach RUD Trail 1470 at 5 miles. Turn right and hike along the trail, descending to a small pond. About 0.1 mile past the pond, turn off the trail and scramble back up to the base of Elephant Head's vertical north face.

Retrace your steps to the RUD Trail and follow it back to your car at Huckleberry Gap.

23 VENUS, JUPITER, AND LUCIFER

Elevations: 7315 feet, 7415 feet, 7474 feet	
Difficulty: S3/T2	
Round trip: 9.8 miles	
Elevation gain: 3206 feet	
Trip time: 6–7 hours	
Time to summits: 3 hours	
Best time of year: July to October	
Map: USGS Devils Peak	
Contact: Rogue River–Siskiyou National Forest, Butte Falls Ranger District	

Special considerations: Prepare for lots of mosquitoes in early season. Snow lingers on the high ridges into July, particularly in the forest or on northern exposures.

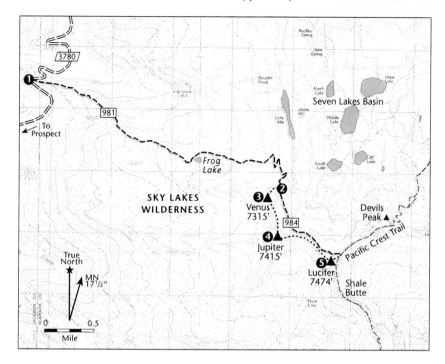

WAYPOINT ROUTE

1. Seven Lakes Trailhead: 5250 feet (10T 558632mE 4723413mN)
2. Leave trail: 3.6 miles, 6960 feet (10T 562805mE 4721725mN)
3. Venus: 3.8 miles, 7315 feet (10T 562583mE 4721585mN)
4. Jupiter: 4.3 miles, 7415 feet (10T 571653mE 4687619mN)
5. Lucifer: 4.9 miles, 7474 feet (10T 571483mE 4688364mN)

The Sky Lakes Wilderness, in the Southern Cascades, is south of Crater Lake National Park and encompasses nearly 120,000 acres of forested wildlands. Sky Lakes is home to the stunning Seven Lakes Basin. Venus, Jupiter, and Lucifer peaks are among the high points just south of the beautiful basin. This scramble is a three-summit traverse with views of peaks along the Cascade crest and of the dense forestlands of the Rogue River and Winema National Forests.

    Trailhead directions: From Prospect drive east on the Prospect–Butte Falls Highway, also called Red Blanket Road. Drive east almost 4 miles and turn left onto Bessie Creek Road, which is also Forest Road 37. FR 37 is paved partially and may be rough on the gravel sections. Continue driving on FR 37, crossing a couple of bridges and passing the Imnaha Campground turn-off. At about 13 miles you will turn left on FR 3780. The trailhead is in about 4.3 miles on the east side of the road and is clearly marked. There is parking on the west side of the road for several cars. There are no services.

    Route description: Seven Lakes Trail 981 ascends eastward away from

The summit of Jupiter is covered with talus, Devils Peak in the background

the road on a rocky, rough track resembling a creek bed in places. The trees are dense, with heavy shrubs and flowers contributing to the thick understory. Wild roses, huckleberry, fir, mountain hemlock, and western white pine are just a few of the species represented.

After climbing steadily for almost 2 miles you will pass Frog Lake. Here the trail flattens out for a short distance before resuming the steady ascent up the ridge.

The trail begins climbing again, winding up the ridge on a few switchbacks to a trail junction with Devils Peak Trail 984. Turn right onto the Devils Peak Trail for a very short hike to the scramble point. Scramble off the trail at about 3.6 miles, west through the trees then southwest up the loose talus and scree ridge of Venus. Bear right up the ridge to stay on more-solid rock, although on this slope "solid" is a rough description.

The smallish summit of Venus has a good view south of Mount McLoughlin. You can also scout the remainder of the route from here, following the obvious ridge south to Jupiter, then curving east to the summit of Lucifer.

Backtrack to descend Venus to the north, then traverse around the summit of Venus on the west side, ascending past the summit to once more get onto the ridge crest. Continue mostly on the crest then cross over to the east side down to the saddle. Do not attempt to scramble across the summit directly south—the ridge is narrow and very exposed.

Ascend the ridge crest to the summit of Jupiter at 4.3 miles, mostly keeping directly on the crest of Jupiter's north ridge. The summit has an east-west orientation and is covered with gray talus and some wildflowers among the rock. As you walk west to explore the longish summit, you will pass a couple of depressions in the talus along with some mountain hemlock. Do not disturb the rocky depressions. They may be old Klamath Indian spiritual sites.

Descend the east ridge about 0.2 mile to the saddle. If you choose to descend back to the trail, this saddle is a good descent point. To ascend to the summit of Lucifer, turn south and ascend the northwest ridge. First scramble up the short rocky section to gain a broad bench, then continue up the steep summit ridge to the top at 4.9 miles.

From the summit the views south reveals the appropriateness of the name "Shale Butte" for the nearby peak. Shale Butte is actually plates of lava that resemble shale. Devils and Lee Peaks are northeast and you can just see into the Seven Lakes Basin to the north. Also enjoy the views of Upper Klamath Lake and Pelican Butte to the southeast.

Descend northeast to the junction of the Pacific Crest Trail and the Devils Peak Trail. Turn left and hike west back to the junction with the Seven Lakes Trail to return to the trailhead. You may also descend directly east to the PCT and then turn north a short distance to reach the junction described above.

In southern Oregon the bulk of Mount McLoughlin dominates most summit views, from the Venus summit.

24 DEVILS PEAK

Elevation: 7582 feet

Difficulty: S3/T2

Round trip: 11.7 miles

Elevation gain: 2442 feet

Trip time: 6–7 hours

Time to summit: 3–4 hours

Best time of year: July to October

Map: USGS Devils Peak

Contact: Rogue River–Siskiyou National Forest, Butte Falls Ranger District

Special considerations: Prepare for lots of mosquitoes in early season. Snow lingers on the high ridges, particularly in the forest or on northern exposures, into July.

WAYPOINT ROUTE

1. Seven Lakes Trailhead: 5250 feet (10T 558632mE 4723413mN)
2. Devils Peak Trail 984: 3.4 miles, 6900 feet (10T 562894mE 4721981mN)
3. Leave trail: 5.0 miles, 7315 feet (10T 564253mE 4720971mN)
4. Devils Peak: 5.3 miles, 7582 feet (10T 564551mE 4721280mN)
5. Leave trail for Lee Peak: 5.3 miles, 7374 feet (10T 564699mE 4721173mN)
6. Lee Peak: 5.6 miles, 7508 feet (10T 565171mE 4721088mN)

The Sky Lakes Wilderness, in the Southern Cascades, is south of Crater Lake National Park and encompasses nearly 120,000 acres of forested wild lands. Sky Lakes is home to the Seven Lakes Basin. Devils Peak, the highest peak in this area, has a forbidding north face; Lee Peak is the second-highest remnant of an old volcano peak. This scramble is a good introduction to the Sky Lakes Wilderness and may be a good entry point for a several-day backpack among the many lakes and tarns in the scenic basins.

Trailhead directions: From Prospect drive east on the Prospect–Butte Falls Highway, also called Red Blanket Road. Drive east almost 4 miles and turn left onto Bessie Creek Road, which is also Forest Road 37. FR 37 is paved partially and may be rough on the gravel sections. Wind through the forest on FR 37, crossing a couple of bridges and passing the Imnaha Campground. At about 13 miles you will turn left on FR 3780. The trailhead is in about 4.3 miles on the left (east) side of the road and is clearly marked. There is parking on the west side of the road for several cars. There are no services.

Route description: Seven Lakes Trail 981 ascends eastward away from the road on a rocky, rough track resembling a creek bed in places. The trees are dense, with heavy shrubs and flowers contributing to the thick understory.

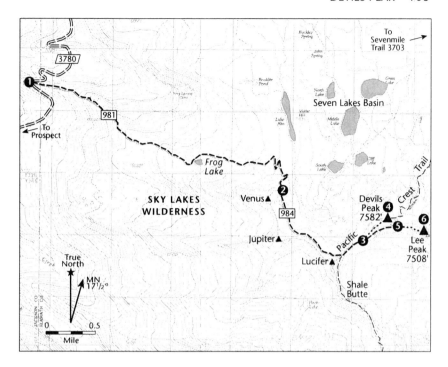

Wild roses, huckleberry, fir, mountain hemlock, and western white pine are just a few of the species represented. As you ascend watch for Shasta red fir.

After climbing steadily for almost 2 miles you will pass Frog Lake. Here the trail flattens out for a short distance before resuming the steady ascent up the ridge. Begin climbing again as the trail winds up the ridge on a few switchbacks to a junction with Devils Peak Trail 984 and turn right (south) onto it.

The Devils Peak Trail travels through the forest to almost reach the ridge crest of Lucifer. Ascend east below Lucifer's summit to reach the junction with the Pacific Crest Trail. Turn left onto the PCT, which drops slightly before climbing once more to reach the scramble point for Devils Peak at 5 miles.

Begin the steep ascent of Devils Peak on the southwest ridge. The ridge leads quickly to the summit in just under 0.3 mile while climbing steadily. As you ascend, bear slightly right to avoid the steeper western slope. The summit of Devils Peak has a good view down into the Seven Lakes Basin. The water of the lakes is a wonderful contrast to the deep green of the surrounding forest.

Enjoy the views and descend the way you came. Continue east on the PCT to the corner of Devils Peak's southeast ridge. Here, instead of going north on the PCT, scramble off the trail at 5.3 miles, heading east and onto the west ridge of Lee Peak.

Ascend the ridge to the summit of Lee Peak at 5.6 miles. Lee Peak's summit gives you a great look at the whole set of peaks to the west. Return to the PCT as you came.

Alternate route: You may also approach the Seven Lakes Basin from the

Devils Peak

Winema National Forest on the east side of the wilderness. Sevenmile Trail 3703 is a wonderful alternative to the westside approach. This may give you earlier access to the Seven Lakes Basin, since the east side generally gets less precipitation. Reach the trailhead by driving west on Nicholson Road from Fort Klamath. In about 3 miles you will enter the Winema National Forest. At the first junction turn left and follow the signs to the "7 Mile" Trailhead.

The Sevenmile Trail heads southwest, quickly passing the wilderness boundary en route to the junction with the PCT at 1.7 miles. Hike the PCT to the lake basin in another 2.5 miles or so. You may want to make the lake basin your base camp for scrambles up all the rim peaks.

Continue southerly on the PCT, past another lake basin trail junction, to reach the various scramble points in the route description. The PCT will take you to the same scramble point for Lee Peak described above (waypoint 5) in 7.2 miles and a 1976-foot gain from the trailhead.

25 MOUNT MCLOUGHLIN

Elevation: 9495 feet	
Difficulty: S3/T2	
Round trip: 11 miles	
Elevation gain: 3909 feet	
Trip time: 5–6 hours	
Time to summit: 3–4 hours	
Best time of year: June to October	
Map: USGS Mount McLoughlin	
Contact: Winema National Forest, Klamath Ranger Station	

Special considerations: In early season you may need crampons and/or ice ax.

WAYPOINT ROUTE
1. Mount McLoughlin Trailhead: 5586 feet (10T 561440mE 4696544mN)
2. Viewpoint: 4.0 miles, 8936 feet (10T 556759mE 4698961mN)
3. Mount McLoughlin: 5.5 miles, 9495 feet (10T 556349mE 4699163mN)

One of the highest Cascade peaks, Mount McLoughlin towers above the densely forested Sky Lakes Wilderness in southern Oregon. This wilderness area features hundreds of glacial tarns, lakes, and ponds surrounded by mountains, ridges, and glacial moraines. Near the southern border of the wilderness, Mount McLoughlin shows the ravages of glacial ice on its northern and eastern exposures. A young volcano by Cascade standards, Mount McLoughlin is a composite volcano, similar to its former neighbor Mount Mazama. The Mount McLoughlin Trail begins in the Winema National Forest and crosses

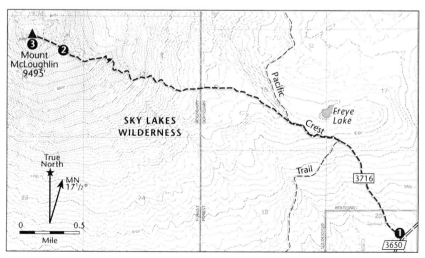

Fourmile Lake and Pelican Butte from Mount McLoughlin

into the Rogue River National Forest halfway to the peak at about 2.3 miles.

Trailhead directions: From White City drive east on State Route 140. At the summit turn left (north) into the Summit Sno-Park, which is marked by a sign. Proceed onto Forest Road 3650, which begins to the right of the parking lot. Drive 2.5 miles to the clearly marked Mount McLoughlin Trailhead. There is room for at least fifteen cars and there is a vault toilet. A Northwest Forest Pass is required.

Route description: Mount McLoughlin Trail 3716 begins ascending almost imperceptibly through the forest of lodgepole pine, Shasta fir, and other conifers. The wilderness boundary comes up quickly, in about 0.3 mile. The trail joins with the Pacific Crest Trail in a mile, and turns right onto the PCT for a short distance. Notice the unmaintained spur off to the right, which leads to Freye Lake. The PCT continues northward at 1.5 miles, while the Mount McLoughlin Trail goes off to the west. This junction is clearly signed. The Mount McLoughlin Trail becomes rockier and begins climbing more steeply at about 2 miles, moving through some rocky sections that require scrambling.

Above 7300 feet there are benches with campsites, and the trail continues to get rockier as the forest gives way to a rocky ridge. At around 8000 feet there is a dramatic view of the northeast side of the mountain, which is a big bowl with a steep scree slope, and colorful rock formations.

Continue to climb and scramble up the rocky slope as the ridge ends below the summit. At around 8900 feet and 4 miles there is a nice viewpoint for photos of Pelican Butte. As you continue to scramble up, notice that the trail drops down to the left, then begins to alternate between boulders and sandy/rocky trail. This can be hard to follow, but keep ascending northwest and you will always wind up back on the trail. Gain the false summit, and go past the old wall to the true summit.

Once there, enjoy views northwest to Willow Lake. In the distance are the Sky Lakes Wilderness peaks. You may also see Mount Thielsen's sharp outline. Fourmile Lake glistens to the east, and to the south are Lake of the Woods and Pelican Butte. Mount Shasta is dominant to the south on a clear day. Upon descending take care not to get caught by the fall line leading south. Stay to the ridge to return to the trail.

26 WHITEFACE PEAK

Elevations: 7652 feet, 7684 feet, 7703 feet

Difficulty: S3/T2

Round trip: 13.4 miles

Elevation gain: 3038 feet

Trip time: 6–8 hours

Time to summits: 3–4 hours

Best time of year: July to October

Maps: USGS Lake of the Woods South, Aspen Lake, Pelican Bay

Contact: Winema National Forest, Klamath Ranger District

Special considerations: The Mountain Lakes Wilderness map covers the area of all three USGS maps and has 20-foot contour lines.

WAYPOINT ROUTE
1. Varney Creek Trailhead: 5500 feet (10T 574101mE 4694326mN)
2. Pass: 5.5 miles, 7416 feet (10T 571485mE 4687954mN)
3. Peak 7652: 6.2 miles, 7652 feet (10T 571082mE 4687058mN)
4. Whiteface Peak: 7.1 miles, 7684 feet (10T 571653mE 4687619mN)
5. Peak 7703: 7.5 miles, 7703 feet (10T 571483mE 4688364mN)

The Mountain Lakes Wilderness is the one of the smallest in Oregon at only 23,071 acres. It is home to a collection of moderate peaks that are fun for scramblers who enjoy the challenge of steep talus slopes and uninterrupted views of the heavily treed wilderness dotted with tiny lakes and tarns. This special wilderness features a lake basin in the caldera from a collapsed volcano, similar to Crater Lake.

Trailhead directions: From Lake of the Woods drive east on State Route 140 until you pass milepost 47. Continue about 0.4 mile and turn right onto Odessa Creek Road 3637 (signed). Proceed for about 2 miles and turn left onto Forest Road 3664, marked with a sign for the Varney Creek Trailhead.

Looking across Eb Lake at the northeast face of Peak 7703

Drive to the end of the road and park. The trailhead is on the right side of the road, with a register and a Forest Service booklet about the area.

Route description: The Varney Creek Trail 3718 quietly leaves the road behind and meanders through a dense forest of Douglas fir, western white pine, mountain hemlock, and ponderosa pine. At about 1 mile the trail crosses the wilderness boundary. To the left a rocky ridge heads away from the trail. The heavily timbered ridge leads up to Mount Harriman, the second-highest peak in the wilderness. Continue on the gentle trail, crossing several footbridges across Varney Creek.

As the trail proceeds and begins to climb, it crosses through several meadows, each with its own character. Many wildflowers are present in summer, including fireweed, paintbrush, mountain bluebell, delphinium, and aster. The trail climbs steeply in places as it continues to the junction with Mountain Lakes Loop Trail 3727 at 4.5 miles. Turn right onto the Mountain Lakes Loop Trail and continue hiking to reach Eb and Zeb Lakes in 0.5 mile. Look beyond Eb Lake and up the long talus slope leading up to Peak 7703. Continue on, and climb steeply up several switchbacks to the caldera rim. The first pass at 5.5 miles (waypoint 2) is the scramble point for both White-face Peak and Peak 7703. Don't stop yet. Continue 0.7 mile farther to the second pass.

Views of Mount McLoughlin from the top of Peak 7703 in the Mountain Lakes Wilderness

This is also the junction of Mountain Lakes Trail 3721 and the Mountain Lakes Loop Trail. Leave the trail here and scramble directly up the northeast ridge to the summit of Peak 7652. Peak 7652 has a blocky false summit, which disappears as you continue up the talus to the rounded summit. There is nothing solid about this talus summit, so take care as you walk around and enjoy the views.

Return back to the trail junction down the ridge and take the trail back to the waypoint 2 pass at 7416 feet. From here, turn south and make your way up the north ridge of Whiteface Peak. After returning to the pass (again), scramble north up the south ridge to the summit of this scramble's highest point—Peak 7703. This scramble is up a steep, unstable talus slope; imagine walking on broken plates ranging in size from automobile tires to dessert plates. Test your footholds before committing your full weight to them. The final pitch is very steep. Scramblers are rewarded by views all around. Enjoy them as you walk around the large, talus summit.

Additional scramble: From Whiteface Peak you could do a long traverse east toward Lake Harriette across the ridges and remaining summits in the area. This scramble would take you in a mile to Peak 7514, east of Lake Harriette. Mostly a descent, the total gain is 235 feet along the way with a slightly exposed saddle approaching the final peak.

27 ASPEN BUTTE

Elevation: 8208 feet	
Difficulty: S3/T2	
Round trip: 13 miles	
Elevation gain: 2541 feet	
Trip time: 6–7 hours	
Time to summit: 3–4 hours	
Best time of year: July to October	
Maps: USGS Lake of the Woods South, Aspen Lake	
Contact: Winema National Forest, Klamath Ranger District	

Special considerations: The Mountain Lakes Wilderness map has the correct location of the trailhead. Mosquitoes in early season.

WAYPOINT ROUTE
1. Clover Creek Trailhead: 5747 feet (10T 571252mE 4683158mN)
2. Mountain Lakes Loop Trail: 3.6 miles, 7121 feet (10T 572045mE 4687205mN)
3. Rock cairn/leave trail: 5.5 miles, 7572 feet (10T 574474mE 4686029mN)
4. Aspen Butte: 6.5 miles, 8208 feet (10T 575289mE 4685005mN)

Deep in the Winema National Forest outside Klamath Falls is the tiny Mountain Lakes Wilderness. One of Oregon's smallest wilderness areas at less than 25,000 acres, Mountain Lakes is rugged and has a lot to offer. The highlight of the wilderness is the caldera left over after a large volcano complex collapsed, similar to Crater Lake. The resulting ridges and peaks surround jewel-like lakes, tarns, and ponds. The hike into the Mountain Lakes up the Clover Creek Trail is challenging and takes you through dense mixed-conifer forest and alpine wildflowers. Once on the rim of the caldera, enjoy the views of the lake basin and surrounding ridges and peaks.

Trailhead directions: From White City drive east on State Route 140. After the pass, and after passing Lake of the Woods, turn right onto Dead Indian Memorial Road. In about 8 miles turn left on County Route 603, also called Clover Creek Road. About 0.5 mile past milepost 5 turn left at the "Clover Creek Trailhead" sign onto gravel Forest Road 3852. The trailhead is at the end of this road in 3.2 miles. The road may have some rough sections. The trailhead

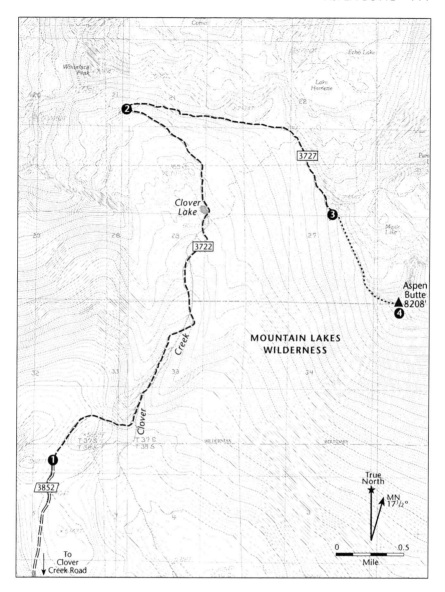

has a register and parking and there is also primitive camping. The trailhead is east from (behind) the register; walk around the road to get there.

Route description: Clover Creek Trail 3722 begins meandering through the mixed-conifer forest and grassy slopes. As it nears Clover Creek beware the mosquitoes and other biting insects. In early season bring insect repellent and use it early and often, or wear appropriate clothing. You may even resort to a mosquito net to keep the bugs out of your mouth! Here the forest is second growth and there is a lot of blowdown and debris on and around the trail.

The view of the Mountain Lakes Wilderness from the summit of Aspen Butte

Clover Creek is on the right and is your best source of water for the first mile or so. The trail begins climbing steeply, continuing along the creek. Wildflowers abound—including fireweed, aster, calypso lily, and bluebell. The trail is rough and although maintained, it is hard to follow in places. Many of the trees have blazes; pay attention to where you are going since it is easy to wander off the trail. At 2.5 miles is Clover Lake.

Approaching the intersection with the Mountain Lakes Loop Trail 3727 (at 3.6 miles), the forest opens up a bit and does not seem so overpowering. Turn right at the junction and proceed along the bottom of a rocky slope that seems to go on forever. The trail contours below two rocky peaks before ascending the ridge south toward Aspen Butte.

At 5.5 miles there is a large cairn on the right indicating the scramble trail to the summit. The unofficial trail basically keeps to the ridge crest all the way to the summit. At the cairn, after leaving the main trail, begin scrambling up the ridge by staying to the left as you ascend. Scramble up the ridge route by crossing through boulder fields. You may use the trail that zigzags through the now-thinning forest.

Soon, most of the trees will be the whitebark pines that do so well at elevations above 7000 feet. At about 0.5 mile from the top, the ridge curves east and you finally get a clear view up to the summit. Keep to the crest as much as possible and continue ascending. You cannot help but notice the nearly vertical exposure across the crest, which drops down quickly to the lake basin.

The summit views are beautiful—Klamath Lake, the Mountain Lakes peaks. Look northwest to see Mount McLoughlin, and enjoy the view of Mount Shasta to the south.

SISKIYOU MOUNTAINS

28 MISLATNAH PEAK

Elevations: 3124 feet, 3720 feet, 4150 feet

Difficulty: S4/T2

Round trip: 13.8 miles

Elevation gain: 4577 feet

Trip time: 12 hours

Time to summits: 8 hours

Best time of year: April through November

Map: USGS Big Craggies

Contact: Siskiyou National Forest, Chetco Ranger District

Special considerations: Wear long pants and sleeves to protect yourself from the thick and burnt brush. Bring sandals to ford Mislatnah Creek. Use the Siskiyou National Forest map or the Kalmiopsis and Wild Rogue Wilderness map for the drive to the trailhead.

WAYPOINT ROUTE
1. Tincup Trailhead: 972 feet (10T 410542mE 4680869mN)
2. Mislatnah Trail 1119: 1.3 miles, 822 feet (10T 411446mE 4680718mN)
3. Mislatnah Peak: 4.6 miles, 3124 feet (10T 413055mE 4684053mN)
4. Peak 3720: 5.9 miles, 3720 feet (10T 412270mE 4685923mN)
5. Saddle: 6.4 miles, 3248 feet (10T 412160mE 4686211mN)
6. Peak 4150: 6.9 miles, 4150 feet (10T 411937mE 4686995mN)

The Big Craggies Botanical Area is in a remote corner of the Kalmiopsis Wilderness of southwest Oregon. A harsh and beautiful place, the wilderness is named for an ancient plant discovered here less than one hundred years ago. *Kalmiopsis leachiana* grows among the rocky outcrops scattered throughout the wilderness and is an endemic species. Its pretty, dark pink flowers are similar to a miniature rhododendron.

Aside from the botanical rarities in this area, the Kalmiopsis is known for its remoteness and for having some high-severity burn areas from the 2002 Biscuit Fire. Once in the wilderness and out of the madrone, fir, and tan oak forest, the slopes are covered with silvery snags. In two years the area has shown a remarkable recovery, and there are plenty of small plants, shrubs, and trees growing.

From the summit of Mislatnah Peak, the view north into the Big Craggies Botanical Area—Peak 4150 and Peak 4619

In the Brookings area, the Big Craggies have a somewhat mythical status as unreachable. This is a rugged scramble that will yield only to the hardiest of adventurers.

Trailhead directions: From Brookings drive east on the North Bank Chetco River Road, also known as County Road 784. Continue until it becomes Forest Road 1376. Stay on FR 1376 until you reach the first spur road. After the third bridge turn left at a T junction where a sign reads "Kalmiopsis 18" and points right. At the next junction, a Y, turn left. At approximately 26 miles you will reach another Y with a sign, "Tincup Trail," and an arrow pointing right. Turn right onto Spur 360. At about mile 28, turn right onto Spur 365 and continue until the end of the road. This is a large trailhead parking area with an outhouse, trailhead sign, and register. A Northwest Forest Pass is required.

Route description: Tincup Trail 1117 leads down through a lush forest of madrone, oak, fir, and pine to Mislatnah Creek. All along the trail you will see spring wildflowers. At the trail junction just before the creek, turn left. You will pass the spot where the old footbridge washed out. A trail leads down to the creek; cross here. Depending upon the time of year, you may need to remove your shoes and wear sandals to cross. In spring the water level may be 2 feet or more in spots.

After crossing, scramble up the short connecting trail to get back on the main trail leading eastward to the junction with Mislatnah Trail 1119 at 1.3 miles. Turn left onto Mislatnah Trail 1119. As the Mislatnah Trail climbs through the forest canopy of oak and madrone, watch for huge red firs.

At almost 1.6 miles is a small spring with lush flowers all around. From the spring the trail goes east, then turns to switchback up the side of a small ridge. This area, the Upper Mislatnah Prairie, has many sections of trail that are washed out. Use your map and compass to stay on course, and bushwhack ahead when the trail fades. You will emerge on the trail after a short distance of bushwhacking through young trees, ferns, or other brush. The prairie area is lush with ferns, thistles, and wild irises in the spring.

Once through the prairie, the trail continues to ascend through the forest northward. Eventually the trail plateaus on the ridge crest, now climbing gently to another spring and then Jacks Camp. The spring at this camp is the last spot to get water.

Here, too, you will pass the wilderness boundary. Through this section of forest you may see bear grass and devils club. After a short distance more in the forest, you will pop out onto a rocky ridge heading northward to Mislatnah Peak. This section of trail leads through overgrown manzanita and climbs to the rocky summit at 4.6 miles, which is also covered with burnt snags and the remains of an old lookout.

After a break, begin the challenging bushwhack to Peak 4150, the second-highest peak in the Big Craggies. This

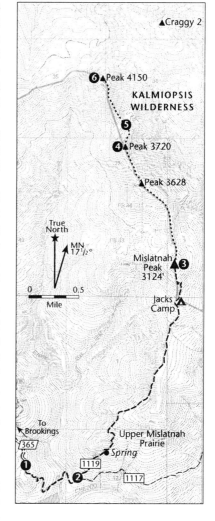

scramble includes numerous ascents and descents through rocky, overgrown terrain. Go north off the Mislatnah summit, following a faint user trail if you see one. You will drop down to a small saddle, then climb back up two small peaks on their southeast sides. After dropping down again to another small saddle, climb up a broad south ridge to the top of Peak 3628. This small summit is unremarkable except for the views north into the heart of the Craggies.

For almost the next 0.5 mile you will be on the ridge crest that ends in a small rocky summit (Peak 3720 at 5.9 miles). From this summit, scramble about 400 feet down a steep slope covered with brush. At the saddle (6.4 miles, 3248 feet), continue north, passing the crumbling vertical rock on the west. Note the flowers blooming amongst the rocks in this area and watch for the small dark green foliage of the *Kalmiopsis*. It is only about a foot high and may be easy to miss. Scramble on the rocks as much as you can and be careful not to step on live plants.

The summit of Peak 4150 is only 0.5 mile farther, but it may seem a lot longer after winding through the heavy brush to ascend about 800 feet. Although this is not the highest peak in the Craggies you will likely want to call it a day here, enjoying the solitude of this remote peak. Return as you came.

Additional scramble: To continue northeast to the summit of Craggy 2 (4619 feet), you will have to again descend a steep brush-covered slope before the 0.5-mile, 1000-foot ascent.

29 GRAYBACK MOUNTAIN

Elevation: 7055 feet

Difficulty: S2/T2

Round trip: 4.5 miles

Elevation gain: 2300 feet

Trip time: 4–5 hours

Time to summit: 2–3 hours

Best time of year: June to October

Map: USGS Grayback Mountain

Contact: Rogue River National Forest, Applegate Ranger District; Siskiyou National Forest, Illinois Valley Ranger District

WAYPOINT ROUTE
1. O'Brien Creek Trailhead: 4565 feet (10T 476241mE 4661890mN)
2. Large meadow: 1.8 miles, 6143 feet (10T 474737mE 4661806mN)
3. Turn north: 2.1 miles, 6683 feet (10T 474408mE 4661653mN)
4. Grayback Mountain: 2.2 miles, 7055 feet (10T 474261mE 4661822mN)

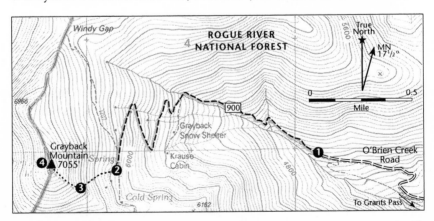

One of southern Oregon's best views is from the summit of Grayback Mountain.

Grayback Mountain is one of the five Siskiyou peaks with an elevation over 7000 feet. The Siskiyou Mountains are biologically diverse and contain more than two dozen coniferous species. This rich forest includes old-growth trees, and species present may include noble fir and/or California fir, Douglas fir, cedar, ponderosa pine, Shasta red fir, and spruce. Scramblers will delight in the abundant wildflowers in late spring or early summer, which may include larkspur, phlox, trillium, Indian paintbrush, avalanche lily, and pasque flower near the summit.

Trailhead directions: From Grants Pass drive south on State Route 199, which will turn into SR 238. Right before entering Applegate and just ahead of the bridge, turn right onto Thompson Creek Road. Drive 12 miles until you see a sign for O'Brien Creek Road. Turn right and follow O'Brien Creek Road until it ends in 3.9 miles at the trailhead, where there is room for several cars. Use caution on this road: although it is gravel there are large potholes, rough patches, and several narrow spots with drop-offs.

Route description: O'Brien Creek Trail 900 begins in the Rogue River National Forest and is a multiuse trail, which allows bikers and horses in addition to hikers. Begin climbing steeply on a dry, rough trail through the forest. As you make your way along the creek, the trail turns sharply left and makes the first of many creek crossings. The forest here still has some old-growth trees but mainly consists of second growth and snags from past fires. Still, watch for big ponderosa pines. At about a mile there is an intersection with the trail leading to where the Krause Cabin stood before it burned down. Turn right, which leads to the Boundary Trail.

Continue approximately another 0.8 mile until the trail emerges into a large meadow. The summit is directly above on the right, hidden from view. Enter the meadow and continue on the trail about 10 or 15 yards, then turn right and start heading up the rocky section of the meadow toward the summit ridge. Here, scramble on the rocks to avoid crushing the fragile wildflowers. Scramble up the steep slope, or traverse, until you reach the prominent rocky ridge. Turn right (north) onto this ridge and head up, scrambling over the blocky gray rocks about 500 feet to the summit. As you scramble up, keep bearing slightly left—and look up to orient yourself.

The summit is massive, covered with the same big blocks as the ridge. Views include the Red Buttes Wilderness just south, as well as Mounts Shasta, McLoughlin, and Ashland. To the northeast, look for the Crater Lake rim peaks.

30 PILOT ROCK

Elevation: 5908 feet

Difficulty: S1/T4

Round trip: 2 miles

Elevation gain: 808 feet

Trip time: 2 hours

Time to summit: 1 hour

Best time of year: June to November

Map: USGS Siskiyou Pass

Contact: Bureau of Land Management, Medford District; Cascades–Siskiyou National Monument. Check with BLM for latest climbing regulations. Pilot Rock may be subject to seasonal closures to protect peregrine falcon nesting sites.

Special considerations: Do not attempt this scramble in wet conditions.

WAYPOINT ROUTE
1. PCT Trailhead: 5100 feet (10T 535679mE 4653052mN)
2. Notch: 0.7 mile, 5691 feet (10T 536391mE 4653121mN)
3. Pilot Rock: 1.0 mile, 5908 feet (10T 536448mE 4653062mN)

The Klamath Mountains dominate southern Oregon and northwest California and include the Siskiyou Mountains. The Siskiyous are significant for both their east-west orientation and because they are a geological divide between the Cascade and Coast Ranges. Uniquely positioned both geographically and geologically, Pilot Rock is near the eastern edge of the Siskiyous and was a prominent landmark for Native Americans and later for pioneers. Pilot Rock is a volcanic remnant and abruptly juts out of the surrounding trees in high contrast to the dense forest. Although short, the scramble to the top of Pilot Rock requires you to use balance and agility. This is an athletic scramble with fine summit views of Mount Shasta and nearby Siskiyou peaks.

Trailhead directions: Drive south on Interstate 5 and take the Mount Ashland exit. Proceed south on the frontage road, going under the highway at 0.8 mile. Turn left onto Pilot Rock Road in 2.1 miles. This is a Forest Service road (40-2E-33) and is an easement through private land. Please respect the private property boundaries, which are all clearly marked. At 2 miles you come to an

Looking up past the scramble route to the top of Pilot Rock

old rock quarry; turn right and go uphill, continuing to the parking area on a rough road. At about 0.8 mile the Pacific Crest Trail crosses the road and there is a parking area. Pilot Rock is visible above the trailhead to the east.

Route description: The trail climbs east toward Pilot Rock through mixed-conifer forest. Spring or early summer wildflowers may include larkspur, columbine, lupine, paintbrush, and wild strawberry. The PCT turns off to the

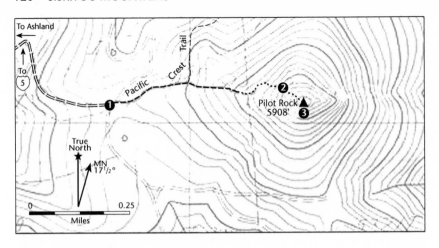

left. Continue straight ahead (east) on the Pilot Rock Trail. It soon begins a short climb on a hard-packed rocky trail.

As you approach Pilot Rock, ascend straight up toward the base on the trail. The trail turns left, but continue straight ahead and up the rocky ledges straight to the base of the monolith. Upon reaching the base, turn left onto a climbers trail and circle clockwise a short distance around the base. The trail becomes steep as it ascends a talus slope and turns right into a small canyon.

As you look up at Pilot Rock, there is a line of weakness on the left side that includes a notch, through which you scramble. First, scramble up the ledge system going slightly diagonally right of the notch above. As you approach the notch, traverse across to the base of the narrow opening (0.7 mile, 5691 feet). Now scramble up and through the notch, into another small canyon area. Continue ascending, scrambling through another small notch, and ascending the ledge systems slightly on the right of the exit point. The summit is up on the right. There is a lot of loose rock. Do not ascend or descend directly above other scramblers. By keeping to the ledges there is less likelihood of rockfall or slides.

Summit views include Mount Shasta and the Trinity Alps to the south in California. You also have fine views of Mount McLoughlin.

EASTERN CASCADES

31 THE DOME

Elevation: 7380 feet

Difficulty: S2/T3

Round trip: 7 miles

Elevation gain: 1471 feet

Trip time: 6 hours

Time to summit: 3 hours

Best time of year: Late June to November

Maps: USGS Campbell Reservoir, Gearhart Mountain

Contact: Fremont National Forest, Bly Ranger District

Special considerations: The Gearhart Mountain Wilderness map covers both USGS maps and has 20-foot contours.

WAYPOINT ROUTE
1. Lookout Rock Trailhead: 6329 feet (10T 680954mE 4703209mN)
2. Below The Dome: 2.7 miles, 7015 feet (10T 677669mE 4704716mN)
3. Start descent back to trail: 3.6 miles, 7814 feet (10T 676826mE 4704993mN)
4. Rejoin the trail: 3.9 miles, 7418 feet (10T 676829mE 4704523mN)

The Gearhart Mountain Wilderness is a gem. Surrounded by the rich old-growth pines of the Fremont National Forest, Gearhart is a unique wilderness with distinctive peaks, cliffs, and monoliths that receives few visitors. One such monolith is The Dome. Rising 400 feet above the trail, The Dome is a weathered hunk of nearly vertical rock. The Dome is a wonderful access point for this scramble among a series of outcrops and cliffs that run west for nearly a mile. The approach hike along the Gearhart Mountain Trail includes abundant wildflowers and stately ponderosa pines. Once above the trees, scramblers will enjoy an unusual perspective on this wilderness playground.

Trailhead directions: From Bly drive east on State Route 140. Turn left (north) onto Campbell Road in less than 0.5 mile. Turn right onto Forest Road 34 and drive 15 miles. Note the Mitchell Monument on the south side of the road at about mile 8. This is a memorial for the group killed in 1945 by an old World War II incendiary device. The memorial site has parking, vault toilets, and picnicking. Continue past the memorial on FR 34 until you reach

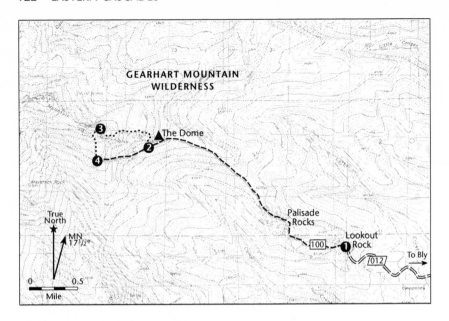

FR 012. Turn left on it and continue to the end to the Lookout Rock Trailhead. There are toilets, nearby camping, ample parking, and the trailhead sign and register. There is no water.

Route description: Gearhart Mountain Trail 100 begins winding through the dense forest heading west-northwest. Huge old-growth ponderosa pines and a mixture of fir trees surround the trail approaching Palisades Rocks. There are many wildflowers in early summer, including lupine and different-colored Indian paintbrush. The trail turns north to wind through this collection of oddly shaped rock outcrops that seem randomly scattered about the land. Continue through the Palisades back into the forest and climb gently northwest to reach The Dome.

The Dome is a rounded mountain that stands at the eastern end of a long rugged ridge. This ridge, your scramble destination, has scattered cliffs, knobs, slabs, and outcrops, which will provide you with as many scrambling variations as you can imagine. As you continue toward The Dome the trail winds through majestic stands of huge, old ponderosa pine. As you pass through a bog, there are even more wildflowers blooming in early summer—enjoy the profusion of color. You may even hear the *whoop, whoop, whoop* of grouse as you make your way through the forest.

You will reach The Dome in about 2.5 miles and then pass it. Continue on the now-level trail about 0.2 mile to a stand of quaking aspens on the right and ascend the steep slope northeast toward the monolith. Leave the trail to ascend a steep, loose gully on the west side of The Dome. The rock is fairly solid on the right side of the gully; keep ascending until you reach the bench just north of The Dome. Here it is worth your time to drop your pack and scramble around to check out the views north and east over the cliffs. From close up, it also becomes more obvious that there is no scramble route up to the top of The Dome.

After enjoying the area, proceed west and begin a series of scrambles above the cliffs west of The Dome. The route is now less defined, as you have many choices about where to ascend next. Keep heading west and bear right anytime you get cliffed out; there is always a chute or notch to scramble through as you continue your ascent.

You will pass through a band of rocky outcrops that are very similar to the Palisades. This is a fun place to drop your pack and pick out several high points to visit. The rock is solid and there are plenty of chimneys and wide slots to scramble through for some wonderful views.

Continue west by going north around any vertical sections until you reach a broad bench with a field of false Solomon's seal. Keep heading west, go north around another outcrop of rock, and ascend to the final group of rocks. After enjoying the views, continue west to a broad open bench above a steep slope heading south.

At 3.6 miles, 7814 feet, descend south to reach the Gearhart Mountain Trail at 3.9 miles. Turn left to return east to the trailhead.

The Dome and Cliffs in the Gearhart Mountain Wilderness

32 GEARHART MOUNTAIN

Elevation: 8370 feet

Difficulty: S3/T2

Round trip: 11.8 miles

Elevation gain: 2581 feet

Trip time: 7–8 hours

Time to summit: 3–4 hours

Best time of year: Late July to November

Maps: USGS Campbell Reservoir, Gearhart Mountain

Contact: Fremont National Forest, Bly Ranger District

Special considerations: The Gearhart Mountain Wilderness map covers both USGS maps and has 20-foot contours.

WAYPOINT ROUTE
1. Lookout Rock Trailhead: 6340 feet (10T 680954mE 4703209mN)
2. West of pass: 4.3 miles, 7940 feet (10T 675450mE 4705295mN)
3. Notch: 4.6 miles, 8075 feet (10T 675182mE 4705108mN)
4. Begin ascent to plateau: 5.0 miles, 7910 feet (10T 674906mE 4705739mN)
5. Gearhart Mountain: 5.9 miles, 8370 feet (10T 674464mE 4706822mN)

Gearhart Mountain is in the Eastern Cascades' Gearhart Mountain Wilderness. Surrounded by the rich old-growth pines of the Fremont National Forest,

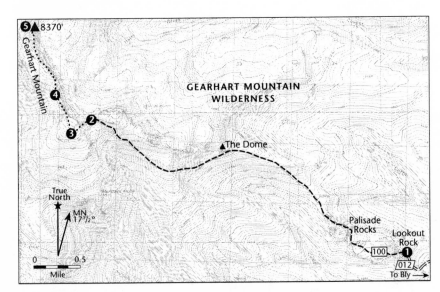

The Gearhart Mountain Wilderness' namesake peak has a distinctive look.

Gearhart is a unique wilderness that receives few visitors. The forest provides habitat for deer, elk, cougar, and coyotes. Wildflowers are scattered throughout the meadows and are particularly stunning in contrast to the melting snow in early season; snow may remain on higher-elevation trails until July. Although mostly heavily forested, the Gearhart Wilderness's few mountains and rocky outcrops offer plenty of scrambling opportunities.

Trailhead directions: From Bly drive east on State Route 140. Turn left (north) onto Campbell Road in less than 0.5 mile. Turn right onto Forest Road 34 and drive 15 miles. Note the Mitchell Monument on the south side of the road at about mile 8. This is a memorial for the group killed in 1945 by an old World War II incendiary device. The memorial site has parking, vault toilets, and picnicking. Continue past the memorial on FR 34 until you reach FR 012. Turn left on it and continue to the end to the Lookout Rock Trailhead. There are toilets, nearby camping, ample parking, and the trailhead sign and register. There is no water.

Route description: Gearhart Mountain Trail 100 begins winding through the dense forest, heading west-northwest. Huge old-growth ponderosa pines and a mixture of fir trees surround the trail as it approaches Palisades Rocks. The trail turns north to wind through this wonderland of oddly shaped rock outcrops that seem randomly scattered about the land. Continue through the Palisades back into the forest and climb gently northwest to reach The Dome—a rounded mountain that stands at the eastern end of a long rugged ridge on the north side of the trail.

Here, the trail flattens out and continues westward where you will again climb, this time to reach a 7900-foot pass south of Gearhart Mountain. After climbing up to the pass, walk west off the trail toward and then past waypoint 2. Turn southwest. Contour around the southern tip of the mountain at about 8000 feet for almost 0.3 mile. You will notice a notch or break in the cliffy section of the mountain. Scramble up the notch (4.6 miles) to get onto the broad southern end of the upper mountain.

Once up on the upper mountain, scramble north and keep to the left of some vertical rock that you encounter in about 0.2 mile. Drop down 100 feet, then scramble back up to the plateau (at 5 miles), which ascends all the way to the summit.

Keep going north to the eastern edge of the summit ridge and scramble to the false summit in about a mile. Along the way you will wind through some scattered rock and trees along the sometimes-flat mountaintop. You might see animal tracks in powdery dirt up here. There are panoramic views from atop the false summit, and you get a good view of your destination just north. Drop down westward and scramble up the final rocks to the summit.

The summit has whitebark pines and a USGS benchmark. Views on a clear day include the Three Sisters to the west and Steens Mountain to the east. Northward you can see Blue Lake, which is the only lake in this wilderness. You may reach Blue Lake by following the Gearhart Mountain Trail north from the pass.

33 TWELVEMILE PEAK

Elevation: 8144 feet	
Difficulty: S1/T2	
Round trip: 3.6 miles	
Elevation gain: 1204 feet	
Trip time: 3 hours	
Time to summit: 1–1.5 hours	
Best time of year: May to October	
Map: USGS Crook Peak	

Contact: Fremont National Forest, Lakeview Ranger District

WAYPOINT ROUTE
1. South Fork Crooked Creek Trailhead: 7050 feet (10T 733480mE 4688638mN)
2. Jeep track: 0.7 mile, 7327 feet (10T 733791mE 4688960mN)
3. Start scramble up ridge: 1.0 mile, 7507 feet (10T 734207mE 4689143mN)
4. Twelvemile Peak: 1.3 miles, 8144 feet (10T 734311mE 4689724mN)

Looking south at the summit of Twelvemile Peak.

Twelvemile Peak is a moderate mountain east of Lakeview in the northern section of the Warner Mountains. Fremont National Recreation Trail 160 runs from north to south through miles of the mountains, which are part of the Fremont and Winema National Forests. The approach to Twelvemile is a study in contrast as the rich pine and fir forest quickly gives way to sage and then to alpine trees, including whitebark pine. The high-desert country here is also home to many sensitive plant species. Twelvemile Peak has a twin summit, and views south show the austere beauty of Drake and Light Peaks.

Trailhead directions: From Lakeview take State Route 140 east approximately 8 miles to Forest Road 3615. Drive northerly on the paved road past the Aspen Cabin, which is available to rent. The South Fork Crooked Creek Trailhead is ahead on the right with ample parking and a vault toilet.

Route description: The trail begins climbing through the forest, using an old jeep track for a short distance. When the old road intersects Fremont Trail 160, turn left onto the trail. Continue climbing through the mixed-pine forest that also has stands of quaking aspens and seasonal wildflowers, including larkspur, Indian paintbrush, and lupine. In some areas, notice the slopes with different types of sagebrush. The trail crosses the jeep track again, but ignore the road and continue on the trail.

At the next jeep track intersection (0.7 mile), leave the trail and take the jeep track as it heads up toward a broad saddle. As you approach a fence line up ahead, turn left (25 yards before it) and leave the jeep track at 1 mile to head up the ridge leading to the summit. This ridge is covered with large rocks that you will scramble up and over to the summit. There are some loose blocks among the rocks, so choose your route with care. There is also some fragile vegetation tucked in with the rocks; avoid crushing it whenever possible. You will notice that many of the rocks have crusty lichen growing on them; the bright colors are a contrast to the grainy rock.

Twelvemile Peak actually has two summits; the first one at 1.3 miles is

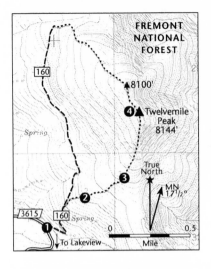

the high point and has great views of the Fremont National Forest, Drake Peak, and Light Peak. From the highest summit, head north to a saddle between the two summits and continue to the 8100-foot summit. As you look back at the higher point, notice the grove of trees on the eastern slope of Twelvemile.

Descend from the second summit, heading north-northeast toward a pine-forested drop-off. When you reach the trees, continue to descend by skirting the trees. This is a steep rocky slope and leads down to the Fremont Trail, which is visible below. As you reach the level ground before the trail, you might notice raised trails in the dirt. These are tunnels left behind by mice that tunnel through the ground under the winter snow. The tunnels remain after the snowmelt. When you reach the Fremont Trail turn left to return to the trailhead.

34 CROOK PEAK

Elevation: 7834 feet

Difficulty: S2/T2

Round trip: 8.2 miles

Elevation gain: 1433 feet

Trip time: 5 hours

Time to summit: 3 hours

Best time of year: May to October

Map: USGS Crook Peak

Contact: Fremont National Forest, Lakeview Ranger District

WAYPOINT ROUTE
1. South Fork Crooked Creek Trailhead: 7050 feet (10T 733480mE 4688638mN)
2. Leave trail: 3.5 miles, 7196 feet (10T 733835mE 4693204mN)
3. Crook Peak: 4.1 miles, 7834 feet (10T 734674mE 4693727mN)

The Fremont National Forest constitutes one of the largest forested areas in Oregon. The Warner Mountains, northeast of Lakeview, are a series of lichen-crusted, rocky peaks surrounded by dense forestland. Fremont National Recreation Trail 160 is an ambitious project that gives hikers and scramblers access to the forest from north to south, allowing them to experience the diversity of the area. The forest is quite a contrast to the rocky, arid plains covered with sagebrush, western juniper, and other species adapted to the harsh environment. You can reach one part of the trail at the South Fork Crooked Creek Trailhead. This area has stands of huge ponderosa pines, which stand out due to the bright color of their bark. In the spring there are abundant alpine wildflowers.

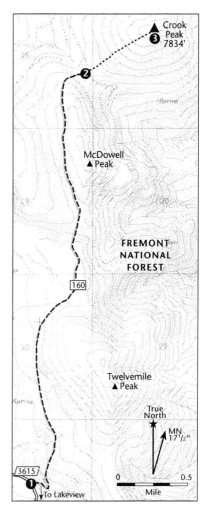

Trailhead directions: From Lakeview take State Route 140 east approximately 8 miles to Forest Road 3615. Drive northerly on the paved road past the Aspen Cabin, which is available to rent. The South Fork Crooked Creek Trailhead is ahead on the right with ample parking and a vault toilet.

Route description: The trail begins climbing through the forest on an old jeep track for a short distance. When the old road intersects the Fremont Trail 160, turn left onto the trail. Ignore any other junctions with old roads and continue northward on the trail. Continue climbing through the mixed-conifer forest that also has stands of quaking aspens and seasonal wildflowers including larkspur, Indian paintbrush, and lupine. Big sagebrush is only one of the many different sages you may encounter along this trail.

The Fremont Trail will continue northward toward Crook Peak for a few miles. The forest of mixed pine and white fir eventually thins and ends as you climb past the northwest ridge of Twelvemile Peak. As you approach McDowell Peak, the trail will take you through an open rocky plain, which is dry and exposed. The trail then traverses along McDowell's west slope. After passing McDowell Peak, you will descend a short distance into the cool forest once more, a welcome change from the hot traverse. The trail then turns east toward Crook Peak.

As you approach Crook Peak's southwest corner, the Fremont Trail will

Looking up the boulder-strewn route to Crook Peak

continue east and then turn north as it nears the mountain. Instead of following the Fremont Trail, leave it at 3.5 miles and begin your ascent by scrambling up the peak's southwest corner. Crook Peak has a broad west ridge, which allows you to pick the most appealing route and just keep ascending to the west end of the summit. This rocky, open ridge climbs steadily upward to the upper mountain.

When you reach the west end of the summit, continue eastward and scramble over the rough rock to the summit. Once on the summit, note the other Warner peaks—McDowell, Twelvemile, Light, and Drake—neatly laid out in a crescent to the south and southeast.

35 DRAKE PEAK

Elevation: 8407 feet

Difficulty: S2/T2

Round trip: 7 miles

Elevation gain: 1929 feet

Trip time: 5 hours

Time to summit: 2.5 hours

Best time of year: May to October

Map: USGS Crook Peak

Contact: Fremont National Forest, Lakeview Ranger District

WAYPOINT ROUTE

1. South Fork Crooked Creek Trailhead: 7050 feet (10T 733480mE 4688638mN)
2. Before pass: 0.8 mile, 7452 feet (10T 734211mE 4688994mN)
3. Light Peak: 2.1 miles, 8325 feet (10T 735120mE 4687209mN)
4. Drake Peak: 3.5 miles, 8407 feet (10T 734311mE 4689724mN)

In south-central Oregon, the Fremont–Winema National Forest covers more than 2 million acres from the slopes of the Eastern Cascades to the high desert's prominent mountains around Lakeview. Drake Peak, at the east end of the Warner Mountains, is in the midst of scenic eastside forest and sagebrush flat. The Drake Peak Lookout (not actually on Drake peak) is an active fire lookout as well as a historic lookout; the latter is available for overnight use. This historic lookout is the highest lookout in Oregon, perched at 8222 feet. Wildflowers are rich and varied in the spring and will also delight you in the fall. The scrambles to Light and Drake Peaks offer visitors an inside look at this unique area.

Trailhead directions: From Lakeview take State Route 140 east approximately 8 miles to Forest Road 3615. Drive northerly on the paved road past the Aspen Cabin, which is available to rent. The South Fork Crooked Creek Trailhead is ahead on the right with ample parking and a vault toilet.

Route description: The trail begins climbing through the forest on an old jeep track for a short distance. When the old road intersects Fremont Trail 160, turn left onto the trail. Continue climbing through the mixed-pine forest that also has stands of quaking aspens and seasonal wildflowers including larkspur, Indian paintbrush, and lupine. Sage of many different sizes will be a

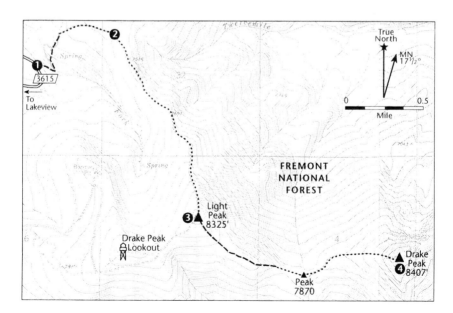

Looking at the Drake Peak summit from Light Peak

constant companion on this hike. The trail crosses the jeep track again; ignore the road and continue on the trail.

At the next jeep track intersection leave the trail and take the jeep track as it heads up to a pass. Just before the pass at 0.8 mile, turn right and head south along the southwest side of the north ridge to Light Peak. The northeast side is steep, with cliffs in some places.

As you scramble up the north ridge to the summit at 2.1 miles, note the groves of twisted whitebark pines on the high slopes. These trees are adept at surviving the wind and snow of the Eastern Cascades winters. You also have a great view of the Drake Peak Lookout to the southwest; there are three separate structures atop the summit. Note as well the good view of the route to Drake Peak itself, to the southeast.

Descend Light Peak's southeast ridge on the dirt trail heading south. Follow this trail until it ends, then continue eastward along a saddle, then past Peak 7870. After crossing another small saddle, ascend the west ridge of Drake Peak. The first 200 feet are just a warm-up for the steeper upper ridge approaching the summit. As you ascend, note the distinct tree line along the north side of the ridge.

Once you reach the summit, enjoy the views east to the high desert. The north side of Drake Peak has beautiful cliffs and dense forest. You can also see the crescent of the Warner Mountains before you. Descend the way you came.

WEST-CENTRAL BLUE MOUNTAINS

36 THE MONUMENT

Elevation: 3241 feet	
Difficulty: S2/T4	
Round trip: 2–3 miles	
Elevation gain: 800 feet	
Trip time: 3 hours	
Time to summit: 2 hours	
Best time of year: August to November	
Map: USGS Gray Butte	
Contact: Smith Rock State Park	
Special considerations: Closed for raptor nesting January 1–July 31.	

WAYPOINT ROUTE
1. Smith Rock: 2708 feet (10T 648464mE 4914020mN)
2. The Monument: 1.1 miles, 3241 feet (10T 648617mE 4915096mN)

Smith Rock State Park came to prominence in the mid-1980s when it gained popularity as a rock-climbing mecca. The crags at Smith meander alongside the Crooked River. The rock at Smith's most popular climbing spots is Smith Rock tuff—a volcanic rock with joints, pockets, and varying texture. At other spots in the Crooked River Gorge are columnar basalt cliffs, which are also popular with climbers. Visiting Smith Rock for the first time, be prepared for an amazing vista from the overlook near the parking area. The view of the river below, surrounded by the varied and dramatic rocks, can seem almost surreal.

Trailhead directions: Drive U.S. Route 97 to Terrebonne just north of Redmond, where you will turn east onto NE Wilcox Avenue (Lambert Drive) and follow the signs to the park. The parking areas are clearly marked, with some overflow parking at the turnaround area where the road ends. A pass for day use may be purchased using the machines and must be displayed on your dash.

Route description: From the parking lot, walk on the path past the viewing area and head down to the river on the trail. Descend on the rocky trail and cross the Crooked River on the footbridge. In the early morning you may

133

Just below the top of The Monument is a great rest spot, Burma Road and The Marsupials in the background.

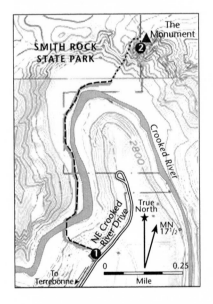

see otters in the river. At the trail junction, turn right, and in 0.75 mile you will reach the northern curve of the Crooked River. The Monument is the imposing pinnacle with the 600-foot south wall just across the juniper- and sage-covered plain to the north.

Walk through the plain to the prominent chute to the left of The Monument. Ascend this steep, loose chute to the upper end of the gully on the ridge. Once on the ridge, turn right onto a trail to the north ridge of The Monument. Once you reach the ridge, scramble along it by keeping to the right side. Then drop down to a small amphitheater with three slots in the rock. The third slot on the right side is your ascent route.

You might choose to leave your pack here. As you scramble up the slot, you will pass a large chockstone as you squeeze yourself upward. When you emerge at the top, turn left and scramble to the base of the summit pinnacle. Turn left again, and scramble north by dropping down for about 30 or 40 feet, then ascend the slab on large pockets to the summit ridge. Turn right to scramble up to the summit. Enjoy the fine views of the central Oregon Cascades, Crooked River Gorge, Staender Ridge, and the Marsupial Crags to the east.

Rather than descend the chute, follow the trail down to the Crooked River and back to the parking area.

134

37 MARSUPIAL CRAGS

Elevation: 4230 feet

Difficulty: S2/T4

Round trip: 4.6 miles

Elevation gain: 1919 feet

Trip time: 5 hours

Time to summit: 3 hours

Best time of year: April to November

Map: USGS Gray Butte

Contact: Smith Rock State Park

WAYPOINT ROUTE

1. Smith Rock: 2829 feet (10T 648500mE 4914003mN)
2. Burma Road: 1.2 miles, 2980 feet (10T 649183mE 4914779mN)
3. Koala Rock–Wombat pass: 1.6 miles, 3417 feet (10T 649465mE 4914443mN)
4. Peak 4230: 2.5 miles, 4230 feet (649859mE 4914992mN)
5. Start Staender Ridge descent: 3.1 miles, 3589 feet (10T 649204mE 4915185mN)

Looking west across Smith Rock, the Three Sisters peaks in the background, from the ridge above The Wombat

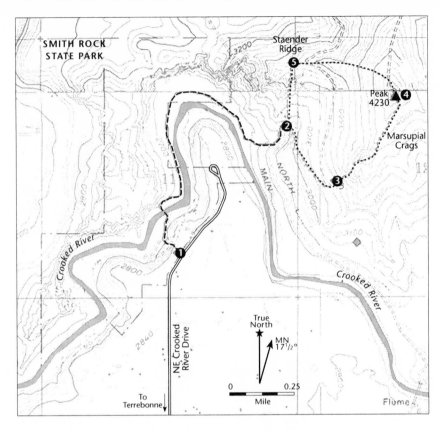

Throughout Oregon, Smith Rock State Park is known as a popular rock-climbing destination. In the mid-1980s, Smith sprang into worldwide prominence as a sport-climbing playland. The cliffs, crags, and rimrock of Smith Rock meander alongside the Crooked River. The rock at Smith's most popular climbing spots is Smith Rock tuff—a soft, volcanic rock with joints, pockets, and varying texture. At other spots in the Crooked River Gorge are columnar basalt cliffs, which are also popular with climbers. Visiting Smith Rock for the first time be prepared for an amazing vista from the overlook near the parking area. The river below, surrounded by the varied and dramatic rocks, can seem almost surreal. The scramble up Koala Rock and up alongside The Wombat will bring you to a quiet area developed during the '50s, '60s, and early '70s. Though visited less often now, the Marsupial Crags and Staender Ridge played an important role in the early development of Smith Rock climbing.

Trailhead directions: Drive U.S. Route 97 to Terrebonne just north of Redmond, where you will turn east onto Wilcox Avenue (Lambert Road) and follow the signs to the park. The parking areas are clearly marked, with some overflow parking at the turnaround area where the road ends. A pass for day use may be purchased using the machines and must be displayed on your dash.

Route description: Walk through the day-use area to the trail that leads down to the Crooked River. Cross the river on the footbridge and turn right at the trail junction. There is a trail sign indicating "Burma Road 1 mile." As you hike along the river you may see river otters and a variety of ducks, including the mallard and goldeneye.

Approaching a mile, you will pass by Little Three Fingered Jack and The Monument. This area is restricted during raptor nesting season. As you glance up at the vertical cliffs, note the huge nests on some ledges.

Follow the trail, which is signed, to the junction with Burma Road at 1.2 miles. Hike along Burma Road heading southeast. As the road switchbacks to the north, hike off the road eastward to the base of Koala Rock, the freestanding monolith right in front of you.

Scramble up the steep slope on the northwest side of Koala Rock. This slope consists of very loose rock and scree. As you pass by the rock, notice the glint of fixed bolts marking the climbing routes up the vertical face. Follow the slope up and around to a small pass at 1.6 miles, between Koala Rock and the huge Wombat.

Drop your pack here. Scramble up the north side of Koala Rock by first working up an open book to a short section of face climbing with huge pockets. The final scramble is up a slab to the top. This is just below the true summit but is a good scrambling destination. Descend back to the pass, keeping left to avoid exposure.

The Wombat overshadows much of the Marsupial Crags.

From the pass, scramble east then north up a rock-filled chute on the east side of The Wombat. As you begin, keep close to The Wombat; continuing up the steep slope, find whatever solid rock is available and use it. You will feel very small as the walls of The Wombat loom overhead. Listen for the trilling of canyon wrens as you ascend. At the top, go around a large rock on its right side and continue to the northern end of The Wombat. From here you may scramble up a few ledges to a nice viewpoint on the northwest corner.

Return to the east side of the monolith. Now you are heading northward to Peak 4230, one of the highest points in the park. Work your way up the ridge, mostly on the ridge crest. You will have to drop down on the right to avoid some cliffy sections; otherwise it is a short scramble to the summit of this broad peak.

From the summit you have a wonderful view of the whole Crooked River Gorge below. The rock walls look even more imposing and dramatic from a distance. Central Oregon's Three Sisters are visible to the west. On a clear day you can follow the Cascade crest right up to Mount Hood's distinctive summit.

Descend north off the peak on a trail for a short distance. In early spring the north side of the mountain will still have patchy snow. Turn northwest and descend the broad west ridge of the peak. This will lead to a user trail that will cut across the road. Then at a four-way junction turn left to descend Staender Ridge by heading south then southeast to cut between Staender Summit and Flattop. Descend the east side of the ridge. There are many opportunities to scramble along side trails to the base of various pinnacles that make up the ridge.

Once past Adit Rock, which is at the southern end of the ridge, continue descending on the more-evident user trail, which will lead to the main trail. Turn right and get back onto the main trail to return to your car.

38 TWIN PILLARS

Elevation: 5500 feet

Difficulty: S2/T3

Round trip: 10.8 miles

Elevation gain: 1849 feet

Trip time: 6 hours

Time to summit: 3 hours

Best time of year: April to November

Map: USGS Steins Pillar

Contact: Ochoco National Forest, Prineville Ranger District

Special considerations: Several fords of East Fork Mill Creek require caution in early season or after a heavy rain.

WAYPOINT ROUTE

1. Twin Pillars Trailhead: 3740 feet (10T 692548mE 4923338mN)
2. Belknap Trail junction: 2.7 miles, 4050 feet (10T 695825mE 4925732mN)
3. Begin ascending: 4.4 miles, 4625 feet (10T 695610mE 4927610mN)
4. Twin Pillars: 5.2 miles, 5500 feet (10T 695937mE 4928332mN)

Just east of Prineville is the Ochoco National Forest. The Ochoco contains three small wilderness areas, each with its own unique scenic beauty. The Mill Creek Wilderness is a popular destination for residents of east-central

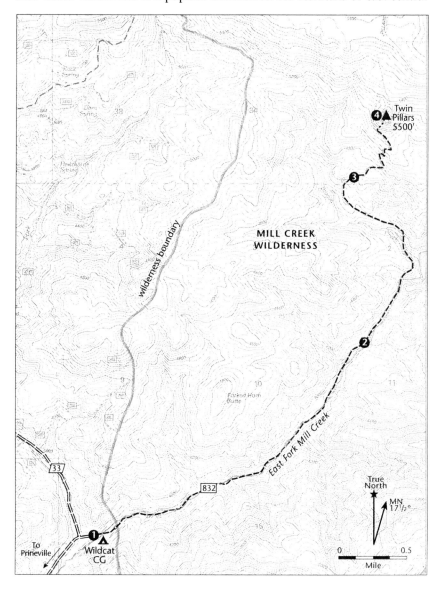

The volcanic remnant next to the Twin Pillars

Oregon. Good roads and a campground make it easy to visit. Huge ponderosa pines dominate the forest and there are many creeks and streams criss-crossing the land. In spring or early summer the wildflower displays are amazing. Two prominent volcanic remnants form the landmarks in this area. Steins Pillar is east of Forest Road 33 on the way to the trailhead. In the north part of the Mill Creek Wilderness the Twin Pillars are a distinctive landmark. These 200-foot-high pillars are also a volcanic remnant. Although the pillars are vertical in some places, there is another remnant nearby to provide scramblers with a true destination.

Trailhead directions: From Prineville drive east on U.S. Route 26 about 9 miles. Turn left onto Mill Creek Road (sign reads "Wildcat Camp"), which will turn into FR 33. Drive northeast on this road for approximately 10 miles until you reach the Wildcat Campground and Twin Pillars Trailhead. Trail parking is just before the campground. Walk through the campground (vault toilets and water available) to a sign at the trailhead and the wilderness boundary.

Route description: Twin Pillars Trail 832 leaves the Wildcat Campground road, crosses a bridge, and heads northeast alongside East Fork Mill Creek. This trail, which bisects the Mill Creek Wilderness from north to south, allows hikers access to much of the wilderness. The trail follows the creek for almost 3 miles and includes many creek crossings. There are no bridges in the wilderness so be prepared to rock-hop, use available down logs, or ford the creek in places.

You will pass the Belknap Trail junction in 2.7 miles. Continue straight along the creek basin. Before you begin climbing to approach the Twin Pillars, you will get fine views of the pillars from the trail. Cross Brogan Creek and climb up to begin an ascending traverse through the forest at 4.4 miles, with Twin Pillars occasionally visible to the northeast.

As the trail begins to level off, you will find yourself south of the Twin Pillars. Leave the trail here and scramble up the rocky slope, around some

Looking through snags at Twin Pillars

downed trees and large rocks, to the base of the pillars. From the base traverse around to the left and continue to scramble up to an obvious saddle between a small remnant and the main pillars.

Scramble west up to the high point (5.2 miles, 5500 feet). From there, turn left and scramble up to the top of the remnant using the south corner. Head up the narrow ramp, continue climbing past the tree, and scramble to the end of the ramp. Turn right and scramble up and over a notch and turn right again to ascend the right side of a narrow gully to a ledge. Enjoy the views and then scramble and downclimb back to the saddle and descend to your car the way you came.

Alternate route: From the Twin Pillars Trail scramble up to the base of the Twin Pillars. Turn right, and begin a counterclockwise circumnavigation of the pillars. This will eventually take you around to the north side. Scramble up a scree- and rock-filled gully to the northwest base of the pillars. Scramble around here to explore some cracks in the rock, and ascend a short steep slab to a viewpoint. Return to the starting point or continue around to reach the north side of the pillars for more scrambling.

The views from the north-side high points are quite a contrast. The Mill Creek Wilderness was almost completely involved in the Hash Rock wildfire, which burned for two months in the summer of 2000. Some slopes are covered with burnt lodgepole amid surviving ponderosa pines.

39 SUTTON MOUNTAIN

Elevation: 4694 feet

Difficulty: S2/T1

Round trip: 4.8 miles

Elevation gain: 1612 feet

Trip time: 4 hours

Time to summit: 2–3 hours

Best time of year: May and June; accessible from January depending on snowfall; summer can be hot and dry

Map: USGS Sutton Mountain

Contact: Bureau of Land Management, Prineville District

Special considerations: Route is within the Sutton Mountain Wilderness Study Area, a designation that allows land managers to preserve an area in its natural state. Please leave all gates as you find them.

WAYPOINT ROUTE
1. Parking: 3075 feet (10T 727898mE 4949464mN)
2. Ridge start: 0.2 mile, 3151 feet (10T 727898mE 4949534mN)
3. Rock pile: 0.5 mile, 3316 feet (10T 727664mE 4949141mN)
4. Pass: 1.8 miles, 4061 feet (10T 726618mE 4947350mN)
5. Sutton Mountain: 2.4 miles, 4694 feet (10T 725934mE 4947803mN)

The rim of Sutton Mountain from the route

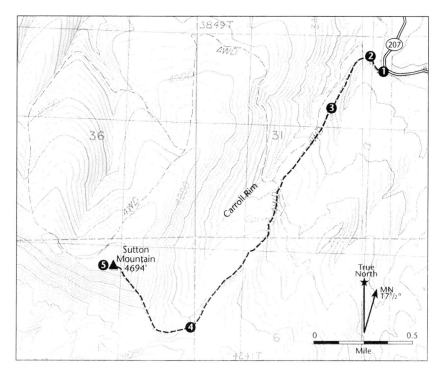

The John Day River area is home to some of the most dramatic landscapes in eastern Oregon, including the John Day Fossil Beds National Monument. Sutton Mountain is not part of the monument geographically, but the Picture Gorge basalt that caps the mountain is visible throughout the monument's various units. This 16-million-year-old rock is evidence of repeated ancient lava flows. Although off the beaten path, Sutton Mountain is a way to get up close to these columns of old basalt. This scramble, below the Carroll Rim, has spring wildflowers throughout. You will likely see Oregon sunshine, hedgehog cactus, prairie stars, and wild onion in the meadows below the summit. After this short scramble you may want to visit the nearby John Day Fossil Beds National Monument, Painted Hills Unit.

Trailhead directions: From Prineville drive east on U.S. Route 26. Turn left and drive north on State Route 207. At milepost 15 park on the right side of the road in a large turnout. You can also drive across the road, through the gate, and park at the corral.

Route description: Cross the road and walk north about 100 feet to a dirt road. Walk through the gate, and up the road. Continue on the road a short distance to a "No Motorized Vehicles" sign. Walk past the sign and turn onto the ridge on the left and scramble up the steep hillside.

Continue up to gain the broad ridge at 0.2 mile, keeping to the top as best you can while avoiding skirmishes with brush or trees. At the large shale rock pile at 0.5 mile, continue upward gently on the ridge, passing the shale mound on the left. This ridge will lead you southwesterly to a pass southeast of the summit. At 1.8 miles you will come to the pass. Turn northward here to continue the approach to the mountain's southwest corner.

Continue west then north toward the southwest corner of Sutton Mountain. Walk to the base of the southwest corner of the summit basalt. Walk along the base of the rimrock to a huge juniper tree, where there is a break in the basalt. Scramble up through this break and turn right along the top ramp. Pick your way along these rocks, which are right below the upper basalt columns. As you continue the wall gets less distinct, eventually petering out. Scramble up and turn left to reach the summit. There are great views of the John Day Fossil Beds Painted Hills from the summit. If you look around you will also find the USGS benchmark.

 WINDY POINT

Elevation: 4578 feet

Difficulty: S3/T2

Round trip: 11.3 miles

Elevation gain: 3800 feet

Trip time: 8 hours

Time to summit: 4 hours

Best time of year: April to November

Maps: USGS Picture Gorge East, Picture Gorge West

Contact: John Day Fossil Beds National Monument, Sheep Rock Unit; Bureau of Land Management, Prineville District

Special considerations: Picking flowers or removing fossils or other materials is not allowed within the monument.

WAYPOINT ROUTE
1. Goose Rock Bridge turnout: 2143 feet (11T 290393mE 4940187mN)
2. Middle Mountain: 1.0 mile, 3389 feet (11T 291664mE 4939972mN)
3. Peak 3493: 2.5 miles, 3493 feet (11T 293489mE 4938969mN)
4. Windy Point: 3.5 miles, 4578 feet (11T 293344mE 4937493mN)
5. Hole in the Ground: 6.0 miles, 3563 feet (11T 292437mE 4934210mN)
6. Descent gully: 6.3 miles, 3359 feet (11T 291981mE 4934084mN)
7. Return trail: 7.5 miles, 2202 feet (11T 290400mE 4934871mN)

Sheep Rock is a prominent landmark in the John Day Fossil Beds National Monument. The peak consists of colorful claystone formations topped by columns of vertical Picture Gorge basalt. Adjacent to the monument's Sheep Rock Unit are public lands with several other peaks, all with unique views of the monument and surrounding lands. The views are stunning from atop Windy Point and afford scramblers a panorama of the monument's geologic

John Day Fossil Beds from Windy Point summit

wonders and surrounding mountain ranges. In spring, the sagebrush steppe is alive with a wide variety of colorful and unusual wildflowers and flowering shrubs. From the bright pink of hedgehog cactus to the deep purple of Nuttall's larkspur, the contrasting shades are sure to add to this scramble, high above the John Day River.

Trailhead directions: Drive east from Mitchell on U.S. Route 26 and turn left onto State Route 19. Drive north, past the John Day Fossil Beds National Monument visitor center and Goose Rock, to the turnout before the bridge. Parking is available on the right.

Route description: This scramble begins by walking north along SR 19 across the Goose Rock Bridge. This is the safest way to cross the John Day River here. Turn right after the bridge at a road entrance. The road is blocked by a gate and has a sign for the monument boundary. There is room to pass the gate on the left side. Once on the road, walk less than 0.1 mile to the west end of the Middle Mountain ridge. Begin ascending next to a washout for the adjacent gully, which looks too rocky and steep to ascend.

Scramble up slope to a band of rock. After scrambling up through this broken rock band, you will find yourself on a small, gently sloping bench. As you get higher, the contrast of the Blue Basin and its colorful formations is striking against the rest of the surroundings. On the ridge, and throughout the scramble, you will see outcrops of rimrock consisting of the broken basalt. This slope is also dotted in places with juniper, purple sage, and mountain mahogany.

After 1200 feet of climbing you will reach the summit of Middle Mountain at 1 mile. Enjoy the views of the Blue Basin and the distant Cascades on a clear day. The remainder of the scramble circumscribes a wide arc through

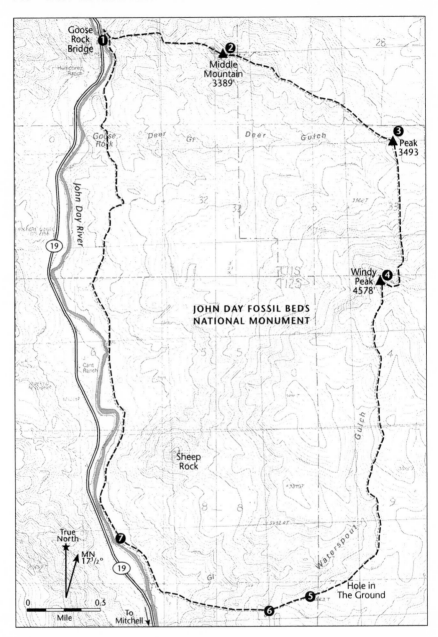

the monument and surrounding public land. The route follows along an indistinct ridgeline leading southward to parallel Waterspout Gulch.

Descend southeast along the ridge from Middle Mountain. You will cross a fence marking the monument boundary. Continue along the ridge, which narrows occasionally as it passes some burnt trees and thriving juniper groves with huge, old trees. Keep to the ridge crest, turning more southward as you

Up-close look at the distinct columns of Picture Gorge basalts in the John Day Fossil Beds National Monument

proceed until ascending to the top of Peak 3493 at 2.5 miles.

The ridge broadens as you descend from Peak 3493 south toward Windy Point. Keep south to ascend the gully east of the very steep rock bands of the northern slopes. Scramble south, up the steep gully, to the summit ridge of Windy Point. Once you gain the ridge, turn west and continue climbing to the summit past the rocks and pretty blooming cacti in the spring. The summit views are expansive on a clear day. The Cascades are visible to the west and north. To the east-southeast are the Aldrich Mountains close by and the Strawberries in the distance. Southwest is Lookout Mountain in the Ochoco Mountains.

After enjoying the views and also the varied rock of the point, descend south off the ridge. For about the next 2 miles, keep to the ridge crest and descend. You will cross the north end of Waterspout Gulch as you begin. For the remainder of the scramble, Waterspout Gulch will be below you to the west.

As you make your way toward Hole in the Ground, note the steep cliffs that are occasionally visible down to the bottom of the gulch. Continue south, then turn west to pass the rocks of Hole in the Ground at 6 miles. After that, continue west and begin descending a gully at 6.3 miles.

This gully is very steep and loose in places, and rattlesnakes like to hang out among the warm rocks of this western slope. Scramble down, avoiding the cliffs on the north side, to the outwash plain where Waterspout Gulch joins the John Day River.

As you cross the plain, turn north until you reach a jeep trail heading north. Sheep Rock, nearly 1200 feet above you, is imposing from down here close to the river. Return to your vehicle by hiking north, keeping on the jeep trails, some faint and some obviously still in use. From waypoint 7 it is 3.8 miles to the parking area.

 41 FIELDS PEAK AND MOON MOUNTAIN

Elevation: 7362 feet, 7043 feet

Difficulty: S2/T2

Round trip: 10 miles

Elevation gain: 2533 feet

Trip time: 6 hours

Time to summits: 3.5 hours

Best time of year: June to November

Map: USGS McClellan Mountain, Big Weasel Springs

Contact: Malheur National Forest, Blue Mountain Ranger District

Special considerations: Fields Peak Trail is popular with hunters in the fall and is open to all-terrain vehicles.

WAYPOINT ROUTE
1. Fields Peak Trail: 6600 feet (11T 319451mE 4910055mN)
2. Fields Peak: 2.3 miles, 7362 feet (11T 320030mE 4911746mN)
3. McClellan Mountain Trail junction: 3.6 miles, 6571 feet (11T 3322112mE 4911365mN)
4. Moon Mountain: 5.0 miles, 7043 feet (11T 322786mE 4912772mN)

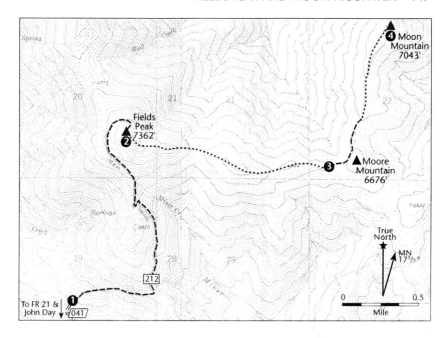

The Aldrich Mountains are a subset of the Blue Mountains west of John Day (the city) and south of the John Day River. Surrounded by the rich mixed conifers of the Malheur National Forest, the Aldrich Mountains are a peak bagger's delight. From the Fields Peak/McClellan Mountain Trailhead you could scramble up to the cluster of peaks near the McClellan Mountain Trail. Fields Peak is the tallest mountain between the Cascades to the west and the eastern neighbor, the Strawberry Range.

Trailhead directions: From the city of John Day take U.S. Route 26 west to Forest Road 21 (aka Fields Creek Road). The turn is marked with a sign that says "Murderers Creek," which refers to a pioneer legend. Turn left onto FR 21 and drive south. The road is lined with beautiful ponderosa pines, and you will pass a primitive campground. Turn left at the sign for Fields Peak/McClellan Trailhead onto FR 21-115. Drive a short distance, continue on FR 2160, then turn east on FR 041 and continue to the parking area for the McClellan Mountain Trailhead.

Route description: Fields Peak Trail 212 starts out as an ATV trail that is dusty, rocky, and dry. In early June there are wildflowers to distract you though, including larkspur and Indian paintbrush, as well as mixed forest that includes ponderosa pine, western larch, and white fir. The trail climbs steeply as it winds its way toward Fields Peak. You have good views of the dense forest and rolling hills as you ascend.

The trail continues through gnarled juniper trees with wildflowers along the trail in spring or early summer. You may see lewisia, false Solomon's seal, and forget-me-nots dotting the trailside. At about 1.5 miles there is a Y and sign—turn left here for the Fields summit.

The rugged ridge leading to the summit of Moon Mountain

The trail climbs on, while it continues contouring around the west side of the mountain. Continue up to the summit at 2.3 miles, where you will find the remains of an old lookout and several other structure remnants (and deep holes—be careful). After checking out the views of the surrounding Aldrich peaks, head down the east ridge.

Begin the descent by heading southeast for about 0.1 mile, then turn east down the ridge to intersect the McClellan Mountain Trail. Keep just below the ridge crest and traverse below a wall of large blocks, being careful not to pull down any large rocks. Follow the faint climbers trail down the ridge to the trail below at 3.6 miles, just adjacent to the sign for "Moore Mountain."

Turn left onto the McClellan Mountain Trail and follow it as it contours around the west side of Moore Mountain (Peak 6676). Continue through the forest until you reach a junction and turn left.

Scramble north on the obvious ridge until you reach the Moon Mountain summit. At 6800 feet you will traverse across a rocky slope above a steep drop-off. Scramble the last 100 feet, up a section of large rocks, to the summit at 5 miles.

Looking north, the views are impressive of the narrow ridge, which leads to Second and First Peaks. Other summit views include the Strawberry Range in the distance to the east. Return to your vehicle on the trails.

CANYON MOUNTAIN

Elevation: 7999 feet

Difficulty: S5/T2

Round trip: 17.6 miles

Elevation gain: 4674 feet

Trip time: 9–10 hours

Time to summit: 5–6 hours

Best time of year: July to November

Map: USGS Pine Creek Mountain

Contact: Malheur National Forest, Prairie City Ranger District

WAYPOINT ROUTE
1. Canyon Mountain Trailhead: 5424 feet (11T 346516mE 4913724mN)
2. Leave trail at Green Mountain ridge: 6.4 miles, 7061 feet (11T351582mE 4911745mN)
3. Green Mountain: 7.1 miles, 7629 feet (11T 350869mE 4910784mN)
4. Viewpoint: 7.9 miles, 7859 feet (11T 350054mE 4910132mN)
5. Saddle: 8.5 miles, 7650 feet (11T 349822mE 4910429mN)
6. Canyon Mountain: 8.8 miles, 7999 feet (11T 349408mE 4910823mN)

Canyon Mountain is a rugged multisummit peak south of Canyon City in the western corner of the Strawberry Mountain Wilderness. Canyon Mountain, like other peaks in the Strawberry Range, has been shaped by glacial ice and erosion. The peak's eastern slopes are nearly vertical and it has a unique twin summit. The Canyon Mountain Trail is a lovely hike with multiple creek crossings, seasonal wildflowers, and old-growth ponderosa pine, lodgepole pine, and Douglas fir. Cold winters and deep snows prevent access into this part of the wilderness until late summer. This scramble features views into seldom-visited parts of the wilderness, from Green Mountain and along the ridge climb to Canyon Mountain.

   Trailhead directions: From the city of John Day drive on U.S. Route 395 south to Canyon City. Turn left on Main Street, which becomes County Road 52. Turn right onto County Road 77. Drive about 0.3 mile, then curve right onto a one-lane road. At the intersection stay left and follow the signs to Canyon Mountain Trail 318. Veer left at the next intersection onto the rutted

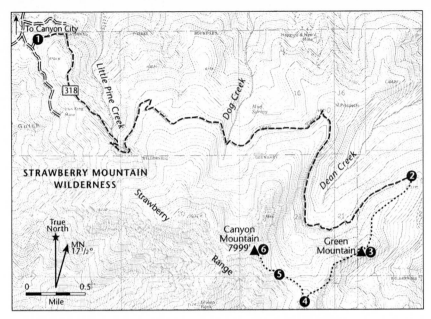

dirt road. This road is in poor condition and is most suitable for all-wheel-drive and/or high-clearance vehicles. If driving a passenger car, you may want to park at the clearing on the right before the road gets bad. This will add a total of 4 miles to the route.

To reach the trailhead follow the main road uphill. At about 0.5 mile the road will take a sharp right (away from the creek) and switchback steeply uphill. Continue about 1.5 miles uphill on the main road, ignoring any side roads or spurs. Fifty feet past a spur on the right, take the next left turn. There is a tree on the right side of this road with an unreadable Forest Service sign. Follow this short road uphill and turn left at the T. This final section of road will take you to a dead end with some parking and the unmarked trailhead.

Route description: Canyon Mountain Trail 318 begins heading east then south above Little Pine Creek and winds gently uphill through the ponderosa pine and Douglas fir forest. As the trail contours around the upper rim of the valley, the views are dramatic. If you are hiking right after the snowmelt, alpine wildflowers dot the trail and include phlox, glacier lily, tiger lily, calypso lily, and gentian.

At 1.6 miles the trail crosses Little Pine Creek. Leaving the creek you cross a dry meadow with little vegetation and great views. Continue contouring through the valley, passing Dog Creek at 6440 feet and 3.3 miles. The trail keeps climbing gently for another 2 miles to Dean Creek.

Continue about 1 more mile on the trail as it passes the ridge to Green Mountain at 6.4 miles. Here, leave the trail and head up the ridge, which is densely forested in places, to the Green Mountain summit at 7.1 miles. As you ascend, scramble southwest while keeping to the ridge crest and contouring around rocky sections as necessary.

Looking across the ridge to the summit of Canyon Mountain

From the Green Mountain summit you are able to see the rest of the route, including the final scramble up to Canyon Mountain. To continue, backtrack off the summit and then contour around the summit on the right side. As you get past the summit block, gain the ridge once more. The ridge here is rocky and, though broad, it has drop-offs alternately on either side. Continue until the cliffy section forces you off the ridge and down on the left side. Contour under the vertical section until you are almost to some tall rock formations straight ahead. Again, veer right to gain the ridge and continue to head southwest until the ridge ends in a viewpoint at 7.9 miles.

Enjoy the views, and then turn right and head northwest to the summit of Canyon Mountain. Stay on the ridge crest, keeping within view of the cliffs on the left as much as possible. You will have to drop down off the ridge crest to go around some steep sections, but you will mostly stay directly on the ridge crest. Descend the ridge to a very small saddle at 8.5 miles, then scramble up the final pitch to the summit of Canyon Mountain.

For the final 50 feet, scramble through the rocks using obvious gullies to the small summit. The views from the Canyon Mountain summit include a lot of dramatic formations and knife-edge ridges. Looking east you can see nearly the whole Strawberry Range.

43 STRAWBERRY MOUNTAIN

Elevation: 9038 feet	
Difficulty: S3/T2	
Round trip: 10.2 miles	
Elevation gain: 3628 feet	
Trip time: 7 hours	
Time to summit: 4 hours	
Best time of year: July to November	
Map: USGS Strawberry Mountain	
Contact: Malheur National Forest, Prairie City Ranger District	

Special considerations: This is a popular big-game hunting area in late summer and fall; wear bright colors during hunting season.

WAYPOINT ROUTE

1. Strawberry Campground: 5775 feet (11T 366581mE 4908501mN)
2. Pass: 4.3 miles, 8280 feet (11T 363421mE 4906943mN)
3. Strawberry Mountain: 5.0 miles, 9038 feet (11T 363180mE 4907744mN)
4. Peak 8452: 6.1 miles, 8452 feet (11T 363673mE 4906776mN)

The Strawberry Mountain Wilderness is alpine country. The Strawberry Range, part of the discontinuous Blue Mountains, has rugged peaks and ridges that will delight any scrambler. The geology of the Strawberry Range is raw and colorful when you observe it up close. Glacial ice has left sharp ridges and peaks surrounding glacial valleys. Summer comes late to the Strawberries, and winter snows linger until mid-July. The wilderness has a mixture of lodgepole and ponderosa pine, true fir, and western larch. Originally named for its color, Strawberry Mountain is the home to mule deer, elk, mountain lion, and a wide variety of birds. After the winter snows melt, the wilderness is full of colorful alpine wildflowers.

Trailhead directions: From Prairie City turn right on Bridge Street. Follow the signs as the road heads south. Bridge Street becomes Forest Road 60 and then FR 6001, which goes to the Strawberry Campground. The trailhead is at the turnaround and is well signed. There is water available at the campground as well as vault toilets.

Route description: Strawberry Basin Trail 375 is a wide, well-maintained trail that winds along a glacier-carved valley. Turn right at the first junction and take the left fork at the Y to get to Strawberry Lake. At the lake, take the left-hand trail around the lake. While you hike along, note the dramatic line of rocky peaks directly across the lake and heading northward. Ignore any other trail junctions while going around the lake. Continue up (left) on the trail at the end of the lake toward Little Strawberry Lake.

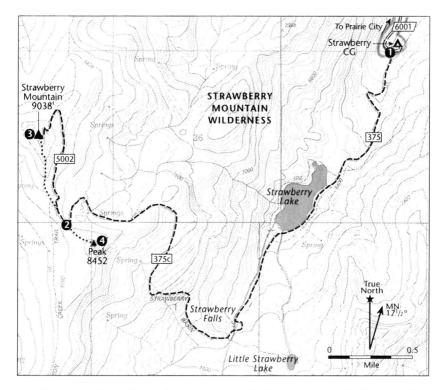

The trail climbs through lodgepole, whitebark pine, and other conifers to reach Strawberry Falls in almost a mile. Enjoy the dramatic falls then climb up several switchbacks to the top of the falls, crossing a bridge as the trail continues. Turn right at the junction onto Strawberry Basin Trail 375C. The grade steepens as the trail narrows and climbs 2.5 miles through a basin en route to the pass just south of Strawberry Mountain. Enjoy the views of the mountain as you hike through the basin, then climb steeply up switchbacks to reach the pass at 4.3 miles.

Hike along the trail a short distance. You will notice the trail veering to the right to go around the south ridge and ascend to the summit. Here, leave the trail and continue north along the south ridge. As you scramble along the ridge stay on the west side and just below the ridge crest as you ascend to the summit. Be very careful, as it narrows slightly and the exposure increases on the west side above 8800 feet.

The Strawberry summit, at 5 miles, has plenty of room to relax, including some rock shelters that make a good lunch spot. From the summit the views include the John Day Valley, Canyon Mountain, Slide Mountain, and the Elkhorn Range. Note the many snags on the west side, sobering reminders of the 1996 fires.

Descend by using Strawberry Mountain Trail 5002. When you reach the pass again, as the trail is going to turn north and descend back to the basin, go straight ahead and off the trail. Scramble up the short ridge about 300 feet

Strawberry Mountain view along the approach

to the summit of the neighboring Peak 8452, at 6.1 miles. You will enjoy great views of the south ridge you just climbed up to Strawberry Mountain.

Descend the short distance back to the pass, where you can pick up the trail.

44 SLIDE MOUNTAIN

Elevation: 8544 feet

Difficulty: S3/T2

Round trip: 10.4 miles

Elevation gain: 3461 feet

Trip time: 7–8 hours

Time to summit: 4 hours

Best time of year: July to November

Map: USGS Strawberry Mountain

Contact: Malheur National Forest, Prairie City Ranger District

Special considerations: This is a popular big-game hunting area in late summer and fall; wear bright colors during hunting season.

WAYPOINT ROUTE
1. Strawberry Campground: 5775 feet (11T 366581mE 4908501mN)
2. Start scramble off trail: 4.4 miles, 7300 feet (11T 368506mE 4907365mN)
3. Above rocky chute: 4.6 miles, 7977 feet (11T 368759mE 4907582mN)
4. Slide Mountain: 5.0 miles, 8544 feet (11T 369239mE 4907564mN)
5. Bench: 5.3 miles, 8267 feet (11T 369260mE 4907298mN)
6. Trail junction: 5.5 miles, 7500 feet (11T 368935mE 4907009mN)

Weathered snag on the summit of Slide Mountain, Graham Mountain in the background

Slide Mountain is a moderate peak in the eastern portion of the Strawberry Mountain Wilderness. The Strawberries are part of the Blue Mountains, a folded and uplifted collection of moderate-elevation peaks in scattered ranges. The extensive lava flows in the wilderness are good examples of a violent volcanic past. The wilderness contains rugged peaks, glacial cirques, and dense forests of ponderosa pine, Douglas fir, lodgepole pine, and juniper.

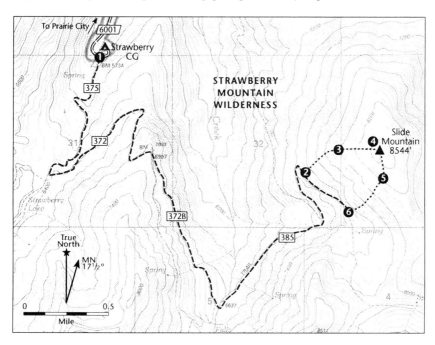

Slide Mountain from the scramble route

Trailhead directions: From Prairie City turn right on Bridge Street. Follow the signs as the road heads south. Bridge Street becomes Forest Road 60 and then FR 6001, which goes to the Strawberry Campground. The trailhead is at the turnaround and is well signed. There is water available at the campground as well as vault toilets.

Route description: Follow Strawberry Basin Trail 375 for about a mile and turn left onto Trail 372 heading toward Slide Lake. Continue on the trail, keeping left at the next two trail junctions. Finally at 3.5 miles you will reach the junction with Skyline Trail 385. Continue straight ahead onto the Skyline Trail. Follow this trail and continue right at another junction. There is a slight detour left around an old-growth tree that blocks the trail. Wind around until you are directly below Slide Mountain on the trail and reach a small rocky section on the left at 4.4 miles, waypoint 2.

Climb up the slope about 400 feet, winding around the few trees, and continue to a band of rock with a gully in the middle. Scramble up and through the gully, keeping to the right side on fairly solid rock. Continue ascending past 7977 feet at about 4.7 miles. As the slope becomes more moderate, you will continue up the rocky slope with whitebark pines scattered about. The next steep pitch mainly involves negotiating the slippery talus to a small bench.

The last 300 feet are up the now blocky rock and talus slope to the summit at 5 miles, which is covered with large rocks and a few surviving whitebark pines. The high point is the northwest corner. Enjoy the views all around of the Wallowas, Elkhorns, and other Strawberry peaks.

To descend, head south toward Graham Mountain and make your way down the talus to a small clearing on a bench at 5.3 miles. At the clearing veer southwest and continue your descent through the forest to the trail. Keep the cliffs on your right and scramble southwest then west, continuing down to the trail. Once on the trail, at 5.5 miles, turn right. From here it is only about 0.3 mile to the point where you left to head up to the summit.

45 INDIAN SPRING BUTTE

Elevation: 8529 feet

Difficulty: S2/T2

Round trip: 4.5 miles

Elevation gain: 1909 feet

Trip time: 4 hours

Time to summit: 1 hour

Best time of year: July to November

Map: USGS Strawberry Mountain

Contact: Malheur National Forest, Prairie City Ranger District

Special considerations: This is a popular big-game hunting area in late summer and fall; wear bright colors during hunting season.

WAYPOINT ROUTE

1. High Lake Trailhead: 7994 feet (11T 364497mE 4903840mN)
2. Indian Spring Butte: 0.7 mile, 8529 feet (11T 364622mE 4904773mN)
3. Gully: 1.2 miles, 8232 feet (11T 365174mE 4905051mN)
4. Viewpoint: 1.6 miles, 8388 feet (11T 365653mE 4905108mN)
5. Last high point: 1.9 miles, 8436 feet (11T 366066mE 4905192mN)
6. Trail junction: 2.1 miles, 8059 feet (11T 366075mE 4904958mN)

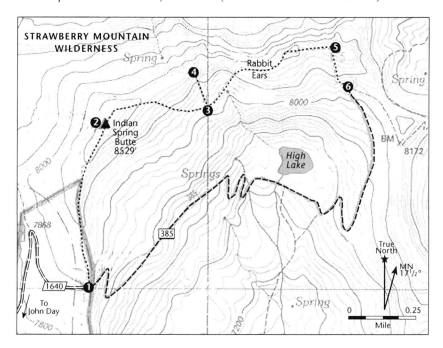

Rabbit Ears and the surrounding lava flows

The Strawberry Mountain Wilderness is a rich mix of alpine ridges, glacial tarns, and beautiful meadows. Indian Spring Butte is a moderate-elevation peak at the southwest end of the prominent lava flow south of the Strawberry Lake basin. This peak, which has easy access from the High Lake Rim, begins this short scramble northeast and leads to the convoluted flow up to the base of Rabbit Ears. Rabbit Ears is a volcanic remnant that has been highly dissected by glaciers and is a prominent landmark. These distinctive twin pinnacles are visible from many points throughout the wilderness. Although you cannot scramble up their vertical sides, the surrounding terrain provides a variety of other scrambling opportunities.

Trailhead directions: From John Day drive south on U.S. Route 395 toward Canyon City. At the junction with County Route 65, turn left. Continue as the name changes to Forest Road 15. Drive past the Parish Cabin and turn left onto FR 16. In about 2.5 miles turn left onto FR 1640 and drive north. Follow this to the end at the High Lake Rim trailhead.

Route description: Begin this short scramble by heading north from the parking area right up the gentle ridge to the summit of Indian Spring Butte. After hiking up the slope a short distance, scramble up along the right side of the two rocky sections that lead to the summit at 0.7 mile.

Head down off the summit of Indian Spring Butte and scramble northeast along the ridge crest. Work your way past some spires and then down to a prominent gully, which dissects the lava flow. Here, scramble up the right side of the gully (at 1.2 miles) to the pinnacles ahead. Work your way up, keeping right, to a small platform below a formation shaped like a semicircular wall of bumpy lava.

Drop your pack for a moment and scramble up to the top of this wall for impressive views of the vertical northwest side of the ridge. When you tire of the views scramble back down, pick up your pack, and return down the gully. Work past a large block of rock by passing it on the right side and continue descending. Once you are past the vertical section, cross back to head north-northeast again. Notice here that there is a short section of nearly vertical cliffs below and to your right.

Do an ascending traverse toward Rabbit Ears. These pinnacles are the vents from an ancient volcano and are responsible for much of the surrounding area's lava flows. Continue working your way along the ridge crest, dropping down to bypass any vertical sections. Always return to the ridge crest as soon as it is possible. Ascend for the best views as you continue to the final high point at 1.9 miles, which is just northwest of High Lake Rim Trail 385. After this last high point, scramble southeast across a talus slope to the junction with the trail at 2.1 miles.

The return hike on the trail is very pleasant, although it is through a forested area that was badly burned in 2002. The view of the whole ridge, including Rabbit Ears, is wonderful from the trail. The view of the ridge above High Lake is particularly dramatic. The trail then leaves the lake and climbs out of the lake basin. The final section is dry and dusty as the trail climbs on a few steep switchbacks to the basin rim and your car.

46 GRAHAM MOUNTAIN

Elevation: 8570 feet

Difficulty: S2/T2

Round trip: 9.4 miles

Elevation gain: 2708 feet

Trip time: 7 hours

Time to summit: 3–4 hours

Best time of year: July to October

Map: USGS Strawberry Mountain

Contact: Malheur National Forest, Prairie City Ranger District

Special considerations: This is a popular big-game hunting area in late summer and fall; wear bright colors during hunting season.

WAYPOINT ROUTE
1. Meadow Fork Trailhead: 5945 feet (11T 369563mE 4900417mN)
2. Mud Lake Trail 379: 0.8 mile, 6351 feet (11T 369738mE 4901705mN)
3. Skyline Trail: 3.9 miles, 7849 feet (11T 369148mE 4906123mN)
4. Leave trail: 4.2 miles, 7767 feet (11T 369535mE 4906115mN)
5. Graham Mountain: 4.7 miles, 8570 feet (11T 36mE905192mN)

The Blue Mountains of eastern Oregon are a complex of small, broken mountain ranges. The Strawberry Range, south of Prairie City, contains diverse forests and enough peaks to satisfy peak baggers of all abilities. The Strawberries have alpine ridges, glacial tarns and lakes, and grassy meadows, which make it a wonderful destination. Graham Mountain is in the eastern section of the Strawberry Mountain Wilderness. The Little Riner Basin is at the end of a U-shaped valley where the mixed-conifer forest of western larch, lodgepole pine, and fir provides a scenic approach. The scramble begins on the west side of a

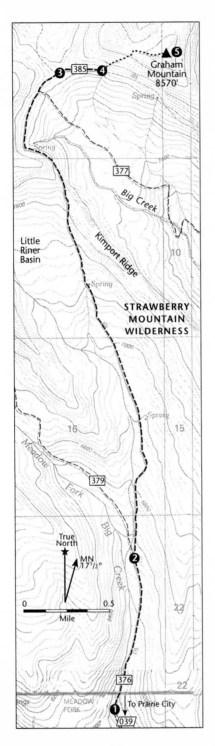

badly burned slope, but ends with a scramble up talus to the upper mountain. Along the way there are good views of Graham Mountain's north-face cliffs and out to the John Day Valley just to the north. Graham's summit is rocky and has wonderful views of the Strawberry peaks and Elkhorn Range to the east.

Trailhead directions: From Prairie City drive south on Forest Road 62 to FR 16. Turn right and drive west on FR 16 for 7.65 miles to FR 924. Turn right on FR 924 and drive north for 2.6 miles. Turn right on FR 1648, past the Murray Campground sign, and drive east for 0.4 mile. Turn left on FR 021, heading north for 1.4 miles. At the Y junction bear left onto FR 039 and continue about 0.5 mile to the trailhead. A Northwest Forest Pass is required.

Route description: Meadow Fork Trail 376 is a great access point for entry into the southeastern Strawberry Mountain Wilderness. The trail climbs steadily along the valley floor, gaining 1400 feet as you pass through the thick forest. Pass the Mud Lake Trail junction at 0.8 mile. After 2.6 miles, the trail enters the Little Riner Basin as it approaches the climb up to the north end of Kimport Ridge. This part of the trail is very striking, as the three ridges rise up in a U shape around the Little Riner Basin.

Follow the trail up to the ridge crest. The trail jogs to the northwest and after passing Big Creek turns northeast toward the junction with Big Creek Trail 377. Continue northeast and then eastward, bearing right at the trail junction with Skyline Trail 385 at 3.9 miles. This will take you to the scramble route just ahead.

Graham Mountain from the summit of nearby Slide Mountain

When you are below the Graham Mountain saddle, at 4.2 miles, scramble northeast off the trail and up the slope of charred snags. Once you reach the saddle, turn right and scramble to the cliffy north side of Graham's summit. Traverse around to the left a short distance to get around the cliffs. Then begin ascending a loose talus slope south to the upper mountain. Once up on the sloping upper summit, turn left to reach the summit.

This summit has some remnants from an old lookout and a couple of USGS survey markers. Enjoy the views of the southern Elkhorn peaks to the northeast and the Aldrich Mountains in the west. The summit has some good examples of whitebark pines, which are very adaptable to the harsh alpine climate.

47 PEAK 8511

Elevation: 8511 feet

Difficulty: S2/T2

Round trip: 8.8 miles

Elevation gain: 2577 feet

Trip time: 7 hours

Time to summit: 3–4 hours

Best time of year: July to October

Map: USGS Strawberry Mountain

Contact: Malheur National Forest, Prairie City Ranger District

Special considerations: This is a popular big-game hunting area in late summer and fall; wear bright colors during hunting season.

WAYPOINT ROUTE

1. Meadow Fork Trailhead: 5945 feet (11T 369563mE 4900417mN)
2. Mud Lake Trail 379: 0.8 mile, 6351 feet (11T 369738mE 4901705mN)
3. Little Mud Lake: 3.4 miles, 7455 feet (11T 369621mE 4904306mN)
4. Peak 8511: 4.6 miles, 8511 feet (11T 368565mE 4905855mN)
5. Meadow Fork Trail 376 junction: 5.0 miles, 7876 feet (11T 369002mE 4906036mN)

The Strawberry Mountain Wilderness, in Oregon's Blue Mountains, contains several unnamed ridges and peaks. Peak 8511 is at the north end of a rocky ridge that divides the Slide Lake basin from the Little and Big Riner Basins. This ridge is shaped like a big capital H, with a south and north peak. This scramble takes you north through the Mud Lake basin along Meadow Fork Big Creek. Hiking the approach to the lake you will pass through a lush forest alongside the fast-moving creek, including a couple of sections with magical waterfalls. There are woodpeckers, elk, and grouse around for observant hikers. The continental climate of the Strawberry Wilderness almost guarantees a short hiking season and beautiful wildflowers in midsummer after the snow melts off.

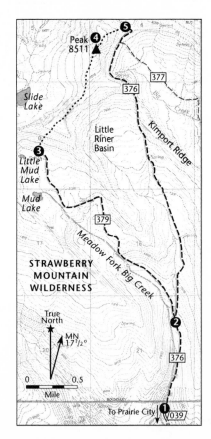

Trailhead directions: From Prairie City drive south on Forest Road 62 to FR 16. Turn right and drive west on FR 16 for 7.65 miles to FR 924. Turn right on FR 924 and drive north for 2.6 miles. Turn right on FR 1648, past the Murray Campground sign, and drive east for 0.4 mile. Turn left on FR 021, heading north for 1.4 miles. At the Y junction bear left onto FR 039 and continue about 0.5 mile to the trailhead. A Northwest Forest Pass is required.

Route description: Meadow Fork Trail 376 begins gently, climbing northward along Meadow Fork Big Creek into the Strawberry Mountain Wilderness. In 0.8 mile turn left onto Mud Lake Trail 379, which follows the creek northward through scenic meadows surrounded by the dense forest of the southern wilderness.

A steep section of trail around 1.6 miles includes a close look at the creek and waterfalls just to the west. Continue along the trail, through another steepish section until you pass Mud Lake, which

From the summit of Peak 8511 the Slide Lake Basin is a sharp contrast.

has a short trail to its east shore.

Continue to Little Mud Lake at 3.4 miles. Just southeast of Little Mud Lake the trail begins to turn westerly. In a short distance, scramble off the trail to the northeast up a broad slope covered in large rocks and some burnt trees. Scramble up to the summit ridge and ascend to the top of the first peak at around 8160 feet. Then continue northeast along the ridge crest to the south ridge of Peak 8511. Note the various formations made by the old lava flows and scramble up the jumble of rough rock to the summit at 4.6 miles.

All along the ridge crest you will have great views down into the Slide Lake basin to the west. Slide Lake gleams like a blue jewel in the midday sun, adding to the beauty of the bowl 1000 feet below. Views from the summit include the nearby Strawberry Range peaks and the Aldrich Mountains out west.

Descend the northeast ridge, which initially narrows enough to force you off to the right side of the crest. Continue to scramble down, turning northeast to reach the junction with Meadow Fork Trail 376 at 5 miles. Here, just north of Big Creek Trail 377, turn to the right and hike the rest of the way out on the trail south through the Little Riner Basin.

48 ROCK CREEK BUTTE

Elevation: 9106 feet

Difficulty: S2/T2

Round trip: 9.7 miles

Elevation gain: 2776 feet

Trip time: 5–6 hours

Time to summit: 3–4 hours

Best time of year: July to November

Map: USGS Elkhorn Peak

Contact: Wallowa–Whitman National Forest, Baker Ranger District

Special considerations: A high-clearance four-wheel-drive vehicle is needed to drive all the way to the trailhead.

WAYPOINT ROUTE

1. Parking/dirt road: 6771 feet (11T 408723mE 4961100mN)
2. Pole Creek Ridge Trail 1624: 1.6 miles, 7491 feet (11T 409321mE 4963072mN)
3. Elkhorn Crest Trail 1611: 2.4 miles, 8040 feet (11T 409618mE 4963761mN)
4. Leave the trail: 4.5 miles, 8370 feet (11T 412492mE 4962667mN)
5. Rock Creek Butte: 4.9 miles, 9106 feet (11T 412801mE 4962990mN)

The summit of Rock Creek Butte gives you unrestricted views north.

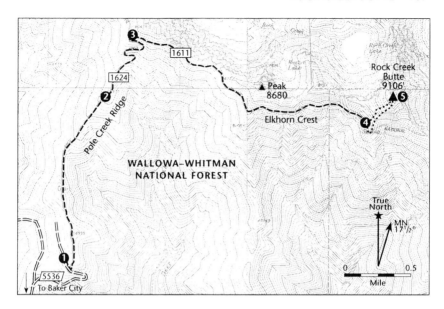

Rock Creek Butte is the highest peak in the Elkhorn Mountains. The Elkhorns, part of the Blue Mountains, are geologically related to the Greenhorn and Strawberry Ranges and are part of the Baker Terrane. Consisting of shattered rock, glacial cirques, and isolated lakes, the Elkhorn Mountains are an ideal place for scramblers looking for peace and quiet. Adjacent to the North Fork John Day Wilderness, the Elkhorns are bisected by the Elkhorn Crest National Recreation Trail. This rocky and exposed trail was blasted into the mountainside and offers through-hikers access to the entire range. Although access to the trail is limited on the southern end due to poor-quality roads, other access points such as Pole Creek are in reasonable shape. This trail is also the highest trail in the Blue Mountains.

Trailhead directions: From Baker City drive south on Main Street, which turns into State Route 7. Drive south, then west, passing McEwan and follow the signs to Sumpter, an old mining town known for the partially restored Sumpter Dredge. At 2.4 miles past McEwan turn right on the Granite Hill Highway, which leads to Sumpter. Just outside the city limits turn right on Cracker Creek Road. Evidence of the Sumpter area's mining history is all around and includes miles of dredge tailings along Powder River and Cracker Creek. Follow Cracker Creek Road about 2.4 miles. Turn right on Forest Road 5536 at the sign reading "Pole Creek Ridge Trail." Follow this to the trailhead if you have a high-clearance or all-wheel-drive vehicle. Otherwise, park at waypoint 1, to the side of the dirt road, and hike up 1.6 miles to the trailhead.

Route description: Pole Creek Ridge rises north of Pole Creek and runs northward toward the crest of the Elkhorns. The hike up to Elkhorn Crest Trail 1611 runs along the ridge crest and is a good warm-up for the eventual steep scramble. Expect to see misshapen whitebark pines as the prominent tree on this beautiful scramble.

Hike north up the remainder of the rough road leading to the Pole Creek Ridge Trailhead. About 100 feet before the road ends the trail begins on the right. The trail mostly follows the ridge as it winds its way north, cresting over three small rocky summits before it switchbacks up to the junction with the Elkhorn Crest Trail.

The Elkhorn Crest Trail leads east along the rocky trail, which at some points seems to barely cling to the mountainside. It is no wonder that you may see mountain goats along the rocky outcrops above the trail; this is their natural habitat. At about 3.5 miles into the approach, you will pass a small path that goes off northeast leading to Peak 8680 (unmarked on the USGS quad). You may scramble up to the summit of this little peak for excellent views of the north side of the Elkhorns. Bucket Lake is directly below the summit if you are looking northeast.

Return to the Elkhorn Crest Trail and continue eastward to Rock Creek Butte. The steep slope of the southern exposure seems quite tame when compared to the broken vertical slope of the north side. Begin the scramble up the southwest slope after leaving the trail just before the southwest ridge at 4.5 miles. This steep scramble ascends almost 900 feet in 0.4 mile. The slope is rocky, but tenacious scramblers will be quickly rewarded by expansive views from the summit, which also has a huge rock cairn. Descend south along the summit and work your way down the southwest ridge back to the Elkhorn Crest Trail.

Alternate route: Scramble up from the junction of the southwest ridge with the Elkhorn Crest Trail. To reach the ridge continue past waypoint 4 for almost 0.1 mile. Although the start looks nearly vertical, there are actually many ledges and blocks to scramble on. Get onto the southwest ridge by scrambling north up fairly solid, blocky rock, then go west for a few feet to get up onto the ridge crest. Follow the ridgeline northeast to the summit block, turning north for the final pitch to the top.

49 ELKHORN PEAK

Elevation: 8931 feet

Difficulty: S3/T2

Round trip: 9 miles

Elevation gain: 3680 feet

Trip time: 5–6 hours

Time to summit: 2–3 hours

Best time of year: July through October

Map: USGS Elkhorn Peak

Contact: Wallowa–Whitman National Forest, Baker Ranger District

Special considerations: This is a popular hunting area in fall; wear bright colors during hunting season.

WAYPOINT ROUTE

1. Twin Lakes Trailhead: 5383 feet (11T 413948mE 4958687mN)
2. Twin Lakes: 3.2 miles, 7708 feet (11T 414252mE 4962033mN)
3. Elkhorn Crest Trail 1611: 3.8 miles, 8268 feet (11T 414492mE 4962264mN)
4. Leave the trail: 4.2 miles, 8166 feet (11T 414830mE 4961920mN)
5. Elkhorn Peak: 4.5 miles, 8931 feet (11T 415102mE 4962187mN)

The Elkhorn Mountains are a small subrange of the Blue Mountains in eastern Oregon. The Elkhorns, a north-south range, are a collection of glacial lakes and valleys that surround dissected mid-elevation peaks. Popular with fall hunters, this remote range gets few visits from hikers. The Elkhorn Crest National Recreation Trail provides hikers with the best access to the mountains and runs north-south through the major section of the range. The northern peaks are in the Anthony Lakes area, where the Elkhorn Crest Trail runs along the eastern edge of the North Fork John Day Wilderness. This important wilderness area protects the headwaters of the John Day River and its rich wildlife population.

Trailhead directions: From Baker City drive south on Main Street, which turns into State Route 7. Continue south and turn right on Deer Creek Road just before McEwan. Follow Deer Creek Road, which changes to Forest Road 6550 and then to FR 030. Continue on FR 030 until it ends at the trailhead. Twin Lakes Trail 1633 is at the north end of the road end.

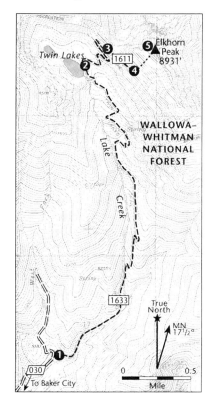

Route description: Twin Lakes Trail 1633 climbs steadily most of the way to the lakes basin below Elkhorn Peak. Winding through the Lake Creek drainage you will pass through heavily forested slopes that provide habitat for wildlife. You may hear elk crashing through the forest or see beaver along Lake Creek in early morning or near dusk.

The mixed forest contains western larch, mountain hemlock, lodgepole pine, and a variety of seasonal wildflowers. Approaching Twin Lakes, look over at the cliffs just southwest of the lakes. There are often families of mountain goats ranging on the cliffs and showing off their agile climbing style. Mountain goats are nonnative, but they thrive in these rugged peaks. You may

Rocky Mountain goats enjoy the solitude of the rugged Elkhorn Mountains.

also see them along the rocky outcrops above the upper trail.

Twin Lakes, at 3.2 miles, is a good spot for a quick break. Continue northward on the trail, which now switchbacks almost a mile up to meet the Elkhorn Crest Trail. This rugged, sometimes exposed trail was blasted into the mountains in an effort to allow through-hikers access to the whole range. Turn right on the Elkhorn Crest Trail for a short approach to the scramble point. At just about any point southwest of the Elkhorn summit, head up the steep slope to the summit of Elkhorn Peak. Once you gain the summit ridge, slightly south of the actual summit, turn left and traverse north to the summit.

The views are the payoff as you gaze down on Goodrich Lake to the east and the whole Elkhorn Range north to the Anthony Lakes area. Descend southeast across the summit ridge then south back to the trail. Turn right to return the way you came.

50 GUNSIGHT MOUNTAIN

Elevation: 8342 feet

Difficulty: S2/T3

Round trip: 3 miles

Elevation gain: 1185 feet

Trip time: 4 hours

Time to summit: 2.5 hours

Best time of year: July to October

Map: USGS Anthony Lakes

Contact: Wallowa–Whitman National Forest, Baker Ranger District

Special considerations: This is a popular summer and fall big-game hunting area; wear bright colors during hunting season.

WAYPOINT ROUTE

1. Anthony Lakes: 7126 feet (11T 402725mE 4978821mN)
2. Hoffer Lakes: 0.7 mile, 7476 feet (11T 402497mE 4977965mN)
3. West ridge: 0.8 mile, 7607 feet (11T 402623mE 4977976mN)
4. Gunsight Mountain: 1.2 miles, 8342 feet (11T 403235mE 4978006mN)
5. Angell Basin: 1.6 miles, 7818 feet (11T 403191mE 4977623mN)

Among the Blue Mountains' easternmost peaks are the Elkhorn Mountains. Surrounded by the dense trees of the Wallowa–Whitman National Forest, the Elkhorns are a highly dissected range of granitic ridges and hundreds of glacial lakes and tarns. The Anthony Lakes area, popular with skiers in the winter, is also a summer and fall destination for campers, hikers, and climbers. This area is just east of the North Fork John Day Wilderness, which protects the headwaters of the North Fork John

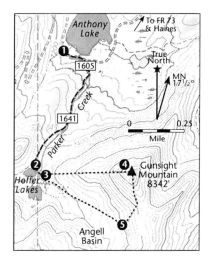

Day and its anadromous fish populations. When hiking in the forests keep an eye out for mule deer or elk. On the rocky ridges you may see mountain goats. From Anthony Lakes gaze across at the rocky summit of Gunsight Mountain—you will see how it got its name!

Trailhead directions: From Haines follow the signs to Anthony Lakes. First drive west-northwest on County Road 1146, which becomes the Anthony Lakes Highway. Once you cross into the Wallowa–Whitman National Forest, the road becomes Forest Road 73. Follow the signs to Anthony Lakes. At Anthony Lakes turn left and drive past the Anthony Lakes Guard Station to the parking for day use in the southwest corner. From the parking area you can access Anthony Lake Shoreline Trail 1605, which is a loop around the lake. There are multiple access points to this loop trail.

Route description: Follow Anthony Lake Shoreline Trail 1605 east to Hoffer Lakes Trail 1641, which is marked. Turn right to head south to Hoffer Lakes on a nicely maintained trail that follows Parker Creek through the dry lodgepole pine and fir forest. The trail climbs, sometimes steeply, then levels off just before the lakes. At Hoffer Lakes, at 0.7 mile, there are beautiful alpine meadows, which are expanding as the lakes' soil deposits accumulate.

When you reach the first and smaller lake, turn left and head southeast, then east cross-country on nearly level ground to the west ridge of Gunsight Mountain at 0.8 mile. Then begin a short steep scramble up the west ridge as it climbs sharply, nearly 1000 feet in just under 0.5 mile.

The ridge is quite pretty, dotted with huge granitic rock outcrops with a

Scrambler working his way up the route on Gunsight Mountain

lot of friction for your steep ascent. The green of the alpine conifers provides a striking contrast to the light gray rock. As you begin the scramble, keep to the right of a large spine of rock, scrambling up the chute along the south side. Continue eastward and up, scrambling up and over more large outcrops and boulders as the pitch increases.

You will ascend through a steep, rock-filled chute for the final pitch to Gunsight's summit. There is some loose rock and sand, so scramble up on the solid rock to the west summit. Then drop back down right and traverse up to the small east summit at 1.2 miles.

Views on a clear day are wonderful. Anthony Lakes is directly below and to the north. The peaks surrounding Angell Basin just south include Angell Peak and Hoffer Butte. East lies Van Patten Butte with its triple-peaked summit.

Descend south down the ridge to 8000 feet, then turn southwest to 7800 feet. You will be on the edge of Angell Basin at about 1.6 miles. Here, turn northwest back to Hoffer Lakes and the trail.

51 VAN PATTEN BUTTE

Elevation: 8729 feet	
Difficulty: S2/T2	
Round trip: 5.4 miles	
Elevation gain: 2322 feet	
Trip time: 5 hours	
Time to summit: 3–4 hours	
Best time of year: July to October	
Map: USGS Anthony Lakes	
Contact: Wallowa–Whitman National Forest, Baker Ranger District	

Special considerations: Road is uneven, with some narrow switchbacks; a high-clearance four-wheel-drive vehicle is needed to drive all the way to the trailhead.

WAYPOINT ROUTE

1. Parking: 6416 feet (11T 406781mE 4979705mN)
2. Van Patten Lake Trailhead: 0.9 mile, 7065 feet (11T 406868mE 4979223mN)
3. Gully: 2.0 miles, 7551 feet (11T 406108mE 4978023mN)
4. Saddle: 2.2 miles, 8221 feet (11T 405777mE 4977625mN)
5. Van Patten Butte: 2.7 miles, 8729 feet (11T 405184mE 4977883mN)

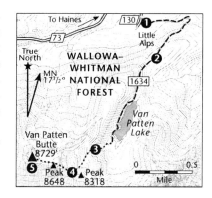

The Elkhorn Mountains are a north-south range in the easternmost Blue Mountains. Uplifted by fault movement millions of years ago, the Elkhorns were also shaped by glacial ice. The Elkhorns are bisected by the Elkhorn Crest National Scenic Trail, which is part of the long-distance national recreation trail system. Van Patten Butte is a craggy summit east of the Anthony Lakes area. At the foot of the 8000-foot crescent formed by Van Patten Butte and Van Patten Ridge lies Van Patten Lake. The lake, at 7396 feet, is a nice place for camping or a cool dip after scrambling up the neighboring peak. You may see mountain goats or other wildlife in the area, particularly in the early morning.

Trailhead directions: From Anthony Lakes drive east on Forest Road 73. Turn right at the Van Patten Lake Trailhead sign. Go south on FR 130 a short distance. You may park, off the road, just past the spur to Little Alps. Walk up the road almost a mile to reach the actual trailhead for Van Patten Lake Trail 1634.

Route description: After your warm-up on the badly rutted road, the trail enters the forest and climbs southward to Van Patten Lake. Although you will reach the lake in less than a mile, there are some steep sections along the trail. At the northern end of the lake is a Y junction. At the junction turn left and stop for a moment to enjoy the view across the lake of the surrounding Van Patten Butte and Ridge, which dominate the southern skyline. Note the broad summit of Van Patten Butte to the southwest; the route to the summit ridge is the prominent gully between the two smaller peaks. After enjoying your view, turn back onto the trail and take the other fork to get onto a well-traveled trail that skirts the west side of the lake.

As you pass the lake, the trail will fade away, leaving you to continue heading south across the dried mud where the lake has receded. The southwest chute or gully is evident on the slope ahead. Head directly for the gully by entering the forest for a short distance. Scramble up some boulders on the right and stay on the boulders as you ascend west-southwest. Traverse left for 50 or so yards to avoid any difficulties then continue southwest on easier

Looking up at the eroded summits of Van Patten Butte

terrain. From the bottom the chute at 2 miles is really pretty—filled with all sizes of whitish-gray boulders and scattered trees. Keep ascending until you reach the saddle at 2.2 miles, between Peak 8318 and the two higher peaks, Peak 8648 and Van Patten Butte at 8729 feet.

From the saddle you will scramble almost directly west to the summit. First, bypass the vertical south corner of the first summit by traversing west on the southern slope of the butte. Once past the cliffy section, begin ascending northwest to a rocky bench around 8600 feet. Go west to the summit across a series of ascending benches strewn with large rocks, a few hardy pines, and silvery snags. The summit is made up of huge blocks of granitic rock dotted with whitebark pines. Enjoy the views of the Blue Mountains west. The surrounding Elkhorn peaks include Gunsight Mountain directly west and Angell and Lees Peaks to the southwest. Descend the way you came.

CHINA CAP

Elevation: 8656 feet

Difficulty: S3/T3

Round trip: 9.3 miles

Elevation gain: 3182 feet

Trip time: 4–5 hours

Time to summit: 3 hours

Best time of year: July to November

Map: USGS China Cap

Contact: Wallowa–Whitman National Forest, Eagle Cap Ranger District, Wallowa Mountains Visitors Center

Special considerations: Pack animals may be on these trails; stay in view and slowly move out of the way to allow animals to pass. Self-issue permits are available at trailheads for entrance into the Eagle Cap Wilderness; please register and read the wilderness regulations.

WAYPOINT ROUTE
1. Buck Creek Trailhead: 5480 feet (11T 455141mE 4999277mN)
2. China Ridge Trail junction: 3.7 miles, 7567 feet (11T 459452mE 4999781mN)
3. Pass: 4.1 miles, 7822 feet (11T 459315mE 5000359mN)
4. Base of rock scramble: 4.4 miles, 8320 feet (11T 459748mE 5000167mN)
5. Summit ridge: 4.5 miles, 8480 feet (11T 459802mE 5000213mN)
6. China Cap: 4.6 miles, 8656 feet (11T 460000mE 5000198mN)

The Wallowa–Whitman National Forest spreads out over 2.5 million acres of northeastern Oregon. The Wallowa Mountains cut across the northern section of the forest. The Eagle Cap Wilderness, where most of the high Wallowa peaks are, was put aside to preserve these rugged ridges, peaks, and glacial valleys. China Cap is a small peak by Wallowa standards, at the southern tip of the China Cap Ridge. The peak is surrounded by dense mixed-conifer forest and has good trail access. As you approach the scramble you may see elk or deer in the forest.

    Trailhead directions: From Union drive east on State Route 203, past Catherine Creek State Park to Forest Road 7785 (aka Catherine Creek Lane).

A fine view of China Cap from the trail approach

FR 7785 is about 2.5 miles past the state park, and there is a green sign on the left side of the road. Turn left onto the unmarked gravel road and drive north to the junction with FR 7787. Follow this to Buck Creek Trailhead, which has large parking spaces for horse trailers. The parking and vault toilet are past the trailhead, which is on the right and clearly marked. A Northwest Forest Pass is required.

Route description: Begin on Elk Creek Trail 1944A, climbing on a dusty trail for 0.7 mile. The junction with the main trail is marked with a sign. Climb north through the forest and past the wilderness boundary sign. Cross

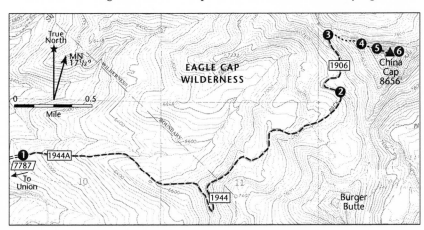

a stream, then travel through a slide area covered with gray rocks. Here is the first good view of China Cap, off to the northeast. Cross another creek bed, which may be dry in late season.

The junction with the China Ridge Trail 1906 is in a few hundred yards, at 3.7 miles. The trail is unmarked, but turns sharply left/north. The main trail right is marked with a rock cairn and leads to Burger Butte. The China Ridge Trail goes through some beautiful meadows on the way to the pass, which is just west of the mountain.

At the sign, as you reach the pass at 4.1 miles, turn right and off the trail to begin your scramble up the ridge to the summit. Leave the trail at the sign, heading east and slightly toward the right side of the ridge. Go a few hundred yards, contouring along or slightly ascending along the west ridge. Ascend through a large grassy open area and continue up to the base of a large rock outcrop on the upper ridge, at 4.4 miles. Scramble up through the rocks, emerging on the summit ridge at 4.5 miles in an open area. Turn right, scramble through some whitebark pines to the summit and sign the summit register. You have a good view to the south of nearby Burger Butte. To the north and northeast are all of the high Wallowa peaks.

 EAGLE CAP

Elevation: 9595 feet

Difficulty: S4/T3

Round trip: 17 miles

Elevation gain: 4771 feet

Trip time: 7–9 hours

Time to summit: 4–5 hours

Best time of year: July to November

Map: USGS Eagle Cap

Contact: Wallowa–Whitman National Forest, Eagle Cap Ranger District, Wallowa Mountains Visitors Center

Special considerations: In early season you will need crampons and ice ax to cross the snowfield. Self-issue permits are available at trailheads for entrance into the Eagle Cap Wilderness; please register and read the wilderness regulations.

WAYPOINT ROUTE
1. Two Pan Trailhead: 5600 feet (11T 470556mE 5010637mN)
2. Lakes Basin Trail 1810 junction: 6.3 miles, 7588 feet (11T 475199mE 5002663mN)
3. Leave trail: 7.4 miles, 8597 feet (11T 475401mE 5001521mN)
4. Above notch: 7.7 miles, 8765 feet (11T 475727mE 5001195mN)
5. Eagle Cap: 8.5 miles, 9595 feet (11T 476417mE 5000982mN)

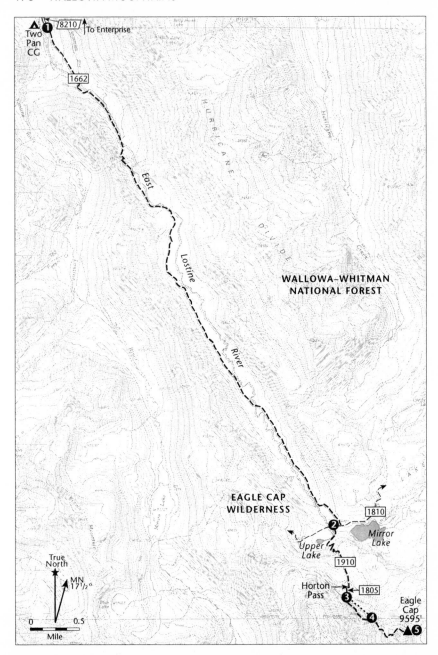

Eagle Cap is the centerpiece of the Eagle Cap Wilderness in far northeastern Oregon's Wallowa Mountains. Eagle Cap originally was thought to be the tallest peak in the Eagle Mountains. Eventually several other peaks turned out to be taller, but Eagle Cap remains the hub of the wilderness. The Wallowa Mountains have seventeen named peaks over 9000 feet high. Although this

Eagle Cap summit from the start of the scramble

is mostly a trail hike, you could not visit the Eagle Cap Wilderness without scrambling to the top of its namesake mountain.

Trailhead directions: From Enterprise drive west on State Route 82 to the town of Lostine. As you enter Lostine, and just before the road turns sharply right, turn left on County Road 551, which becomes Forest Road 8210. Drive south to the trailhead. The road is gravel the last 12 miles or so and may be rough in spots. On the way to the trailhead you will pass the Lostine Guard Station where a bubbling water fountain has drinking water 24 hours a day. In summer the station is staffed. At the trailhead are vault toilets, plenty of parking, and camping. You may park on the right at the end of the road. A Northwest Forest Pass is required.

Route description: From the Two Pan Trailhead information sign, get onto East Fork Lostine Trail 1662 by heading right and following the sign for "Lostine Trails." In a short distance you will pass a Y where the stock trail joins the hiker trail from the trailhead. The trail starts ascending almost right away, passing the wilderness boundary in less than 0.25 mile. In a mile the trail turns to the right to cross the river on a single-log bridge. Then the trail resumes climbing, switchbacking up sharply as it ascends through subalpine forest.

At 3 miles you enter the canyon and pass a lake on the left. For the next 2 miles the trail meanders through the Lostine Canyon, passing by the rocky remnants of slides as well as lush alpine meadows with seasonal wildflowers and a number of small lakes on the left. Eagle Cap comes into view and dominates your views to the south for the next couple of miles. Enjoy it.

This canyon, carved out by glaciers, is a good spot to camp for backpackers. The trail crosses the East Fork Lostine River again on a low bridge at 4.7 miles. Enjoy the last views of the mountain for a little while. The trail soon enters the forest and climbs to the junction with Lakes Basin Trail 1810 at 6.3 miles.

Turn right at the trail sign, hike a short distance, then turn left onto East

Eagle Cap from the Lostine River valley

Eagle Trail 1910, which climbs up to and over Horton Pass. You are now in the Lakes Basin Management Area. The Lakes Basin has rules in place to preserve the fragile alpine lake environment from overuse damage; please adhere to all restrictions. If you choose to backpack in the Eagle Cap area, set up camp outside the Lakes Basin to reduce your impact. The setting is stunning, with Eagle Cap looming to the south and luscious meadows and alpine lakes all around. Proceed on Trail 1910, passing Upper Lake on the right as the switchbacks begin. Most likely there will be backpackers fishing in the lake. There will also be a lot of wildflowers depending on the season, particularly on the lower slopes.

At the next junction there is a sign, "Eagle Cap Summit." An arrow points left and directs you onto Trail 1805, which climbs steeply to the Eagle Cap summit. Turn around and take in the views—they are tremendous. Climb some switchbacks up to the ridge, turning left to follow the ridgeline trail.

As you ascend and are at about 8700 feet, the trail will switchback right. At this corner, notice the cliffs along the summit ridge, with a snowfield below them. As you follow the cliffs toward the summit, notice a break in the vertical rock. You can leave the trail here (at 7.4 miles) and scramble across the snowfield, keeping well below the rocky cliffs. If it is still early season, be prepared here to use your crampons and ice ax for a more secure crossing. Aim directly for the obvious notch and scramble through it. Once you are above the notch at 7.7 miles, get back on the trail, which is up ahead less than 25 feet.

Turn left on the trail and follow it to the summit. You could directly ascend the ridge, but there are a number of whitebark pines and the rock is very loose. Help preserve this popular mountain by using the trail. Climb steadily through the dwarf trees. The summit is large and predictably rocky and windy. Sign the summit register, enjoy the views, and descend on the trails.

54 SACAJAWEA PEAK

Elevation: 9838 feet

Difficulty: S4/T3

Round trip: 13 miles

Elevation gain: 4924 feet

Trip time: 8–9 hours

Time to summit: 5 hours

Best time of year: July to November

Map: USGS Eagle Cap

Contact: Wallowa–Whitman National Forest, Eagle Cap Ranger District, Wallowa Mountains Visitors Center

Special considerations: Self-issue permits are available at trailheads for entrance into the Eagle Cap Wilderness; please register and read the wilderness regulations.

WAYPOINT ROUTE
1. Hurricane Creek Trailhead: 5152 feet (11T 475985mE 5017340mN)
2. Thorp Creek Trail: 1.8 miles, 5445 feet (11T 475998mE 5014591mN)
3. Creek bed: 4.7 miles, 7460 feet (11T 477826mE 5011324mN)
4. East ridge: 5.8 miles, 8234 feet (11T 478044mE 5010047mN)
5. Summit: 6.5 miles, 9838 feet (11T 477007mE 5009965mN)

The ridge route to the summit of this classic Wallowa peak

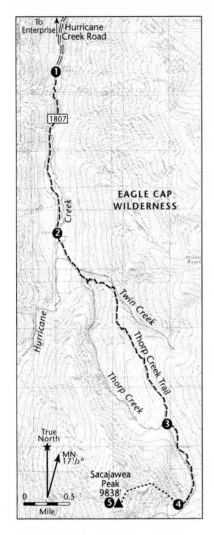

Sacajawea Peak is the tallest mountain in the Wallowa Mountains. At least it is the current tallest peak, the alternate tallest peak being the Matterhorn at 9824 feet. For some reason the designation of the tallest peak in the Wallowas is frequently under dispute, although it matters little. Scrambling to the summit of Sacajawea will reward you with dramatic views across the banded slopes of one of the Wallowas' most distinctive high peaks. The dragontail north ridge looks quite rugged and dramatic from the summit and has a daunting reputation as an extreme scramble. To the north the white slopes of Matterhorn gently climb toward its rounded summit. Along the way, enjoy the drama of the diverse forest in the Hurricane Creek canyon and the serene Thorp Creek valley below the Hurwal Divide. Although many animals enjoy this rich habitat, most scramblers will see only mountain goats, deer, and a variety of birds from the trail.

Trailhead directions: From Enterprise drive south on Hurricane Creek Road. After passing the Hurricane Creek Campground on the left, follow the signs to the trailhead at the end of the road. There is a vault toilet and trailhead self-register. The trail begins at the south side of the parking area. A Northwest Forest Pass is required.

Route description: Follow Hurricane Creek Trail 1807 south to the junction with the Thorp Creek Trail (no sign) at 1.8 miles. Along the way you will pass through some aspen groves that are stunning in the fall contrasted against the mixed conifers. The vine maples also offer fall color. The trail follows Hurricane Creek past some dramatic views of the Hurricane Divide to the west and the Hurwal Divide to the east. At waypoint 2 (at 1.8 miles), leave the Hurricane Creek Trail for the (unmaintained) Thorp Creek Trail and descend slightly to cross Hurricane Creek. This may be a tricky crossing in spring when the creek is swollen with melted snow. Cross on logs or bring along sandals. After crossing the creek, continue southeast and cross a clearing as the trail heads toward Twin Creek.

Scrambling up the distinctive rock of Sacajawea Peak

The trail soon begins to climb through the forest toward a broad but steep ridge leading to the Thorp Creek valley. This badly eroded section of trail may be hot and dusty as it climbs above the Thorp Creek canyon. Approaching 3 miles, the trail flattens slightly for a much-needed break. The trail then continues climbing steeply until about 4 miles. Continue southward while gently ascending through the U-shaped valley to the junction with the east ridge of Sacajawea Peak.

After about 4 miles the trail fades; continue south. Hiking along the dry creek bed (at 4.7 miles) is easiest; continue until you almost reach the end of the valley. The Hurwal Divide begins to loom sharply to the east and there is a dramatic headwall ahead to the south. For the last 0.3 mile before the east ridge junction (at 5.8 miles), you will begin to climb more steeply.

Turn west to gain the ridge, keeping to its right side and scrambling up through a band of intrusive rock. There may be mountain goats up on the ridge in early morning. The rock seems to change constantly as you ascend the ridge. Continue scrambling up, either on a route you choose or on a faint, braided, climbers trail heading roughly northwest then west.

Mountain goats on the ridge to Sacajawea Peak

As you reach the long ridge to the summit, turn southward for the final ascent. The views from Sacajawea are wonderful. The Matterhorn is impressive just to the south. Another highlight is the view of the sharp ridge of the Hurricane Divide to the west and the Hurwal Divide to the east. Both of these high ridges contain granitic intrusions and dramatically colored bands of rock.

CHIEF JOSEPH MOUNTAIN

Elevation: 9616 feet

Difficulty: S5/T3

Round trip: 13.4 miles

Elevation gain: 5596 feet

Trip time: 12 hours or 2 days

Time to summit: 6–7 hours

Best time of year: July to October

Map: USGS Chief Joseph

Contact: Wallowa–Whitman National Forest, Eagle Cap Ranger District, Wallowa Mountains Visitors Center

Special considerations: You will have to ford Hurricane Creek. Trekking poles may help with the steep descents. Self-issue permits are available at trailheads for entrance into the Eagle Cap Wilderness; please register and read the wilderness regulations.

WAYPOINT ROUTE
1. Hurricane Creek Trailhead: 5152 feet (11T 475985mE 5017340mN)
2. Thorp Creek Trail: 1.8 miles, 5445 feet (11T 475998mE 5014591mN)
3. Leave trail: 4.0 miles, 7378 feet (11T 477566mE 5012171mN)
4. Cliffs above saddle: 6.0 miles, 9257 feet (11T 479108mE 5013656mN)
5. Point Joseph: 6.7 miles, 9616 feet (11T 479572mE 5014494mN)

The Wallowa Mountains lie at the eastern end of the Blue Mountains of northeast Oregon. Protected largely by the vast Eagle Cap Wilderness, the Wallowas offer scramblers opportunities to enjoy miles of isolated ridges, dramatic glacial valleys, and high-elevation peaks. The Hurricane Creek Trail runs down a majestic canyon between Hurwal Divide and Hurricane Divide. This canyon offers scramblers access to both ridges and the Wallowas' highest peak—Sacajawea. The Thorp Creek Trail is not on many maps but is the approach for routes up to Hurwal Divide, Chief Joseph Mountain, and Sacajawea Peak.

Trailhead directions: From Enterprise drive south on Hurricane Creek Road. Follow the signs to Hurricane Creek Campground. Continue past the

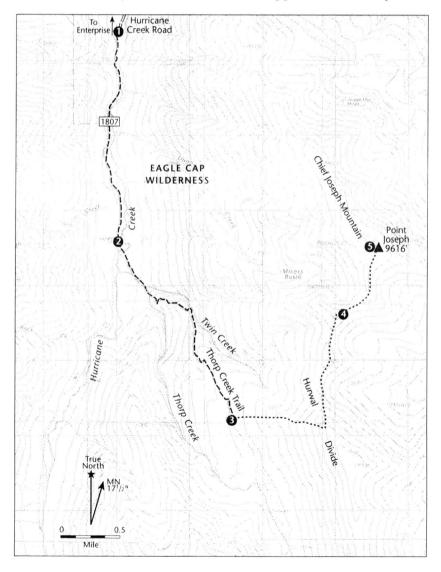

Scrambler making the descent from the summit of Chief Joseph Mountain

campground on the forest road until it ends at the trailhead. There is a parking area, trailhead sign and self-register, and vault toilet at the road end. A Northwest Forest Pass is required.

Route description: Head south on the rocky and dusty Hurricane Creek Trail 1.8 miles to the Thorp Creek Trail junction. This section of the Hurricane Creek Trail is very scenic, with numerous creeks and streams that drain into Hurricane Creek. You will hike past aspen groves, open meadows, and pine, hemlock, and fir forest. Enjoy the views of the high ridges rising on either side of the glacial valley. Turn left at waypoint 2 for the Thorp Creek Trail (at 1.8 miles), which is on the USGS quad but not on the Wallowa Mountains map. This trail is not maintained. Follow the trail east through the trees then drop down to cross Hurricane Creek. Look for logs to cross on or bring sandals during early season.

Continue east and then turn right through a meadow and ascend on a faint trail, which crosses Twin Creek before getting steep. The trail soon begins to climb more sharply on switchbacks to gain the ridge. This section of trail is rocky, dusty, and dry.

Once above Thorp Canyon you will continue on the trail southeast while contouring above the canyon and climbing more gently. You may turn this into a two-day trip by continuing on the Thorp Creek Trail into the Thorp Creek valley to camp in the scenic valley below Sacajawea Peak. For the scramble, at about 4 miles, 7400 feet, leave the trail and turn east to head through the trees a short distance. Enter the clearing and continue east while scrambling up the slope to intersect a broad ridge (northwest).

Once you are on the ridge, scramble up the steep loose talus to about 9200 feet. You may begin contouring northward while below this elevation, eventually ending up on the southern end of the long series of ridges to Chief Joseph Mountain.

186

Descend to a saddle, then begin the first of a series of three short ascents, each leading to a higher point until the final summit elevation of 9616 feet on Point Joseph. There are some intriguing natural features along the way. Oddly enough, there is a distinct difference in the appearance of the slopes on either side of the ridge crest. The westside slopes are green and have wildflowers growing in abundance. The eastside slopes are rocky, dry, and mostly devoid of obvious plant life. As you descend from the summit north of Peak 9093 you will find yourself above what appear to be cliffs (at about 6 miles, 9257 feet), which lead to a saddle. Downclimb the right side to the saddle, then continue northward.

At almost any point along the ridges you are likely to see mountain goats roaming around. If you are quiet and still enough you may get to watch a whole family emerge over a ridge crest. There are also bighorn sheep in the area, but they seem to be more difficult to spot.

Once you make the final ascent up a short gully to Point Joseph, enjoy the views. The surrounding high Wallowa peaks include nearby Sacajawea Peak, Matterhorn, and the Hurwal Divide. Farther south is the wilderness's namesake—Eagle Cap. Wallowa Lake glimmers in the sunshine and looks awfully inviting after the dry ascent. The long northward ridge of the mountain stands out against the sky and is a good spot for goat watching. You may even have overhead visitors as hang gliders make their way above you on the summer thermals, having launched off Mount Howard just a couple of miles to the east. There is a summit register of sorts in a metal container.

Return the way you came.

56 HURWAL DIVIDE

Elevation: 9776 feet

Difficulty: S4/T2

Round trip: 10.8 miles

Elevation gain: 4719 feet

Trip time: 6–7 hours

Time to summit: 3–4 hours

Best time of year: July to October

Map: USGS Chief Joseph

Contact: Wallowa–Whitman National Forest, Eagle Cap Ranger District, Wallowa Mountains Visitors Center

Special considerations: Self-issue permits are available at trailheads for entrance into the Eagle Cap Wilderness; please register and read the wilderness regulations.

Scrambling up the ridge to the Hurwal Divide, Chief Joseph Mountain in the background

WAYPOINT ROUTE

1. Hurricane Creek Trailhead: 5152 feet (11T 475985mE 5017340mN)
2. Thorp Creek Trail: 1.8 miles, 5445 feet (11T 475998mE 5014591mN)
3. Leave trail: 4.0 miles, 7378 feet (11T 477566mE 5012171mN)
4. Summit ridge: 4.9 miles, 9273 feet (11T 478886mE 5012006mN)
5. Hurwal Divide: 5.4 miles, 9776 feet (11T 479320mE 5011581mN)

The Wallowa Mountains lie at the east end of the Blue Mountains of northeast Oregon. Protected largely by the vast Eagle Cap Wilderness, the Wallowas offer scramblers opportunities to enjoy miles of isolated ridges, dramatic glacial valleys, and high-elevation peaks. The Hurricane Creek Trail runs down a majestic canyon between the Hurwal Divide and the Hurricane Divide. This canyon offers scramblers access to both ridges and the Wallowas' highest peak—Sacajawea. The Thorp Creek Trail is not on many maps, but it is the approach for routes to Hurwal Divide, Chief Joseph Mountain, and Sacajawea Peak. The high point of the Hurwal Divide has unparalleled views of Chief Joseph and of the standard scramble route to Sacajawea's summit. Looking northeast off the divide summit you can also see the Zumwalt Prairie, which provides habitat for a wide array of birds.

Trailhead directions: From Enterprise drive south on Hurricane Creek Road. Follow the signs to Hurricane Creek Campground. Continue past the campground on the forest road until it ends at the trailhead. There is a parking area, trailhead sign and self-register, and a vault toilet at the road end. A Northwest Forest Pass is required.

Route description: Head south on the Hurricane Creek Trail 1.8 miles to the Thorp Creek Trail junction. This section of the Hurricane Creek Trail is very scenic, with numerous creeks and streams that drain into Hurricane Creek. You will hike past aspen groves, open meadows, and pine, hemlock, and fir forest. Enjoy the views of the high ridges rising on either side of the glacial valley. Turn left at waypoint 2 for the Thorp Creek Trail (at 1.8 miles), which is on the USGS quad but not on the Wallowa Mountains map. This trail is not maintained. Follow the trail east through the trees then drop down to cross Hurricane Creek. Look for logs to cross on or bring sandals during early season.

Continue east and then turn right through a meadow and ascend on a faint trail, which crosses Twin Creek before getting steep. The trail soon begins to climb more sharply on switchbacks to gain the ridge. This section of trail is rocky, dusty, and dry.

Once above the Thorp Creek canyon you will continue southeast on the trail while contouring above the canyon and climbing more gently. At about 4 miles and 7400 feet you leave the trail, and then turn east to head through the trees a short distance. Enter the clearing and continue east while scrambling up the slope to intersect a broad ridge.

Once on the ridge, scramble up the steep loose talus to a bench at the end of the summit ridge. At the bench, turn more southeast up the ridge (waypoint 4). Look around for mountain goats as you make your way up the

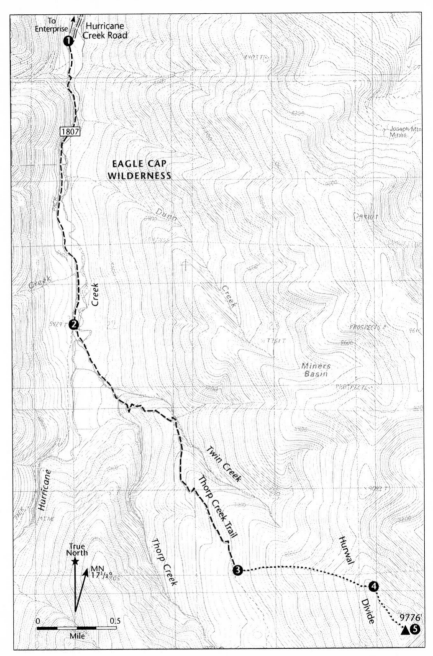

final summit ridge. It is worth peering over the ridge crest to see if goats are lounging on the other side.

Continue up and scramble to the summit. From the summit, the views are a panorama of the high Wallowas, with Sacajawea Peak and Matterhorn especially impressive to the south. From this high vantage point you can pick

Descending the ridge of the Hurwal Divide

out a route to Point Joseph, the summit of Chief Joseph Mountain. Across the valley is the colorful and rugged ridge top of the Hurricane Divide. Although you may not find a summit register, there is a large cairn on the summit.

 MATTERHORN

Elevation: 9832 feet

Difficulty: S4/T2

Round trip: 16.8 miles

Elevation gain: 5195 feet

Trip time: 10–12 hours

Time to summit: 6–8 hours

Best time of year: July to November

Map: USGS Ice Lake

Contact: Wallowa–Whitman National Forest, Eagle Cap Ranger District, Wallowa Mountains Visitors Center

Special considerations: Self-issue permits are available at trailheads for entrance into the Eagle Cap Wilderness; please register and read the wilderness regulations.

WAYPOINT ROUTE
1. Wallowa Lake Trailheads: 4500 feet (11T 483337mE 5012440mN)
2. Ice Lake: 6.6 miles, 7849 feet (11T 478923mE 5008489mN)
3. Trail junction: 7.0 miles, 7859 feet (11T 478323mE 5008463mN)
4. Rock cairn: 7.5 miles, 8520 feet (11T 477727mE 5008581mN)
5. Bench: 8.0 miles, 9023 feet (11T 477175mE 5008502mN)
6. Matterhorn: 8.4 miles, 9832 feet (11T 476607mE 5008077mN)

Matterhorn is a striking limestone and marble mountain rising majestically above Ice Lake. Named for its likeness to the European peak, the Wallowa Matterhorn is a landmark in its own right. The Wallowa Mountains, at the eastern end of the broken and uplifted Blue Mountains, are more similar to the Rockies than other Oregon mountains. The Wallowas have short summers and long, cold winters with plenty of snow. The high Wallowas have numerous rugged summits and include seventeen named peaks over 9000 feet high. Matterhorn is the second-tallest peak in the Wallowas. The Eagle Cap Wilderness, one of Oregon's largest, protects much of the Wallowa Mountains. Enjoy the alpine wildflowers, glacial lakes and tarns, and deep canyons of this northeastern Oregon gem.

Trailhead directions: From Enterprise follow State Route 82 east to Wallowa Lake. Past the lake, turn left at the junction for the Wallowa Lake Trailheads. Continue on the road until it ends at the trailhead parking area, with parking on the right side of the road. There are restrooms and water. The trailhead register is on the left side of the dead end. Follow signs to the right for the West Fork Wallowa River Trail.

Route description: The West Fork Wallowa River Trail 1820, a well-used pack trail, begins climbing immediately. Follow it through the forest of western

Ice Lake and surrounding peaks from atop Matterhorn

larch, Douglas fir, and Engelmann spruce. Vine maples, various berries, and seasonal wildflowers also line the trail as it climbs gently for 2.5 miles to reach a junction. Just before the footbridge, the West Fork Trail meets up with Ice Lake Trail 1808 at 5530 feet. Turn west onto the Ice Lake Trail and cross the river.

The Ice Lake Trail climbs relentlessly alongside Adam Creek. There are many switchbacks, some very steep as the trail passes through increasingly alpine forest. As you climb, note the dramatic views down to the creek and of rock debris from slides. The trail becomes more level as you approach Ice Lake, reaching it at 6.6 miles. There is camping on the east and south sides of the lake, on benches; cross the creek to the left for camping along the eastern side or continue south. If you are backpacking, try to use existing campsites.

To reach the climbers trail to the Matterhorn summit, hike west along the north side of Ice Lake. You will quickly reach a washed-out section; use caution when crossing this steep slope. At 7 miles, leave the lakeside at the trail junction at the lake's northwest corner. Ascend the left side of a rather broad ridge on an intermittent climbers trail. The trail begins alongside a creek, then crosses the creek, and continues until you cross a second creek. Turn right and ascend the climbers trail alongside the second creek. The path is alternately dirt or rough and rocky, but it never quite disappears. There are rock cairns in the distance to roughly mark the route. Please do not add to the cairns or leave any new ones.

As you continue to ascend you will pass through a gully and cross a

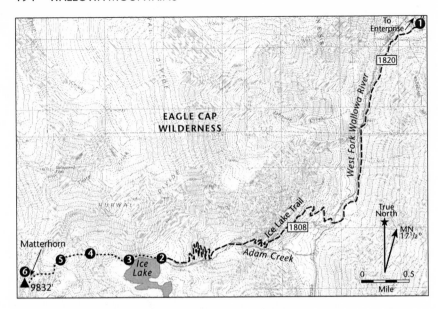

meadow. Continue west, past a rock cairn at 7.5 miles, 8520 feet, and climb up a granitic bench at 8 miles. You will continue ascending on a series of benches. Finally, scramble up a brick-red scree and talus slope, on switchbacks at the top. Bear left, continue traversing across the grayish granitic rock, turn right, and head up to the summit.

The summit is broad and the views expansive. Enjoy the panorama of the Wallowa peaks. Eagle Cap is notable for its distinctive shape. The peaks below, which nearly encircle Ice Lake, are very dramatic.

58 PETES POINT

Elevation: 9675 feet	
Difficulty: S5/T3	
Round trip: 17 miles	
Elevation gain: 5420 feet	
Trip time: 10–12 hours	
Time to summit: 5–6 hours	
Best time of year: July to November	
Map: USGS Aneroid Mountain	

Contact: Wallowa–Whitman National Forest, Eagle Cap Ranger District, Wallowa Mountains Visitors Center

Special considerations: Self-issue permits are available at trailheads for entrance into the Eagle Cap Wilderness; please register and read the wilderness regulations.

WAYPOINT ROUTE

1. Wallowa Lake Trailheads: 4500 feet (11T 483337mE 5012440mN)
2. Aneroid Lake: 5.9 miles, 7510 feet (11T 484301mE 5005748mN)
3. Climbers trail: 7.8 miles, 8441 feet (11T 483843mE 5003941mN)
4. Bench: 8.2 miles, 9082 feet (11T 483259mE 5003992mN)
5. Petes Point: 8.5 miles, 9675 feet (11T 482743mE 5003803mN)

The Wallowa Mountains' rugged Eagle Cap Wilderness contains enough peaks to keep scramblers happy for months. Petes Point is a unique-looking peak between Tenderfoot and Polaris Pass. Scramblers who venture into the area south of Aneroid Lake will enjoy a wide variety of alpine wildflowers, limber and whitebark pines approaching the alpine zone, and uninterrupted quiet. Mountain bluebirds may accompany you on your scramble and many other birds populate this part of the Wallowa Mountains. Northwest and southwest from the summit are dramatic views of the Lakes Basin and of Matterhorn and Sacajawea Peak.

Petes Point and scrambler from near Dollar Lake

Trailhead directions: From Enterprise take State Route 82 east to Wallowa Lake. Past the lake, turn left at the junction for Wallowa Lake Trailheads. Continue on the road until it ends at the trailhead parking area, with parking on the right side of the road. There are restrooms and water. The trailhead register is on the left side of the dead end. Follow signs to the right for East Fork Wallowa River Trail 1804.

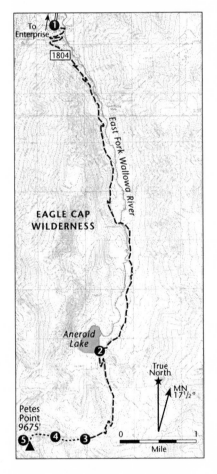

Route description: There are two trailheads here; bear left for the East Fork Wallowa River Trail. The trail begins climbing immediately. This is a well-used pack trail and the first 4 miles or so are very rocky and incredibly dusty. The bushes and trees lining the trail are coated in powdery brown dust from the many hikers and horses that travel this route daily.

Follow the trail through the rich forest mix of conifers and broadleaf trees. At the first junction, a road goes off to the left—do not take that route; instead bear right. The trail passes a beautiful waterfall just before passing a dam at 2 miles. Continue past the dam and note the wilderness boundary at 2.25 miles. Enjoy the views back to Wallowa Lake as you switchback up.

There is a bridge over the river at 3.8 miles. As you ascend you will pass open rocky slopes and boggy areas with many wildflowers. Early in the day, look for wildlife off in the rocky open areas on the right—you may see a family of deer at the end of the meadow.

Continue up the dusty trail, which climbs more gently once past the split at around 4 miles. Follow the signs and ascend on the right-side trail. Above this, the trail passes several meadows and reaches Aneroid Lake at 5.9 miles. If you are backpacking, follow the signs for eastside or westside camping areas on benches surrounding the lake. Please respect the private cabins at the lake.

To reach the east ridge of Petes Point, continue on the trail past Aneroid Lake, bearing left past the pathway to the private cabins (well-signed). You will soon reach the junction with the Bonny Lakes Trail and bear right.

As you approach Petes Point the east ridge is prominent on the horizon and there are many wildflowers in the meadows on the way, including aster, penstemon, and monkeyflower. When you reach about 8300 feet, with the ridge to your right, head across a meadow to the base of the ridge. You may notice a faint climbers path at about 7.8 miles, 8441 feet. Begin ascending the ridge, scrambling up to the first bench at 8.2 miles, 9082 feet. Continue scrambling up the ridge on rough red rock while gaining a series of short benches.

At 9300 feet the rock changes dramatically to hard white rock. Scramble up a short section of vertical outcrops with a clear break in the center. Here, there is some exposure on either side of the ridge as you work past the rock band. Continue to ascend and turn south to stay on the ridge. When you reach the rocky outcrops, pass them on their right; the left side offers lousy rock with a lot of exposure. Continue south to the summit.

Sign the register and enjoy the summit view of high Wallowa peaks. Matterhorn, Sacajawea, and Hurwal Divide are to the northwest. To the southwest are Eagle Cap and Glacier Mountain.

ANEROID MOUNTAIN

Elevation: 9702 feet

Difficulty: S5/T3

Round trip: 17 miles

Elevation gain: 5338 feet

Trip time: 10–12 hours

Time to summit: 5–6 hours

Best time of year: July to November

Map: USGS Aneroid Mountain

Contact: Wallowa–Whitman National Forest, Eagle Cap Ranger District, Wallowa Mountains Visitors Center

Special considerations: Self-issue permits are available at trailheads for entrance into the Eagle Cap Wilderness; please register and read the wilderness regulations.

WAYPOINT ROUTE
1. Wallowa Lake Trailheads: 4500 feet (11T 483337mE 5012440mN)
2. Aneroid Lake: 5.9 miles, 7510 feet (11T 484301mE 5005748mN)
3. Rock cairn: 7.6 miles, 8147 feet (11T 485638mE 5004261mN)
4. Upper ridge: 8.2 miles, 8780 feet (11T 486039mE 5004900mN)
5. Aneroid Mountain: 8.6 miles, 9702 feet (11T 486378mE 5005309mN)

The Wallowa Mountains are the dominant range of northeastern Oregon. Aneroid Mountain is the easternmost peak of the high Wallowas. Nearby Aneroid Lake is a popular destination for day hikers and backpackers, and

Aneroid Mountain has an easy approach from the lake area. The symmetric mountain dominates the surrounding high meadows and offers commanding views north of East Peak and Mount Howard. This scramble has delightful alpine wildflowers on the approach, whitebark and limber pine on the ridge, and views of the many lakes and tarns in this region of the wilderness. Expect solitude, too; once you leave the Aneroid Lake area you probably will not encounter many other people.

Trailhead directions: From Enterprise drive east on State Route 82 to Wallowa Lake. Past the lake, turn left at the junction for the Wallowa Lake Trailheads. Continue on the road until it ends at the trailhead parking area, with parking available on the right side of the road, and restrooms and water. The trailhead register is on the left side of the dead end. Follow signs to the right for East Fork Wallowa River Trail 1804.

Route description: There are two trailheads here; bear left for the East Fork Wallowa River Trail. The trail begins climbing immediately. This is a well-used pack trail and the first 4 miles or so are very rocky and incredibly dusty. The bushes and trees lining the trail are coated in powdery brown dust from the many hikers and horses that travel this route daily.

Follow the trail through the rich forest mix of conifers and broadleaf trees. At the first junction a road goes off to the left—do not take that route; instead bear right. The trail passes a waterfall just before passing a dam at 2 miles. Continue past the dam and note the wilderness boundary at 2.25 miles. Enjoy the views back to Wallowa Lake as you switchback up.

There is a bridge over the river at 3.8 miles. As you ascend you will pass open rocky slopes and boggy areas with many wildflowers. Early in the day, look for wildlife in the rocky open areas on the right—you may see a family of deer at the end of the meadow.

Continue on the dusty trail, which climbs more gently once past the split at around 4 miles. Follow the signs and ascend on the right-side trail. Above this the trail passes several meadows and reaches Aneroid Lake at 5.9 miles. If you are backpacking,

Aneroid Mountain

follow the signs for eastside or westside camping areas on benches surrounding the lake. Please respect the private cabins at the lake.

From Aneroid Lake continue on the East Fork Trail to the junction with Bonny Lakes Trail 1802. Turn left onto the Bonny Lakes Trail, heading to Dollar Lake Pass. The trail ascends through a meadow with a wide variety of wildflowers; enjoy them for a few minutes before continuing on. The ascent ends in a meadow, where you will turn off the trail at Dollar Lake Pass at a rock cairn (7.6 miles, 8147 feet). Turn left to head across the meadow to the southwest ridge of Aneroid Mountain. Once you reach the ridge, scramble up and go across a bench and through a stand of limber and whitebark pines.

Work your way through the trees and ascend to a rocky outcrop that has a wide break in the center for you to scramble up through. Here, scramble up the rocks, taking care not to dislodge them as you climb. Ascend past the next bench, working left through the trees and up through a notch in another blocky section. After emerging from this rocky section, keep ascending to the upper part of the ridge at 8.2 miles, 8780 feet. Keep climbing and head for the right side of a short vertical section; scramble through a weak spot.

Scramble up the remaining rocks by using one of the chutes or blocky sections. Traverse past the false summit to the summit. Sign the register and enjoy the views. The views down to the Bonny Lakes area below and to the southeast make a striking reward.

60 EAST PEAK

Elevation: 9360 feet

Difficulty: S2/T2

Round trip: 4.3 miles

Elevation gain: 1650 feet

Trip time: 3 hours

Time to summit: 1.5 hours

Best time of year: July to October

Map: USGS Aneroid Mountain

Contact: Wallowa–Whitman National Forest, Eagle Cap Ranger District, Wallowa Mountains Visitors Center

Special considerations: Please follow all Eagle Cap Wilderness regulations.

WAYPOINT ROUTE
1. Mount Howard, leave trail: 0.3 mile, 8273 feet (11T 485991mE 5011668mN)
2. Saddle: 0.8 mile, 8101 feet (11T 486086mE 5011482mN)
3. Climbers trail to ridge: 1.3 miles, 8640 feet (11T 486052mE 5010095mN)
4. East Peak: 2.1 miles, 9360 feet (11T 486197mE 5009094mN)

Northeastern Oregon's Wallowa Mountains is a land of contrasts. Long ago glacial ice left behind sharp ridges, peaks, lakes, and valleys. The forest changes as you climb, with lodgepole pine and fir giving way to whitebark pine and dwarf juniper. For some visitors, the summit of Mount Howard is as high as they want to go. For others, the tram is just the starting point high atop Mount Howard. East Peak is a worthwhile introduction to the high Wallowas. The scramble up the ridge is challenging and has wonderful views.

Trailhead directions: From Joseph just south of Enterprise, drive east then south on State Route 82 to Wallowa Lake. At the Y turn right to reach the Mount Howard Tram, where there is a parking lot. After purchasing your tram ticket, enjoy the short ride up to Mount Howard. When you exit the tram station you will be on the Mount Howard Trail system. There is a large map of the nature trail on a sign ahead of you. Follow it to the point at which you leave the trail for East Peak.

Route description: From the tram station, turn right onto the trail and walk about 0.3 mile along the nature trail to a point between the summit overlook and the highlands overlook. Look southeast and follow the slope down to a saddle. Walk off the trail at about waypoint 1 (0.3 mile, 8273 feet) and scramble down the short slope to the saddle at 0.8 mile, where you join a user trail. The saddle has a couple of old outhouses back in the trees.

Continue along the user trail, heading south to ascend along the west side of a small peak. Then continue south along the east side of another small peak on the way to a trail that contours along the east side of East Peak. As you walk along this trail you will approach a small grove of white-bark pines; look up west to the ridge above. A climbers trail at 1.3 miles leads up to the ridge crest from just ahead of these trees. Climb the loose slope up to the ridge and turn left.

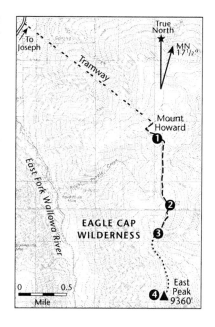

The rest of the scramble is along this ridge all the way south to the East Peak summit. Scramble along the crest as much as you can, although loose rock and some exposure will cause you to drop down occasionally.

The summit offers nice views of surrounding peaks. The dominant view is northwest toward Hurwal Divide and Chief Joseph Mountain; both peaks have beautifully banded summit ridges that stand out against the sky. Aneroid Mountain is just to the south.

You can see for miles from the summit of East Peak.

61 PEAK 9495

Elevation: 9495 feet

Difficulty: S2/T2

Round trip: 6.1 miles

Elevation gain: 1902 feet

Trip time: 3–4 hours

Time to summit: 2 hours

Best time of year: July to October

Map: USGS Aneroid Mountain

Contact: Wallowa–Whitman National Forest, Eagle Cap Ranger District, Wallowa Mountains Visitors Center

Special considerations: Please follow all Eagle Cap Wilderness regulations.

WAYPOINT ROUTE

1. Mount Howard, leave trail: 0.3 mile, 8273 feet (11T 485991mE 5011668mN)
2. Saddle: 0.8 mile, 8101 feet (11T 486086mE 5011482mN)
3. Start descent across gully: 2.4 miles, 8567 feet (11T 486417mE 5008746mN))
4. Peak 9495: 3.1 miles, 9495 feet (11T 486649mE 5007869mN)

From the summit of Peak 9495 you can see alpine lakes and peaks of the Eagle Cap Wilderness.

The Wallowa Mountains form the focal point for much of far northeastern Oregon. Small towns exist on the edges of the mountains and serve as supply points for campers, hikers, backpackers, and others who venture into the wilderness. Long ago, glacial ice left behind sharp ridges, peaks, lakes, and valleys. The forest changes as you climb, with lodgepole pine and fir giving way to whitebark pine and dwarf juniper, and you will also encounter alpine wildflowers and lush springs. For some visitors, the summit of Mount Howard is as high as they want to go. Mount Howard, just east of Chief Joseph Mountain, is named for the U.S. army officer who was the nemesis of Chief Joseph of the Nez Perce. The summit of Mount Howard is a good starting point for a scramble south to Peak 9495, which local climbers call Hidden Peak.

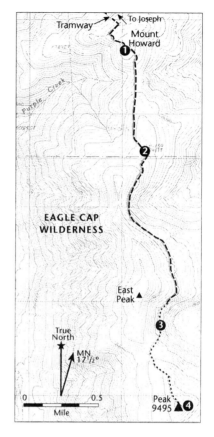

Trailhead directions: From Joseph, drive east then south on State Route 82 to Wallowa Lake. At the Y, turn right to the Mount Howard Tram station, where there is parking. After purchasing your tram ticket, enjoy the short ride up to Mount Howard; the views from the tram are amazing. When you exit the tram station you will be on the Mount Howard Trail system. There is a large map of the nature trail on a sign ahead of you. Follow it to waypoint 1.

Route description: The route to Peak 9495 begins along the route to East Peak. From the tram station, turn right onto the nature trail and walk about 0.3 mile to a point between the summit overlook and the highlands overlook. Look southeast downslope to a saddle that is your short-term destination. Walk off the trail at about waypoint 1 (0.3 mile, 8273 feet) and scramble down the short slope to the saddle at 0.8 mile, 8101 feet. The saddle has a couple of old outhouses back in the trees, if you need them. At the saddle, join a user trail that leads toward East Peak.

Continue along the user trail heading south to ascend along the west side of a small peak. Then continue south along the east side of another small peak on the way to a trail that contours along the east side of East Peak. After you pass the climbers trail up to the East Peak ridge, continue along the trail, which contours at about 8700 feet, above McCully Creek.

As you make your way south, you will pass a spring with lovely wildflowers;

phlox, many-stalked clover, and dwarf yellow fleabane are just a few that populate these slopes in summer. Passing below the summit of East Peak, you will then approach a wide rocky gully.

Drop into the gully at 2.4 miles and cross the talus and scree slope. You may want to cross the slope up high, but the talus is really loose and the slope is steeper. Crossing lower down seems more straightforward. After crossing the gully, head up to a saddle between Hidden Peak and East Peak. There is a large boulder propped on the right side of the saddle.

From the saddle, turn south-southeast and climb the ridge to the summit. The summit view looks right across to Aneroid Mountain, just to the south. There is a summit register stored in an ammunition container.

SENTINEL PEAK

Elevation: 9401 feet

Difficulty: S5/T3

Round trip: 20.4 miles

Elevation gain: 4275 feet

Trip time: 11–12 hours

Time to summit: 5–6 hours

Best time of year: July to November

Map: USGS Aneroid Mountain

Contact: Wallowa–Whitman National Forest, Eagle Cap Ranger District, Wallowa Mountains Visitors Center

Special considerations: Self-issue permits are available at trailheads for entrance into the Eagle Cap Wilderness; please register and read the wilderness regulations.

WAYPOINT ROUTE
1. Tenderfoot Trailhead: 6485 feet (11T 491887mE 5002453mN)
2. Polaris Trail 1831 junction: 8.6 miles, 8198 feet (11T 484064mE 5003438mN)
3. Polaris Pass: 9.3 miles, 8697 feet (11T 482431mE 5001981mN)
4. Summit ridge: 10 miles, 9086 feet (11T 482269mE 5001390mN)
5. Sentinel Peak: 10.2 miles, 9401 feet (11T 482331mE 5000907mN)

The eastern end of the Eagle Cap Wilderness is adjacent to the Hells Canyon National Recreation Area. The trails on this side of the Wallowa Mountains are not as popular as those near Wallowa Lake and should be appealing to scramblers seeking a more quiet wilderness experience. The Tenderfoot Trail is north of the Imnaha Divide and begins between sharp ridges along the drainage for Big Sheep Creek. The trail then leaves the creek to contour above

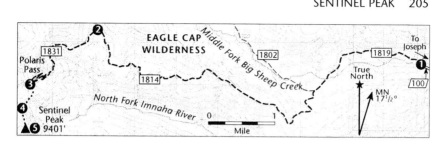

the North Fork Imnaha River canyon, providing wonderful views of the peaks around Polaris Pass as you approach Sentinel Peak.

Trailhead directions: From Joseph drive east 8 miles, then turn right onto Wallowa Mountain Road. Drive south 12.5 miles past Salt Creek Summit. In another 2.8 miles turn right onto Forest Road 100 and drive about 3.1 miles to the trailhead. There is a large parking area with no services. The trailhead sign and wilderness self-register are at the west end of the parking area.

Route description: Tenderfoot Trail 1819 begins by descending through burnt snags and fire debris to cross Big Sheep Creek. After the crossing, ascend past more snags, young lodgepole pine, and a few western larch. There are also groves of quaking aspens along the early section of the trail.

Continue on the trail and keep left at the next two trail junctions. The third junction is with Bonny Lakes Trail 1802; stay left and continue on the Tenderfoot Trail for the next 5 miles. Enjoy the views as the sometimes-faint

Looking west to Sentinel Peak and Petes Point from the Tenderfoot Trail

Looking northwest from the Sentinel Peak summit at the peaks surrounding Ice Lake

trail contours above the dramatic North Fork Imnaha River canyon. As you continue westward there are also great views of Petes Point and Sentinel Peak.

At yet another trail junction, turn right (away from the river) to head toward Tenderfoot Pass using North Fork Imnaha Trail 1814. This section of trail becomes faint in one area. As it fades, keep going straight ahead, cross a small creek, then look ahead a short distance to a prominent rock cairn. Hike past the cairn as the trail resumes and crosses another small creek.

At the junction with Polaris Trail 1831 (at 8.6 miles), turn left. The trail contours around a rocky bowl, then climbs on steep switchbacks to Polaris Pass at 9.3 miles.

At the pass, leave the trail and scramble south then southwest along the ridge. Drop down to some rocks and scramble around them on the left, keeping to the crest as much as possible. Traverse a short distance, then work around a steep rocky section on the left side of a rust-colored rock band to the sandy band. Here, scramble up and across to the right side. Continue through the rocks again on the left side. Stay on this side of the rocks to gain the summit ridge at 10 miles. Once on the summit ridge, stay on the crest all the way to the summit. The last pitch to the summit is very steep.

The summit of Sentinel Peak is quite small. There are impressive views of all the surrounding high Wallowa peaks. Eagle Cap is the most prominent peak to the west, and Cusick Mountain is to the southwest.

63 KRAG PEAK

Elevation: 9048 feet

Difficulty: S2/T3

Round trip: 14.4 miles

Elevation gain: 5327 feet

Trip time: 12 hours or 2 days

Time to summit: 2–3 hours from Crater Lake, 6–7 hours in a day

Best time of year: July to November

Maps: USGS Krag Peak

Contact: Wallowa–Whitman National Forest, Eagle Cap Ranger District, Wallowa Mountains Visitor Center

Special considerations: Pack animals may be on these trails; stay in view and move slowly out of the way to allow animals to pass. Self-issue permits are available at trailheads for entrance into the Eagle Cap Wilderness; please register and read the wilderness regulations.

WAYPOINT ROUTE

1. New East Eagle Trailhead: 4453 feet (11T 474206mE 4988109mN)
2. Little Kettle Creek Trail 1945: 0.6 mile, 4572 feet (11T 474610mE 4988872mN)
3. Crater Lake north side: 5.6 miles, 7822 feet (11T 478419mE 4989376mN)
4. Turn west: 6.0 miles, 7911 feet (11T 478367mE 4990006mN)
5. Saddle above cirque: 6.6 miles, 8523 feet (11T 477509mE 4989740mN)
6. Krag Peak: 7.2 miles, 9048 feet (11T 477174mE 4990162mN)

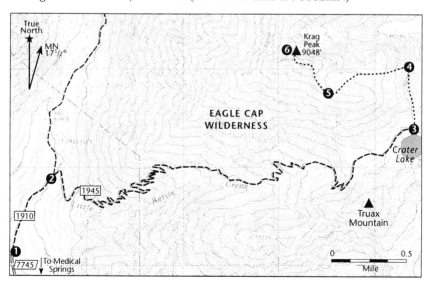

The talus-covered slopes of Krag Peak across a lovely tarn

The Wallowa–Whitman National Forest spreads out over 2.5 million acres of northeastern Oregon. The Wallowa Mountains cut across the northern section of the forest. The Eagle Cap Wilderness, where most of the high Wallowa peaks are, was put aside to preserve these rugged ridges, peaks, and glacial valleys. The southern tip of the wilderness contains a cluster of high Wallowa peaks. Red Mountain, towering above Cliff Creek, has distinctive coloring and a long south ridge. Northwest of Crater Lake is Krag Peak. It has a nearly vertical north side, and the south ridge scramble is up a steep slope littered with slippery talus and precarious boulders. The scramble to the summit requires balance and agility. This route is for intrepid scramblers who will appreciate the majestic views of the nearby high Wallowa peaks.

Trailhead directions: From Medical Springs drive east on Forest Road 67, also called Big Creek Road. Follow the road east to the junction with FR 77. Turn right onto FR 77 and drive to the junction with East Eagle Road, or FR 7745. Follow this road north to the parking area for the East Eagle Trail. There are two parking areas; the first one is the new parking area and is where this route description begins. There is a vault toilet to the left of the trailhead, which is clearly marked. A Northwest Forest Pass is required.

Route description: East Eagle Trail 1910 begins by crossing an open meadow northward toward the junction with Little Kettle Creek Trail 1945. Turn right onto the Little Kettle Creek Trail, which is marked with a sign. Although the trail begins gently ascending through the cool mixed-conifer forest, get ready. The trail soon emerges from the dense canopy of trees and begins ascending seemingly endless switchbacks that lead to the rich valley below Krag Peak's southwest slopes.

As you ascend take a moment to enjoy the rich natural beauty of the area. You may see hummingbirds in the trees and bushes bordering the trail. There are dozens of varieties of wildflowers in early summer; you could easily lose count. Stands of aspens along the way offer a nice diversion from the dry, dusty trail. Eventually you will pass through a couple of groves of fir trees before reaching the ascent through the flower-filled meadows above the creek.

There are a couple of creek crossings, which are good places to filter water in early summer. Continue eastward, cross two wide rock slides, and climb up to Crater Lake on another set of switchbacks. Before you reach the lake you will pass some tarns on the west side.

Crater Lake is a decent destination if you are backpacking. You may see a variety of birds in the forested area around the lake, including mountain blue-birds or northern flickers. There are a few spots around the lake to camp; look carefully to find places to practice low-impact camping.

From the north side of Crater Lake at 5.6 miles you will scramble off the trail northward for about 0.5 mile. As you pass through the trees you may see glacier lilies and patches of blooming pink mountain heather. Turn west at about 6 miles and ascend westward until you reach a broad bench ending in a pretty glacial tarn.

From here you will see a cirque below Krag Peak's south slope. Cross the cirque heading southwest to the southern end of the obvious saddle. Once on the saddle, at about 6.6 miles, turn north toward the upper mountain.

Ascend the upper mountain by crossing the saddle, then scrambling north-northwest up the slope, which has loose talus, rickety boulders, and shattered rock everywhere. You may choose to go up one of the loose, rock-filled gullies—but it may be difficult to get very far on the moving rock.

Try to ascend north on the short spurs of relatively solid rock, hopping from one solid section to another as you climb. This is more secure than the gullies, yet there is still plenty of loose rock so use extreme caution. Scramble up this slope one person at a time for maximum safety.

Once you reach the false summit, turn westward and then north to the small main summit. The views from Krag Peak are magnificent. North you can see Marble and Cusick Mountains. To the east is Red Mountain and Granite Mountain.

Descend back to the saddle very cautiously, keeping to the rocky spurs as much as possible. From the saddle, reverse your route to return to Crater Lake.

64 CORNUCOPIA PEAK

Elevation: 8643 feet

Difficulty: S2/T2

Round trip: 9.6 miles

Elevation gain: 3022 feet

Trip time: 5–6 hours

Time to summit: 3 hours

Best time of year: July to October

Maps: USGS Krag Peak, Cornucopia Peak

Contact: Wallowa–Whitman National Forest, Eagle Cap Ranger District, Wallowa Mountains Visitors Center

Special considerations: The Cliff Creek Trail may be very difficult to follow in some places. USGS maps and a compass are necessary for navigation. An ice ax is needed if you choose to travel on snow. Self-issue permits are available at trailheads for entrance into the Eagle Cap Wilderness; please register and read the wilderness regulations.

WAYPOINT ROUTE
1. Summit Point Trailhead: 6435 feet (11T 481212mE 4980177mN)
2. Open meadow: 1.8 miles, 7409 feet (11T 480256mE 4982684mN)
3. Leave trail: 3.9 miles, 7589 feet (11T 479345mE 4985317mN)
4. Peak 8720: 4.4 miles, 8720 feet (11T 479604mE 4985891mN)
5. Cornucopia Peak: 5.9 miles, 8643 feet (11T 481322mE 4985013mN)
6. Descent point saddle: 6.4 miles, 8166 feet (11T 480561mE 4984757mN)
7. Rejoin trail: 6.9 miles, 7256 feet (11T 480133mE 4984178mN)

Cornucopia Peak is in the southern portion of the Wallowa Mountains. Barely inside the Eagle Cap Wilderness, the area around Cornucopia was the site of a gold strike in the late nineteenth century. The town of Cornucopia sprang up, grew, and was deserted in the mid-twentieth century when the gold strike ran out. Largely a privately owned ghost town now, the town has recently seen some new life as a private development. Cornucopia Peak stands out against its surroundings with its bright gray granite slopes and broad summit ridge. The summit once had a fire lookout that was built in 1924. The meadows and creeks around the mountain make this scramble a lovely destination in a less-crowded part of the wilderness.

Trailhead directions: From Richland drive north on State Route 86 toward Halfway. In about 6 miles turn left onto Forest Road 77. Drive FR 77 about 11 miles to the junction with FR 7715 near McBride Campground. Follow FR 7715 north to the Summit Point Trailhead, with plenty of parking. The trailhead information sign and wilderness self-register are at the north

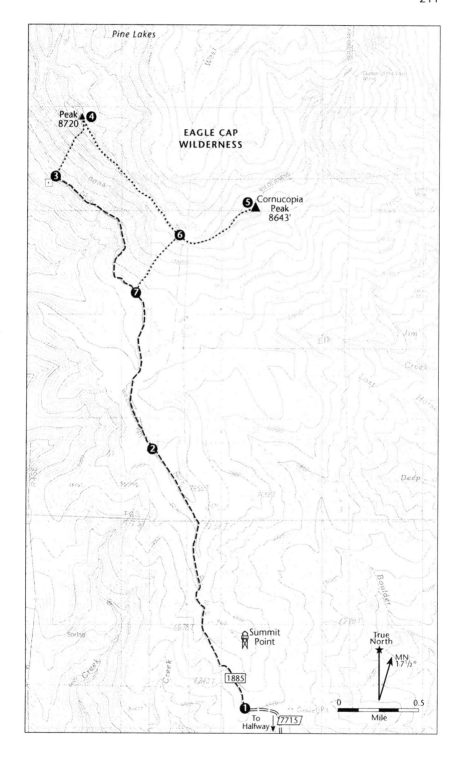

Pine Lakes

EAGLE CAP
WILDERNESS

Peak
8720 ④

③

⑥

⑤ Cornucopia
Peak
8643'

⑦

②

Summit
Point

1885

①
To
Halfway 7715

True
North

MN
17½°

0   0.5
Mile

Looking northeast, from the approach, at the distinctive Cornucopia Peak

end of the parking area. A Northwest Forest Pass is required.

Route description: Cliff Creek Trail 1885 is an entry point for backpackers looking for solitude. The trail climbs for the first 1.5 miles, winding north mostly along a ridge that runs west of Summit Point. Although this first section of trail is rocky and dry, you will pass through groves of quaking aspens and fields of wildflowers. Some fields of lupine extend as far as you can see. The ridge crests at about 1.8 miles, 7400 feet, as the trail enters a broad expanse of open meadow.

The trail continues north, descending slightly across the meadows, as it gets closer to the western slopes of Cornucopia Peak. After a short ascent above a steep drainage you will reach the scramble point (at 3.9 miles) for the summit northwest of Cornucopia. This 8600-foot-plus peak is on the extensive ridge that extends almost 2 miles in a crescent shape.

Scramble northward up a steep slope to reach the summit ridge in almost 0.5 mile. Once on the main ridge turn north to reach the summit of Peak 8720. The summit displays a prominent rock cairn and has great views down to the Pine Lakes basin to the north.

To reach the summit of Cornucopia Peak descend the ridge to the south for nearly a mile before the steady ascent begins. Ascend the west ridge along the ridge crest. You will find a well-beaten path that winds along the ridge to the summit. You may use the trail or remain on the ridge crest. In early summer, snow patches remain on the northern exposures, making travel tricky at times. If you choose to travel on snow make sure you carry an ice ax and watch for melted-out snow close to the rock.

Enjoy the summit of Cornucopia Peak, which has expansive views north into the wilderness. Granite and Red Mountains are hard to miss to the north above Pine Lakes.

To reach the descent point, scramble westward back to the saddle, which is at about 6.4 miles, 8166 feet. Descend southwest for almost 0.5 mile across the south slope of the mountain to a meadow, which you can continue across to reach the trail. Return on the trail to the trailhead.

 ## DIABLO PEAK

Elevation: 6147 feet

Difficulty: S2/T2

Round trip: 9.8 miles

Elevation gain: 1890 feet

Trip time: 6–8 hours

Time to summit: 3–4 hours

Best time of year: May to November

Maps: USGS Diablo Peak; Bureau of Land Management, Lakeview District, North Half, Lakeview Resource Area Recreation Guide

Contact: Bureau of Land Management, Lakeview District

Special considerations: There may be blowing sand on the sand dunes. Diablo Peak is in a Wilderness Study Area, a designation used to preserve the primitive value of a place. Use the BLM recreation map to navigate the WSA roads.

WAYPOINT ROUTE
1. Park off road: 4255 feet (10T 691919mE 4759307mN)
2. Ridge junction: 1.8 miles, 4328 feet (10T 694873mE 4760204mN)
3. Cat Camp Draw: 3.2 miles, 4844 feet (10T 696398mE 4759361mN)
4. Gully: 3.9 miles, 5462 feet (10T 697675mE 4758764mN)
5. Plateau: 4.4 miles, 5682 feet (10T 697230mE 4759325mN)
6. Diablo Peak: 4.9 miles, 6147 feet (10T 698609mE 4759668mN)

Summer Lake is a popular birding area known for its migratory flocks of waterfowl and shorebirds. Hot springs in the area also attract visitors. Surrounded by sand dunes and sagebrush flats, the area's peaks are rugged and isolated—chances are you will scramble all day without seeing another person. Diablo Peak is part of the Diablo Mountain Range in the high lava plains of the Northern Basin and Range. Natural features include tall sagebrush, desert wildflowers, and volcanic rock. This scramble has a bit of everything and will take you across sand dunes, over volcanic ridges, and up to the blocky summit of Diablo Peak.

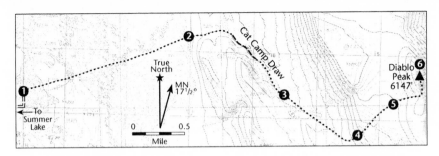

Trailhead directions: From the town of Summer Lake, drive north on State Route 31. Turn right (east) on County Road 4-17 (past the rest area and before the old church). Drive 5.9 miles east to a fork and turn right. Continue 1.9 miles southeast until you see double green gates to a ranch on the right. Turn left on a dirt BLM road and park in about 150 to 200 yards (waypoint 1), or park anywhere along the west side of the road with a pullout area and access to the route. The road is the WSA boundary; please do not park on the east side.

Route description: This scramble begins when you step down to the sand dunes heading east. Out in this remote area there are few discernible trails. Looking eastward you can barely make out a low ridge with two rock promontories and a red slash on the left side. Hike about 1.8 miles across the nearly level dunes to the ridge, then scramble up the lower left side below the outcrop and continue east up a series of steps.

Descend into Cat Camp Draw at 3.2 miles, where you will intersect a jeep

The expansive view from atop Diablo Peak

track. Follow the jeep track roughly up the draw. It is easier to follow this track for about 0.3 mile and then to climb the draw slightly and contour around. The draw will lead you southeast, eventually flattening out as you near its end. Continue to contour and ascend southeast along the draw, winding your way until you almost reach the end.

As you ascend past 5200 feet, turn northeast and head up a gully (at about 3.9 miles) that climbs the moderate slope to the upper plateau at 4.4 miles. Continue northeast past the head of the gully and continue across the plateau to the south ridge. Note your position when you emerge on the upper plateau—it is quite featureless and you will need to know where to descend on your return route.

The south ridge is a moderate pitch to the summit. As you reach the ridge, turn left and scramble to the top. As you pick your way along the rocks, note the impressive drop-off on the east side and the amazing panoramic views. Look north and south to see the rest of the Diablo Rim peaks.

 ABERT RIM

Elevation: 6370 feet

Difficulty: S2/T3

Round trip: 8.8 miles

Elevation gain: 2075 feet

Trip time: 6–8 hours

Time to summit: 2–3 hours

Best time of year: May to November

Maps: USGS Lake Abert South; Bureau of Land Management, Lakeview District, South Half, Lakeview Resource Area Recreation Guide

Contact: Bureau of Land Management, Lakeview District

Special considerations: Abert Rim is in a Wilderness Study Area, a designation used to preserve the primitive value of a place.

WAYPOINT ROUTE
1. Park in turnout: 4295 feet (10T 730366mE 4716097mN)
2. Junction with fence: 0.2 mile, 4307 feet (10T 730024mE 4715865mN)
3. Poison Creek: 1.0 mile, 4743 feet (10T 731104mE 716137mN)
4. Junipers: 1.2 miles, 5079 feet (10T 731364mE 4715968mN)
5. Reach rim plateau: 1.6 miles, 5904 feet (10T 731704mE 4715487mN)
6. Scramble end: 4.4 miles, 6370 feet (10T 72933mE 4712645mN)

Abert Rim is a fault-block mountain common to the Northern Basin and Range. Oriented along a north-south axis, the mountain has a nearly vertical west side and gently sloping east side. The rim extends for more than 30 miles

Abert Rim rises dramatically from the surrounding landscape.

along Lake Abert and south to the Fremont National Forest. One of the largest fault scarps in the state, Abert Rim offers scramblers solitude and a unique scrambling experience. Though the west side of the rim rises 2000 feet above Lake Abert, the blocky basalt rimrock allows scramblers access to the top via a creek drainage. Along the way you will enjoy abundant wildflowers in early season, particularly near springs and the creek bed. Sagebrush, juniper, and the occasional pine are the dominant shrubs and trees.

Trailhead directions: Drive north on U.S. Route 395 from Valley Falls. At 8 miles is Poison Creek, but the mouth of the creek is on private land. To park, look for a turnout south of the creek about 0.4 mile. Park at the turnout on the lake side (west) of the road.

Route description: Walk south along the road 0.2 mile to get around the private land (fenced and marked "No Trespassing"). Follow the fence line east about 0.5 mile, then turn back north-northeast, staying clear of the private property. Continue in this direction, gradually ascending to about 4700 feet, contouring until you almost run into Poison Creek (waypoint 3). Do not bother going down to the creek; it is too overgrown. Instead, pick a line on the right side and begin your ascent.

Scramble up the boulder field while keeping to the right and heading for

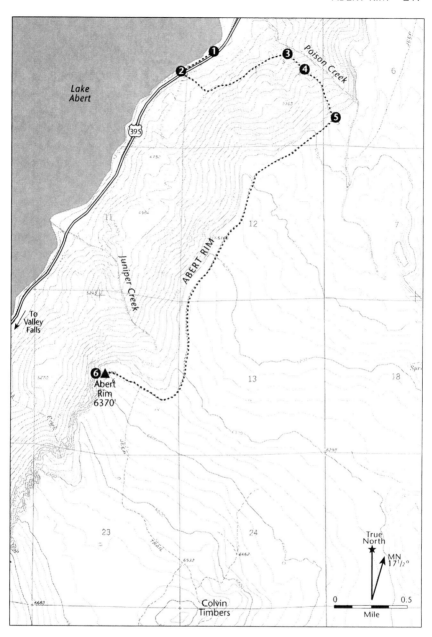

Lake
Abert

395

To
Valley
Falls

Juniper Creek

ABERT RIM

Poison Creek

6

7

11

12

18

13

24

23

6 ▲
Abert
Rim
6370'

Colvin
Timbers

True
North
★
MN
17½°

0   0.5
Mile

the juniper trees at 1.2 miles. Keep an eye out for horned lizards on the rocks.
The lake views are stunning from this point. Continue climbing, passing large
rocks and old snags. Stay on the right of large rock outcrops and aim for a
spot on the rim to the right of Poison Creek. Continue ascending, passing a
grove of quaking aspens on the left. Note also the impressive band of basalt
columns that line the upper left rim edge.

The final scramble to the rim is through large blocks of vertical basalt and will take you to the edge of the summit plateau, which gently slopes eastward. Just remember to look back occasionally, and also mark a waypoint or take a bearing when you emerge on the rim plateau (waypoint 5). The plateau is huge and it would be easy to get disoriented. You can walk south along the rim to view the expansive, gently sloping east side of the rim.

To reach the high point walk southwest, contouring along the rim to Juniper Creek at about 2 miles. Continue along the rim another 0.8 mile to reach a high point southwest of the creek at 6370 feet. In the summertime watch for eagle, or a variety of hawks riding the thermals around the rim. At any point along the rim, views of the alkaline Lake Abert are wonderful. A wide variety of birds summer at the lake. When you return to your car you might want to watch along the lake for grebes and ruddy ducks.

Additional scramble: If you want to explore the plateau, there are many opportunities for more scrambling once you are on top. From waypoint 6 you may also visit Colvin Timbers, an isolated stand of old-growth ponderosa pines, 1.5 miles to the southeast. From any of the points along the rim, views of Lake Abert—a briny remnant of a Pleistocene lake—are spectacular. Wildlife on the rim may include deer, a variety of birds, and rattlesnakes. Wildflowers include aster, mariposa lily, and wood rose.

 WARNER PEAK

Elevation: 8017 feet	
Difficulty: S2/T2	
Round trip: 10 miles	
Elevation gain: 2264 feet	
Trip time: 5 hours	
Time to summit: 2–3 hours	
Best time of year: June to October	
Map: USGS Warner Peak	

Contact: Fish and Wildlife Service, Hart Mountain National Antelope Refuge

WAYPOINT ROUTE
1. Hot Springs Campground: 5900 feet (11T 279053mE 4708416mN)
2. Leave the trail: 4.0 miles, 6819 feet (11T 275700mE 4704462mN)
3. Turn west-southwest: 4.7 miles, 7907 feet (11T 274689mE 4704582mN)
4. Warner Peak: 5.0 miles, 8017 feet (11T 274659mE 4704229mN)

Hart Mountain is a huge fault block rising several thousand feet above the Warner Valley. Home to protected herds of pronghorn antelope, it gets few visitors annually. The rugged west face of the mountain is quite a contrast to

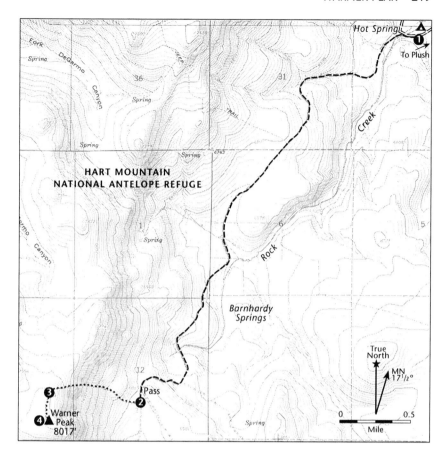

the many lakes in the Warner Valley below. Watch for golden eagles circling lazily on summer thermals. The refuge, with the aid of various conservation and outdoor organizations, has been removing barbed-wire fencing for the last several years, making this a wonderful place for viewing pronghorn herds, bighorn sheep, sage grouse, and mule deer. Park headquarters are minimal; however there is a pay phone and a public restroom with running water. There are also hot springs near the campground.

Trailhead directions: From Lakeview drive east on State Route 140 to the Plush/Hart Mountain turnoff. Turn left and follow this road through Plush (which is your last chance for gasoline and a general store) about 25 miles to Hart Mountain. The paved road changes to gravel eventually, but it is well maintained as it climbs from the Warner Valley to the refuge entrance and headquarters. From the refuge headquarters, drive south about 1.7 miles to a fork in the road. Turn right and continue to the campground and hot springs. At the campground there is a turnoff for the hot springs. Continue left for camping. The trailhead is near the end of the campground.

Route description: This scramble uses seasonal jeep roads for easy access

From the top of Warner Peak you have great views of the Warner Valley to the west.

to a high pass below Warner Peak. Along the way you may see or hear sage grouse or mule deer, particularly in early morning. Follow the road west out of the campground. This track will pass a seasonal gate (closed to vehicles from December 1 to August 1) and continue ascending through quaking aspen groves and beautiful wood roses in the spring and early summer.

The trail follows Rock Creek before turning west and heading to Barnhardy Springs. In 2.3 miles you will descend to cross a creek, then climb slightly passing Barnhardy Springs to the east. In contrast to the dry jeep roads, you will enjoy the relief of the aspen groves and will pass several more on the way to the pass. Continue to 3.3 miles until you pass a gate and another jeep track going off to the left. Here, at the pass, look west to the ridge leading to Warner Peak. You will be almost directly below a rocky chute that leads up to the edge of a saddle.

Head cross-country at 4 miles (waypoint 2); pick your way around the thick sagebrush while aiming for a small bench. After crossing the bench continue toward the gully and head up its left-hand side. It is very steep and you may have to switchback a bit to keep from slipping on the scree.

You may continue up the left side all the way to the saddle edge. Turn southerly toward the Warner summit at 4.7 miles. You will then pass through a grove of mountain mahogany at 4.8 miles. From the trees, it is a short scramble up to the summit.

From the summit, walk westward toward the rim of the scarp. The views to the Warner Valley over Potter Canyon and Hart Canyon are dramatic. Hart Lake, elevation 4473 feet, looks like a pond from this vantage point.

68 HAWKS MOUNTAIN

Elevation: 7234 feet

Difficulty: S2/T1

Round trip: 4 miles

Elevation gain: 1624 feet

Trip time: 2–4 hours

Time to summit: 1–2 hours

Best time of year: May to October

Maps: USGS Hawks Mountain; Bureau of Land Management, Lakeview District, South Half, Lakeview Resource Area Recreation Guide

Contact: Bureau of Land Management, Lakeview District

Special considerations: Hawks Mountain is in a Wilderness Study Area, a designation used to preserve the primitive value of a place. You will need the BLM recreation map to get around in this remote area.

WAYPOINT ROUTE

1. Park at jeep road junction: 5570 feet (11T 331790mE 4662201mN)
2. Ham Waterhole: 1.0 mile, 5800 feet (11T 331441mE 4660544mN)
3. BLM gate: 1.3 miles, 6050 feet (11T 331180mE 4660122mN)
4. Hawks Mountain: 2.0 miles, 7234 feet (11T 330705mE 4659111mN)

From the summit of Hawks Mountain you have a 360-degree view of the surrounding open spaces.

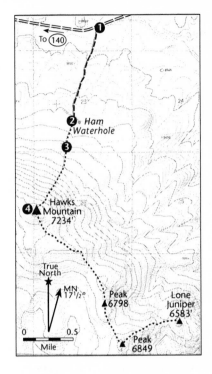

The Hawks Valley is a striking and remote grassland ringed with ancient mountains. Part of the proposed Oregon Grasslands Wilderness in the Northern Basin and Range, Hawks Mountain is one in a chain of low peaks that gently rises up out of the grass. Scramblers who visit here will not forget the sweeping views and solitude. You can expect a contemplative hike among some of the oldest rocks in the state. North of Hawks Mountain is Lone Mountain, aptly named and consisting of rugged, ancient lava flows. Although grazing has negatively affected this area, there is still plenty of austere natural beauty. Wildlife thrives despite the harsh environment and may include pronghorn, feral horses, bighorn sheep, and mule deer.

Trailhead directions: From Adel drive east on State Route 140 about 37 miles to milepost 65. Turn left on the dirt road just before the Sheldon National Wildlife Refuge and the Nevada border. Drive about 8.2 miles to a junction and keep right, heading northeast. The road continues northeast 5.6 miles, then winds through a pass between Bald Mountain to the north and Acty Mountain to the south. Stay on the main dirt road and continue as the road descends south then southeast into Hawks Valley to the parking spot. (Note: If you reach the Moss Waterhole, turn around and go back 0.5 mile.)

Route description: From the parking spot off the main road, hike south along an old jeep track toward Hawks Mountain. This hard-packed and overgrown road leads across the gently sloping grasslands toward the Ham Waterhole. If you have a high-clearance vehicle you may be able to drive all the way to the old waterhole.

Keep hiking past the dry Ham Waterhole at 1 mile, up to a metal gate at 1.3 miles. Proceed through the gate and scramble up the open slope to the summit. The slope is moderately steep and rocky in places. Watch for the rock outcrops hidden in the grass, and scramble over or around them. Occasionally glance at the ground to avoid stepping in the many animal dens dug into the hillside. Continue up to the broad, windswept summit. This area can be extremely windy so prepare for blowing sand and/or dust.

The summit views are of uninterrupted rolling hills and desert highlands. Lone Mountain, a complex of peaks, is the closest mountain range to the north.

Additional scramble: Continue to explore the area by heading for some of the lower peaks to the southeast. Descend off the summit southeasterly along the ridge past Peak 6798 then south to Peak 6849. After a look around, turn east to head for Lone Juniper (6583 feet). This is a mostly downhill ridge scramble, which loses about 650 feet. The route is 9 miles round trip with the Lone Juniper addition.

 LONE MOUNTAIN

Elevations: 6675 feet, 6903 feet

Difficulty: S2/T3

Round trip: 4.8 miles

Elevation gain: 1498 feet

Trip time: 4 hours

Time to summits: 2–3 hours

Best time of year: May to October

Maps: USGS Hawks Mountain; Bureau of Land Management, Lakeview District, South Half, Lakeview Resource Area Recreation Guide

Contact: Bureau of Land Management, Burns District

Special considerations: Lone Mountain is in a Wilderness Study Area, a designation used to preserve the primitive value of a place. The BLM map will help you get around in this remote area.

On the Lone Mountain descent Juniper Spring provides a welcome relief from the surrounding grasslands.

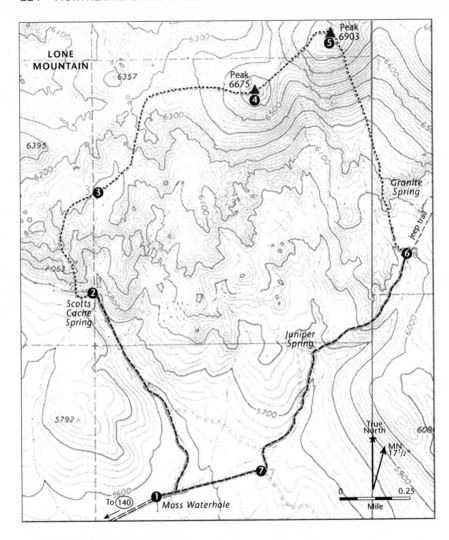

WAYPOINT ROUTE

1. Moss Waterhole: 5581 feet (10T 332814mE 4662364mN)
2. Scotts Cache Spring: 0.9 mile, 5816 feet (10T 332372mE 4663504mN)
3. Midway on bench: 1.4 miles, 6077 feet (10T 332485mE 4664102mN)
4. Peak 6675: 2.1 miles, 6675 feet (10T 333395mE 4664672mN)
5. Peak 6903: 2.5 miles, 6903 feet (10T 333847mE 4664976mN)
6. Jeep trail: 3.4 miles, 5995 feet (10T334188mE 4663720mN)
7. Main road: 4.5 miles, 5655 feet (10T 333381mE 4662500mN)

Between Lakeview and Fields there are broad expanses of grasslands inter-
rupted by solitary mountain ranges. Lone Mountain, adjacent to Hawks Mountain and just west of the Pueblos, is one of those mountains. The mountain is

*A scrambler enjoys a moment atop one of the many huge rocky outcrops
en route to the summit of Lone Mountain Peak 6675.*

really a complex of medium-elevation peaks, jumbled lava flows, and lush springs. Lone Mountain really is alone, and getting there is half the fun. Whether approaching from Fields or Adel, you are unlikely to see anyone out here. Lone Mountain is a scramble up a boulder-strewn canyon, which winds up on a ridge to the first summit. The rock is solid, and the springs boast lush trees, grasses, and flowers—a stark contrast to the overgrazed grasslands of the Hawks Valley just west of the mountain.

Trailhead directions: From Adel drive east on State Route 140 about 37 miles to milepost 65. Turn left on a dirt road just before the Sheldon National Wildlife Refuge and the Nevada border. Drive about 8.2 miles to a junction and keep right, heading northeast. The road continues northeast 5.6 miles, then winds through a pass between Bald Mountain to the north and Acty Mountain to the south. Stay on the main dirt road and continue as the road descends south then southeast into the Hawks Valley. Drive east on the road to the Moss Waterhole, which is on the south side of the road. There is space to park near the waterhole.

Route description: Cross the main road and walk northward on the dirt road to Scotts Cache Spring at 0.9 mile. You will reach the spring quickly on the level road. At the spring, scramble west around a fence (the spring has a small pocket of private land that is fenced). Once on the west side of the spring, scramble north then northwest along the canyon, keeping to the left side.

Scramble northward past 6000 feet and turn northeast for about 0.5 mile along a gently sloping bench. Begin ascending again at about 1.6 miles, scrambling north up to the broad west ridge leading to the summit of Peak 6675. At the ridge, and just before a fence, turn east and scramble up the final 300 feet to the summit at 2.1 miles. From here you can see Hawks Mountain, the Pueblo Mountains, and Beatys Butte to the north.

When you are ready, scramble east then northeast up to the summit of Peak 6903 at 2.5 miles. After enjoying the views, descend south almost a mile, past Granite Spring, to a jeep trail at 3.4 miles. Take the jeep trail southwest to Juniper Spring, an old cooperative project between the BLM and the Oregon Game Commission. Enjoy the cool contrast of the spring.

From the spring, follow the jeep trail south to the main road at 4.5 miles. At the main road, turn right and walk the final 0.3 mile back to the Moss Waterhole where you parked your car.

70 WEST PUEBLO RIDGE

Elevation: 8420 feet	
Difficulty: S3/T3	
Round trip: 10.1 miles	
Elevation gain: 2705 feet	
Trip time: 8 hours	
Time to summit: 4 hours	
Best time of year: June to November	
Maps: USGS Ladycomb Peak, Van Horn Basin	
Contact: Bureau of Land Management, Burns District	

WAYPOINT ROUTE
1. Stergen Meadows: 6239 feet (11T 362343mE 4664717mN)
2. Ten Cent Meadows: 3.1 miles, 6787 feet (11T 360922mE 4661568mN)
3. Bench: 3.6 miles, 7045 feet (11T 360185mE 4661686mN)
4. Upper ridge: 4.1 miles, 7764 feet (11T 359424mE 4661815mN)
5. Chute: 4.5 miles, 8190 feet (11T 358707mE 4662396mN)
6. Peak 8420: 5.0 miles, 8420 feet (11T 358828mE 4662506mN)

The Pueblo Mountains of southeast Oregon are actually two ranges separated by a broad meadow. While the eastern range actually has the Pueblo Mountain summit, the western range consists of a long ridge crest oriented along a north-south axis. You may want to begin in the south and scramble along the whole West Pueblo Ridge, an endeavor that would likely take a few days. This scramble, to the top of the ridge crest's high point at Peak 8420, is a good way to sample the remote feel of these mountains with a worthy endpoint and great views. You might think you would run into a lot of animals in this remote area. There are some remaining sage grouse, and plenty of chukars—

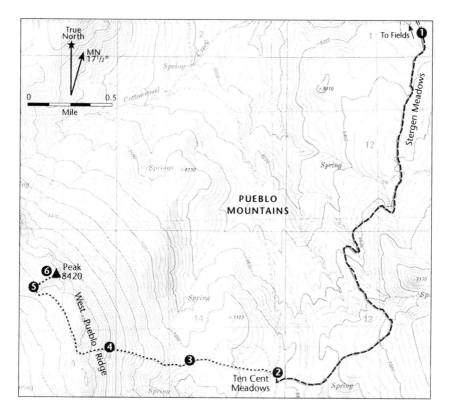

although you will hear them more than see them. Herds of pronghorn range through the mountains, and you may see them in the distance.

Trailhead directions: From Fields drive south on State Route 205. Just past the turnoff for Whitehorse Road, turn west onto Arizona Creek Road, a dirt road that is rough in some places. Drive west on Arizona Creek Road until just before it crosses Arizona Creek. You may park either before crossing in a pullout area, or cross the creek and pull out along the road afterward. You may also continue along the road until you reach the north end of Stergen Meadows (waypoint 1).

Route description: If you parked at Arizona Creek, walk 2 miles until you reach Stergen Meadows, which is after the road turns southward. From Stergen Meadows walk south on the road. Although not the most forgiving surface for hiking, by using this road to get to Ten Cent Meadows you eliminate a tedious bushwhack through sagebrush and mahogany trees. This environment is also fragile, and using the existing road conserves the area's already at-risk natural resources.

After the 3-mile walk on the jeep road from Stergen Meadows, you will approach Ten Cent Meadows. Descend slightly to the meadow, still following the old road to end up at or near waypoint 2 at 3.1 miles. From here, go west across the flats and then up the draw on the left side, to go through a notch.

Scramble up the chute to the upper ridge of the West Pueblo's highest peak

There are mountain mahogany groves along here. Pass through and cross a broad bench that intersects a four-wheel-drive road at 3.6 miles.

Continue climbing the slope through the sage and rocks toward the saddle. The last 250 feet of this slope is slippery scree; try to hug the rocks that are on your left to avoid the loosest rock. You may even scramble up the last bit on the relatively solid rock. Once you reach the upper ridge at 4.1 miles, turn right to head north to the summit block in the near distance. Pass the broad high point on the west side by keeping nearly to the ridge crest and scrambling westward when dropping down to avoid vertical sections.

Once you reach the summit block, traverse westerly along the base until you reach a chute at 4.5 miles, which climbs up blocky rock to the short summit ridge. Scramble up the chute, being sure to not dislodge loose rock on your partner. When you emerge on the summit ridge, turn northeast and make your way up the steep ridge to the summit. The summit is small and you may find a small summit booklet hidden inside a couple of old tin cans. Not many people make it up here, as the summit log will attest.

The views are expansive all up and down the ridge crest, both north and south. You can also see all the way to Tumtum Lake through the Arizona Creek drainage to the northeast. In the fall the bright yellow of aspen groves along the creeks will catch your eye. Return to the top of the chute and carefully scramble down. Reverse your route to return to your car.

The unique landscape of the Pueblo Mountains, looking across at the West Pueblo Ridge peaks from the eastside approach

71 PUEBLO MOUNTAIN

Elevation: 8632 feet

Difficulty: S3/T2

Round trip: 8.6 miles

Elevation gain: 3300 feet

Trip time: 6 hours

Time to summit: 3 hours

Best time of year: June to November

Maps: USGS Ladycomb Peak, Van Horn Basin

Contact: Bureau of Land Management, Burns District

Special considerations: The Pueblos are in a Wilderness Study Area, a designation used to preserve the primitive value of a place.

WAYPOINT ROUTE

1. Park: 5422 feet (11T 364888mE 4665804mN)
2. Scramble off jeep road: 2.0 miles, 6051 feet (11T 363070mE 4665009mN)
3. West side of ridge: 3.0 miles, 7874 feet (11T 363775mE 4663096mN)
4. Pueblo Mountain, north summit: 4.0 miles, 8562 feet (11T 363928mE 4662673mN)
5. Pueblo Mountain, south summit: 4.3 miles, 8632 feet (11T 363585mE 4661928mN)

The summit of Pueblo Mountain.

The Northern Basin and Range contains many little-known mountains. Some have unusual names, like the Stinkingwater or Sheepshead Mountains. The Pueblo Mountains contain ancient rocks, lava flows, aspen-filled canyons, and a noticeable lack of development. South of Steens Mountain, the Pueblos offer intrepid scramblers many opportunities for uninterrupted quiet. Although scarred by old mining claims, the Pueblos will hopefully remain undeveloped for hikers and climbers to enjoy in the future. Populated by a wide range of animals and plants, keep an eye out for bear, mule deer, pronghorn herds, cougar, and smaller mammals. Enjoy the seasonal wildflowers, springs, and meadows of this remote area. Although in the high desert, the Pueblos are home to western juniper, mountain mahogany, and groves of quaking aspen.

Trailhead directions: From Fields drive south on State Route 205. Just past the turnoff for Whitehorse Road, turn west onto Arizona Creek Road. To your east, the north end of Tumtum Lake is right across from Arizona Creek Road. This is a dirt road and is rough in some places. Drive west on Arizona Creek Road until just before Arizona Creek. Park in a pullout just before the road crosses the creek.

Route description: Walk along the jeep road for about 2 miles. At waypoint 2, just east of and below a rocky outcrop running south upslope, turn south to ascend the steep slope. Keep the rocks to your right as you ascend, picking the route with the fewest obstacles—those being large sagebrush. Once on the ridge (waypoint 3), head left and ascend above the drainage to the south.

Scramble southeast across the talus slope that is steep and loose in places. You are basically ascending the western side of the north ridge. Once on the north ridge you will turn more south and scramble up to the summit plateau. The north summit is the first one you will ascend at 4 miles; continue over it to the south.

The south summit is the high point. The views are only limited by weather—on a clear day you can see north to The Peaks and to distant Steens Mountain. Eastward are the Trout Creek Mountains and the Oregon Canyon Mountains. From this solitary summit you will have a fine view of the seasonal, heart-shaped Tumtum Lake. *Tumtum* is a Native American jargon word for *heart*.

Pueblo Mountain from the Pueblo Valley floor

Descend the way you came. If you want a less steep alternative, descend the ascent route until about 7200 feet. This will put you south of the drainage that runs northwest to Stergen Meadows. You may descend through the drainage to intersect the jeep track there. Once you hit the road, just hike north then east to return to your starting point.

72 ALVORD PEAK

Elevation: 7132 feet

Difficulty: S2/T2

Round trip: 4.8 miles

Elevation gain: 2655 feet

Trip time: 5 hours

Time to summit: 3 hours

Best time of year: June to November

Maps: USGS Fields; Bureau of Land Management, Burns District, South Half

Contact: Bureau of Land Management, Burns District

Special considerations: The BLM map will help in navigating the roads. Practice "Leave No Trace" in the Steens Mountain Wilderness Study Area.

Looking up at the summit of Alvord Peak from the scramble route

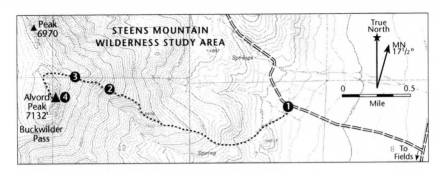

WAYPOINT ROUTE

1. Parking: 4329 feet (11T 362553mE 4689380mN)
2. Upper slope: 1.4 miles, 5950 feet (11T 360443mE 4689636mN)
3. Turn west: 1.7 miles, 6560 feet (11T 360047mE 4689784mN)
4. Alvord Peak: 2.6 miles, 7132 feet (11T 359747mE 4689543mN)

In Oregon's southeast nothing is as widely known as Steens Mountain. Less well known are the many other peaks in the immediate area. Just south of Steens Mountain lies a series of moderate peaks with nearly vertical eastern cliffs and gentle western slopes. Alvord Peak is the highest peak along a north-south ridge called The Peaks. The Peaks stretch for about 7 miles, beginning near Buckwilder Pass and running northerly toward Whiskey Hill. Alvord Peak is an accessible peak just north of Buckwilder Pass. The mountainside is barren except for sagebrush and other desert shrubs. Horned lizards, prong-horn antelope, and bighorn sheep are animals you may encounter on this remote scramble.

Trailhead directions: From Fields drive north on the Fields–Denio Road (State Route 205), which becomes gravel about 2 miles north of Fields. Once it becomes gravel, drive about 3.5 miles to a dirt road, turn left (west) toward Burke Spring, and drive 1 mile to a gate blocking further vehicle access. Park here.

Route description: From the parking area, walk through the small gate. Just west is the broad ridge that leads to the summit. Cross the drainage right away and hike west through the sagebrush. You will actually be scrambling just north of the ridge crest and will pass a rocky outcrop at 5600 feet, keeping it on your left (south). Watch for bighorn sheep in this area as you continue up the ridge. The ridge peters out and becomes part of the upper slope at around 6000 feet and 1.4 miles. Keep scrambling up the slope, passing through 6500 feet on your way west to the gully. Continue west (at 1.7 miles) to the upper mountain and to below the summit block.

On the right side there is a notch between a small block on the right and the main summit block on the left. Go up the sagebrush-filled gully leading to the notch and gain the bench just north of the summit. Turn left and scramble up the ridge to the summit.

From the summit the views are excellent. The Pueblo Mountains and the West Pueblos are to the south; to the southeast are the Trout Creek Mountains.

A scrambler atop Peak 6970 in the Steens Mountain WSA near Alvord Peak

Looking north you will see the broad outline of Steens Mountain in the distance. In the foreground are the summits of The Peaks.

Additional scramble: As an alternate route back to your car, consider sampling more of The Peaks by hiking north along the ridge toward the three nearby summits. Peak 6970 is the highest of the three and is about 0.6 mile from Alvord Peak. Descend off Alvord Peak and scramble north toward the summits. You will want to skip the first (southerly) summit, which requires rock-climbing gear to ascend safely. After passing the first summit, ascend the southwest chute to the middle summit. Descend the northwest side and continue along the west side of the ridge. Scramble up the rocks to the top of Peak 6970 and enjoy the views.

Descend to the south. Once you reach the saddle between Peak 6970 and Alvord Peak, turn east down the drainage. This will nearly parallel your ascent route, but eliminates hiking farther south just to intercept that route.

73 STEENS MOUNTAIN

Elevation: 9733 feet

Difficulty: S5/T3

Round trip: 24 miles

Elevation gain: 4588 feet

Trip time: 12–15 hours

Time to summit: 7–9 hours

Best time of year: July to November

Maps: USGS Fish Lake, Wildhorse Lake; Sportsman Series, Baca Lake, Oregon BLM map

Contact: Bureau of Land Management, Burns District

Special considerations: The BLM map has updated road information. Steens Mountain is preserved as a Wilderness and cooperative management area. Practice "Leave No Trace."

WAYPOINT ROUTE
1. Trailhead: 5251 feet (11T 358766mE 4723894mN)
2. Cross left fork Big Indian Creek: 7.7 miles, 6891 feet (11T 368374mE 4723749mN)
3. Turn southeast: 8.2 miles, 7494 feet (11T 369259mE 4723812mN)
4. Scramble toward springs: 8.8 miles, 8560 feet (11T 369913mE 4724052mN)
5. Through notch: 9.0 miles, 8895 feet (11T 370099mE 4724087mN)
6. Steens summit: 11 miles, 9733 feet (11T 370758mE 4721352mN)

In eastern Oregon, Steens Mountain is the most well-known Basin and Range uplift. The raw, nearly vertical east face towers more than 5000 feet above the Alvord Desert and playa, dominating the landscape. From the west, the gentle slopes lure visitors to its layered interior, which is exposed in the

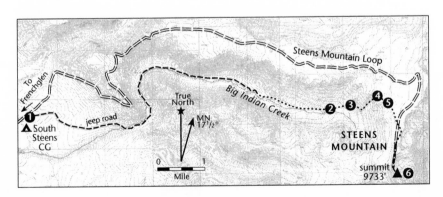

Looking across the high plain to Steens Mountain

rugged gorges carved by glacial ice and corrosive rivers. Steens Mountain is a classic north-south fault block and consists of many layers of distinct lava flows. The scramble up the imposing headwall of Big Indian Gorge will reward adventurous scramblers with a sense of accomplishment. Although you are able to drive to the top of Steens Mountain, scrambling up the gorge gives you a unique perspective on this Oregon natural wonder.

Trailhead directions: From Frenchglen drive south on State Route 205 (Catlow Valley Road). Turn left at the prominent sign onto Steens Mountain South Loop Road. Follow this unpaved road to the South Steens Campground, which is on the right. There are vault toilets and water at the campground. Walk east to the end of the campground just beyond the group site. The trail begins at the fence on an old jeep road. There is a register that includes trail conditions about 0.1 mile up the trail.

Route description: The route to the summit of Steens Mountain begins quietly with a walk up an old jeep road for almost 2 miles. After two creek crossings, the trail begins climbing and passes an old cabin. At about 3 miles there is yet another creek crossing and the trail now turns to head up the steep-walled gorge.

Enjoy the views for the next few miles. The trail winds up through the Big Indian Gorge below impressively steep and dramatic formations along the colorful walls. The trail is now taking you east and will not stray much for the next few miles. After passing through several groves of trees, the trail winds eastward, climbing gently. The aspens are beautiful when displaying their bright fall colors. Note the decades-old Basque sheepherder carvings on some tree trunks.

At 7.7 miles you will cross the left fork of Big Indian Creek. Continue heading east toward the headwall at the end of the gorge and the drainage that is a prominent break in the nearly vertical wall. Hike through a last aspen grove and then through a meadow easterly toward the break. Continue east, traversing rocky benches and a couple of ravines as you work your way southeast to the drainage; at this point, the whole east end of the gorge is in view. After crossing the third ravine, continue traversing to the point where you intersect a ridge on the left side of the drainage. Turn left and scramble up the ridge until it peters out, then work your way into the drainage by scrambling to the right and up some rock.

Now you are in the drainage that leads to the summit plateau. Continue straight up through another rocky section. Keep ascending, heading toward a vertical section of rocks in the middle of the drainage. You will pass these on the right side while heading up toward an eventual notch in the blocks above. Begin scrambling across toward the springs, crossing over at about 8.8 miles, 8560 feet.

Scramble up the right side of the drainage, avoiding the boggy springs as much as possible. After you pass the springs you will scramble up and into the now narrow right side of the drainage. Note that the rocks become quite blocky on the right, and there is an obvious notch. Keep right and scramble up to and through the notch at 9 miles. This will deposit you on the gentle sloping area.

Keep heading south-southeast as you ascend, crossing the plateau. You will eventually run into the road. Cross the road to check out the amazing views down the steep east side of the mountain and out to the Alvord Desert more than 5000 feet below.

Contour south along the edge of the mountain or go back to the road to reach the Steens summit. The final summit pitch is on the path from a small parking area. From the summit you will enjoy amazing views. Looking west on a clear day you can see Mount McLoughlin.

You may return on the same route. However, due to the length of the ascent it may be easier to descend using the Steens Mountain Loop Road. The gravel and dirt road leads back to the South Steens Campground in about 13 miles.

74 PEAK 7698

Elevation: 7698 feet

Difficulty: S2/T2

Round trip: 6.6 miles

Elevation gain: 2560 feet

Trip time: 6 hours

Time to summit: 3.5 hours

Best time of year: July to November

Maps: USGS Alvord Hot Springs; Sportsman Series, Baca Lake, Oregon BLM map

Contact: Bureau of Land Management, Burns District

Special considerations: USGS quad lists peak as 7571 feet. The peak is in a Wilderness Study Area, a designation used to preserve the primitive value of a place. No services are available. The BLM map has updated road information. Low-clearance vehicles are not recommended.

WAYPOINT ROUTE

1. Park: 5150 feet (11T 371777mE 4711733mN)
2. Whitehorse Creek view: 0.5 mile, 5455 feet (11T 372043mE 4711577mN)
3. South ridge: 2.5 miles, 7014 feet (11T 370014mE 4712763mN)
4. Peak 7698: 3.3 miles, 7698 feet (11T 369575mE 4713943mN)

In southeast Oregon's Northern Basin and Range, nothing blots out the sky like the vertical cliffs of Steens Mountain's east side. Gazing up at the summit—

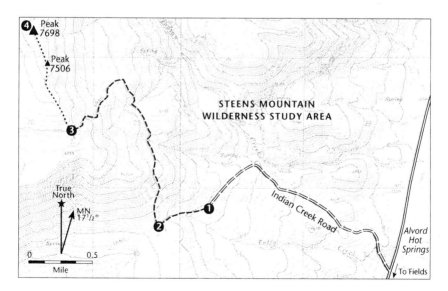

Great views of the Alvord Desert from the route to Peak 7698

nearly 6000 feet above you from the Alvord Desert—is overwhelming. From this vantage between Little and Big Alvord Creeks, the massive size of the mountain is not in question, and the dark basalt is quite a contrast to the light-colored desert surrounding you. For a closer look at the rugged east side of Steens, the scramble to Peak 7698 offers unique vistas and a different perspective. Along the way to the summit, you will enjoy tall sage, gnarled juniper, and stands of aspen. You will also hear, but not likely see, chukars clucking in the low area along the route.

Trailhead directions: Drive north from Fields on the Fields–Denio Road (State Route 205). Just about 2 miles north of Fields, bear right at the fork (left is the continuation of SR 205) and continue on the gravel road, which is also called East Steens Road. Once you pass Andrews, continue to drive north for about 8.5 miles. Just before the Alvord Hot Springs and a cattle guard in the road, turn left onto Indian Creek Road, a dirt road that provides access to the area around Indian and Dry Creeks. Follow this road past the first junction and turn left at the Wilderness Study Area marker at the second spur. There is room to park in about 0.5 mile, just when the road becomes rough and rocky.

Route description: There really are no trails out here in the high desert around Steens Mountain. However, there are a lot of dirt roads in convenient locations such as this. Hike up the road to the pass above Wildhorse Creek at 0.5 mile, 5455 feet. Walk to the west side of the pass for the best views down to the creek and west across the pristine landscape.

Turn north on the dirt road, climbing steeply for about 0.5 mile until the road levels out for a while. As you amble along the level road, enjoy the views of rugged cliffs above the creek at around 1.3 miles, as well as views eastward across the desert. Continue another 0.5 mile north to 6378 feet and a spur leading southwest toward the south ridge of Peak 7698. As you make your way to the south ridge enjoy the aspen groves, sagebrush, and gnarled junipers scattered across the slopes. On a warm summer day you may also see raptors circling lazily on thermals.

Go south for about another 0.5 mile to 2.5 miles, 7014 feet. Here you will be on the south end of a broad ridge leading to the summit. Turn northwest and scramble up along this ridge to the long, double summit. The south summit, Peak 7506, is nothing more than a pile of rocks. Continue north to the true summit at 7698 feet.

Look north to the forbidding cliffs of Steens Mountain. With the right light, you will be able to make out the radio antennas on the summit. Either way, the views are impressive. To the northwest you can see across Wildhorse Canyon, which may provide adventurous scramblers another route to Steens. Across the canyon to the west are aspen groves and rolling green bench lands.

 FLAGSTAFF BUTTE

Elevation: 6029 feet

Difficulty: S1/T3

Round trip: 2.5 miles

Elevation gain: 1050 feet

Trip time: 4 hours

Time to summit: 2 hours

Best time of year: May to December

Maps: USGS Trout Creek Canyon; Bureau of Land Management, Vale District Recreation Guide; Trout Creek Sportsmen Series

Contact: Bureau of Land Management, Burns District

Special considerations: For driving near Flagstaff Butte use the BLM map, which shows private property and BLM roads.

WAYPOINT ROUTE
1. Park: 4900 feet (11T 385444mE 4674164mN)
2. West ridge: 0.9 mile, 5753 feet (11T 385838mE 4672740mN)
3. Flagstaff Butte: 1.25 miles, 6029 feet (11T 386270mE 4672551mN)

Flagstaff Butte rises dramatically above the surrounding rangelands.

Flagstaff Butte is the prominent peak north of the Trout Creek Mountains in Oregon's Basin and Range region. These ranges contain some of the oldest rocks in the state. A small mountain by Cascade standards, Flagstaff Butte is a worthy scramble in a unique place. The views here are filled with sagebrush and grasslands. Big and Little Trout Creeks irrigate nearby land, and that green provides the only relief from the miles and miles of high desert landscape.

Trailhead directions: From Fields drive south on the Fields–Denio Road (State Route 205). Turn left onto gravel Whitehorse Ranch Road and drive about 12.1 miles to a dirt track on the north side of the road. Turn left onto the track and drive about 2 miles to a small pullout on the right side. Park carefully just off the road. Due to fire danger, do not park anywhere else.

Route description: Hike south toward a small rise in the sagebrush and continue to Flagstaff Butte's west ridge at 0.9 mile. Ascend to the ridge on a rocky slope that begins as talus and changes to larger rocks just below the ridge crest. Scramble up the rocks the last 100 feet to the ridge crest that winds its way to the broad summit.

Once on the ridge, turn east and scramble along the crest toward the first high point. This is a butte, after all, and it has a series of increasingly high points on the way to the summit. Gain the first point, and then continue to work east toward the main summit. Scramble down when necessary to go around short vertical sections. Near the eastern end of the ridge, gain the main summit of the butte. This plateau has fine views northeast to Whitehorse Ranch, a historic ranch that also is known for hot springs. Just south is Big Trout

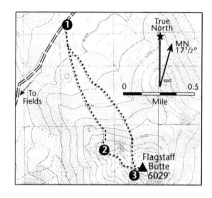

Creek, which cuts a bright green swath across the mostly brown plain.

Descend toward a saddle you passed on the way over. Descend the large bowl below the saddle to the sagebrush-covered plain. Return to your car across the plain. As you hike out, notice the mining claims in the area, marked by white plastic pipes that contain copies of the actual claim. Return to the main road by continuing northward then east on the dirt road. This will give you a 360-degree view of Flagstaff Butte.

Mount Thielsen from the Pacific Crest Trail

Appendix A:
Equipment Lists

These are basic lists that will get you started. Equipment lists may be personalized and modified for your own particular preferences.

For an extensive discussion of clothing, gear, and equipment see Chapter 2, Table 2-3 in *Mountaineering: Freedom of the Hills*, 8th edition.

THE TEN ESSENTIALS: A SYSTEMS APPROACH
1. Navigation (map and compass)
2. Sun protection (sunglasses and sunscreen)
3. Insulation (extra clothing)
4. Illumination (headlamp or flashlight)
5. First-aid supplies (including whistle)
6. Fire (firestarter and matches/lighter)
7. Repair kit and tools (including knife or multitool)
8. Nutrition (extra food)
9. Hydration (extra water)
10. Emergency shelter

PERSONAL GEAR
Backpack
Insect repellent
Camera equipment (including film, batteries, memory cards, filters)
Trekking poles
Water bottles or hydration reservoir
Instant hand warmers (nice for unexpected temperature drops)
Lightweight bivy sack or emergency Mylar blanket
Plastic surveyor's tape (to mark a route; always remove it)
Toilet paper and sealable plastic bags
Watch, altimeter, and/or GPS receiver
Foot-care kit—moleskin, new skin, duct tape
Small notebook and pencil (in a plastic bag)
Insulated sit pad (some lightweight packs have removable pad)

CLOTHING
Sturdy boots
Gaiters
Wool or wool-blend socks
Sock liners
Long underwear
Fleece jacket
Fleece pants

Lightweight balaclava
Fleece or wool cap
Waterproof/breathable pants and hooded jacket
Two pairs of gloves—one liner-type, one heavyweight (windproof is handy)
Hat with brim
Lightweight pants or shorts
Short-sleeved shirt or lightweight long-sleeved shirt

EQUIPMENT
Ice ax
Crampons (your boots must be compatible with your crampons)
Climbing helmet (do not substitute a bicycle helmet)
Rope

BACKPACKING
Backpack—internal or external frame
Tent and ground cloth
Sleeping bag and pad
Water filter or treatment method
Pot with lid
Cup, bowl, and spoon
Food
Stove and fuel
Camp clothes or shoes
Garbage bag

GEAR THAT IS NICE TO HAVE
Binoculars
Bandana
Cell phone
Two-way radios
Lens cleaner/antifog cream or solution for glasses/goggles

Appendix B:
Contact Information

WEATHER AND TRAVEL INFORMATION
National Weather Service
www.wrh.noaa.gov
Oregon Department of Transportation
Road conditions, construction report
(800) 977-6368
www.tripcheck.com

LAND MANAGEMENT AGENCIES
Bureau of Land Management
www.blm.gov/or
Burns District
  28910 Highway 20 West
  Hines, OR 97738
  (541) 573-4400
Lakeview District
  1301 South G Street
  Lakeview, OR 97630
  (541) 947-2177

Medford District
  Cascade–Siskiyou National
  Monument
  3040 Biddle Road
  Medford, OR 97504
  (541) 618-2200
Prineville District
  3050 NE 3rd Street
  Prineville, OR 97754
  (541) 416-6700

U.S. Fish and Wildlife Service
Hart Mountain National Antelope Refuge
  PO Box 21
  Plush, OR 97637
  (541) 947-3315
  www.fws.gov/sheldonhartmtn/Hart

U.S. Forest Service
www.fs.fed.us/r6
Columbia River Gorge National
  Scenic Area
  902 Wasco Avenue, Suite 200
  Hood River, OR 97031
  (503) 308-1700
  www.fs.fed.us/r6/columbia/forest

DESCHUTES NATIONAL FOREST
Bend–Fort Rock Ranger District
  1230 NE 3rd Street, Suite A-262
  Bend, OR 97701
  (541) 383-4000
Crescent Ranger District
  136471 Highway 97 North
  Crescent, OR 97733
  (541) 433-3200

Sisters Ranger District
    Pine Street and Highway 20
    Sisters, OR 97759
    (541) 549-7700
FREMONT NATIONAL FOREST
Bly Ranger District
    PO Box 25
    Bly, OR 97622
    (541) 353-2427
Lakeview Ranger District
    Highway 395 N
    HC 64, Box 60
    Lakeview, OR 97630
    (541) 947-3334
MALHEUR NATIONAL FOREST
Blue Mountain Ranger District
    431 Patterson Bridge Road
    John Day, OR 97845
    (541) 575-3000
Prairie City Ranger District
    PO Box 337
    Prairie City, OR 97869
    (541) 820-3800
MOUNT HOOD NATIONAL FOREST
Hood River Ranger District
    6780 Highway 35
    Parkdale, OR 97041
    (503) 352-6002
Zigzag Ranger District
    70220 E Highway 26
    Zigzag, OR 97049
    (503) 622-3191
OCHOCO NATIONAL FOREST
    Lookout Mountain Ranger
    District
    3160 NE 3rd Street
    Prineville, OR 97754
    (541) 416-6500
ROGUE RIVER NATIONAL FOREST
    Applegate Ranger District
    6941 Upper Applegate Road
    Jacksonville, OR 97530
    (541) 899-3800
Prospect Ranger District
    47201 Highway 62
    Prospect, OR 97536

(541) 560-3400
SISKIYOU NATIONAL FOREST
    Chetco Ranger District
    539 Chetco Avenue
    Brookings, OR 97415
    (541) 412-6000
Illinois Valley Ranger District
    26568 Redwood Highway
    Cave Junction, OR 97523
    (541) 592-4000
UMPQUA NATIONAL FOREST
Diamond Lake Ranger District
    2020 Toketee Ranger Station
        Road
    Idleyld Park, OR 97447
    (541) 498-2531
Tiller Ranger District
    27812 Tiller Trail Highway
    Tiller, OR 97484
    (541) 825-3201
WALLOWA–WHITMAN NATIONAL
FOREST
Baker Ranger District
    3165 10th Street
    Baker City, OR 97814
    (514) 523-4476
Eagle Cap Ranger District
    Wallowa Mountains Visitors
    Center
    88401 Highway 82
    Enterprise, OR 97828
    (541) 426-4978
WILLAMETTE NATIONAL FOREST
    Middle Fork Ranger District
    46375 Highway 58
    Westfir, OR 97492
    (541) 782-2283
McKenzie Ranger District
    57600 McKenzie Highway
    McKenzie Bridge, OR 97413
    (541) 822-3381
WINEMA NATIONAL FOREST
Klamath Ranger District
    2819 Dahlia Street
    Klamath Falls, OR 97601
    (541) 885-3400

National Park Service

John Day Fossil Beds National Monument
Sheep Rock Unit
  32651 Highway 19
  Kimberly, OR 97848
  (541) 987-2333
  www.nps.gov/joda
Crater Lake National Park
Steel Information Center
  PO Box 7
  Crater Lake, OR 97604
  (541) 594-3100
  www.nps.gov/crla

Oregon Department of Forestry

Tillamook State Forest
Forest Grove District
  801 Gales Creek Road
  Forest Grove, OR 97116
  (503) 359-7401
  egov.oregon.gov/ODF/tillamookstateforest/index.shtml

Oregon State Parks

Smith Rock State Park
  9241 NE Crooked River Drive
  Terrebonne, OR 97760
  (541) 548-7501 or (541) 480-1683
  www.oregonstateparks.org/park_51.php

OTHER CONTACTS

LEAVE NO TRACE
  www.LNT.org
  Visit this informative website to learn about how to lower your impact on the natural world.
OREGON PEAKS
  www.climber.org/data/peaks/ORpeaks.html
  This website lists approximately 2000 Oregon peaks and includes the NAD27 latitude and longitude, relevant USGS quad, elevation, and a topographic map link.
USGS/CASCADES VOLCANO OBSERVATORY
  vulcan.wr.usgs.gov
  This website has a lot of useful information on the Cascades, including news and current seismic conditions.

Appendix C:
Bibliography and Recommended Reading

Backer, Howard D. and others, eds. *Wilderness First Aid: Emergency Care for Remote Locations.* Sudbury, MA: Jones and Bartlett Publishers, 1998.

Barstad, Fred. *Hiking Oregon's Eagle Cap Wilderness.* 2nd ed. Guilford, CT: The Globe Pequot Press, 2002.

Bishop, Ellen Morris. *In Search of Ancient Oregon: A Geological and Natural History.* Portland: Timber Press, 2003.

Bishop, Ellen Morris, and John Eliot Allen. *Hiking Oregon's Geology.* Seattle: The Mountaineers Books, 1996.

Cox, Steven M., and Kris Fulsaas, eds. *Mountaineering: The Freedom of the Hills.* 7th ed. Seattle: The Mountaineers Books, 2003.

Evanich, Joseph E., Jr. *The Birder's Guide to Oregon.* Portland: The Portland Audubon Society, 1990.

Ferguson, Sue A., and Edward R. LaChapelle. *The ABCs of Avalanche Safety.* 3rd ed. Seattle: The Mountaineers Books, 2003.

Jensen, Edward C., and Charles R. Ross. *Trees to Know in Oregon.* Rev. ed. Corvallis: Oregon State University Extension Service and Oregon Department of Forestry, 1999.

Kerr, Andy. *Oregon Desert Guide: 70 Hikes.* Seattle: The Mountaineers Books, 2000.

Letham, Lawrence. *GPS Made Easy: Using Global Positioning Systems in the Outdoors.* 4th ed. Seattle: The Mountaineers Books, 2003.

McArthur, Lewis A., and Lewis L. McArthur. *Oregon Geographic Names.* 7th ed. Portland: Oregon Historical Society Press, 2003.

Randall, Glenn. *The Outward Bound™ Map and Compass Handbook.* Rev. ed. New York: The Lyons Press, 1998.

Sullivan, William L. *Oregon: Trips and Trails.* Eugene: Navillus Press, 2003.

Thorson, T. D., and others, eds. *Ecoregions of Oregon.* Reston, VA: U.S. Geological Survey, 2003.

USGS/Cascades Volcano Observatory. *vulcan.wr.usgs.gov.*

Weiss, Hal. *Secrets of Warmth: For Comfort or Survival.* Seattle: The Mountaineers Books, 1999.

Wuerthner, George. *Oregon's Wilderness Areas: The Complete Guide.* Englewood, CO: Westcliffe Publishers, Inc., 2002.

Index

About the Author

Photo by Pete Sandrock

Barbara I. Bond is a freelance writer and active member of Mazamas. She teaches in their basic, intermediate, and advanced rock schools and has served on their Executive Council as well as other committees. Barbara enjoys participating in many endurance activities, including long-distance hiking, trail running, and road biking.

Having had an early introduction to the outdoors, Barbara camped and hiked in California's Sierra Nevada and Santa Cruz Mountains as a youth. She now enjoys an active life that includes biking, camping, hiking, and skiing with her family. She has climbed extensively not only in Oregon and California, but also in Arizona, New Mexico, Tanzania, Switzerland, Italy, and France.

Barbara currently lives in Portland, Oregon with her family.

THE MOUNTAINEERS, founded in 1906, is a nonprofit outdoor activity and conservation club, whose mission is "to explore, study, preserve, and enjoy the natural beauty of the outdoors. . . ." Based in Seattle, Washington, the club is now one of the largest such organizations in the United States, with seven branches throughout Washington State.

The Mountaineers sponsors both classes and year-round outdoor activities in the Pacific Northwest, which include hiking, mountain climbing, ski-touring, snowshoeing, bicycling, camping, kayaking, nature study, sailing, and adventure travel. The club's conservation division supports environmental causes through educational activities, sponsoring legislation, and presenting informational programs.

All club activities are led by skilled, experienced instructors, who are dedicated to promoting safe and responsible enjoyment and preservation of the outdoors.

If you would like to participate in these organized outdoor activities or the club's programs, consider a membership in The Mountaineers. For information and an application, write or call The Mountaineers, Program Center, 7700 Sand Point Way NE, Seattle, WA 98115; 206-521-6001. You can also visit the club's website at www.mountaineers.org or contact The Mountaineers via email at info@mountaineers.org.

The Mountaineers Books, an active, nonprofit publishing program of the club, produces guidebooks, instructional texts, historical works, natural history guides, and works on environmental conservation. All books produced by The Mountaineers Books fulfill the club's mission.

Send or call for our catalog of more than 500 outdoor titles:

The Mountaineers Books
1001 SW Klickitat Way, Suite 201
Seattle, WA 98134
800-553-4453
mbooks@mountaineersbooks.org
www.mountaineersbooks.org

The Mountaineers Books is proud to be a corporate sponsor of The Leave No Trace Center for Outdoor Ethics, whose mission is to promote and inspire responsible outdoor recreation through education, research, and partnerships. The Leave No Trace program is focused specifically on human-powered (nonmotorized) recreation.

Leave No Trace strives to educate visitors about the nature of their recreational impacts, as well as offer techniques to prevent and minimize such impacts. Leave No Trace is best understood as an educational and ethical program, not as a set of rules and regulations.

For more information, visit *www.LNT.org*, or call 800-332-4100.

OTHER TITLES YOU MIGHT ENJOY FROM THE MOUNTAINEERS BOOKS:

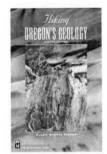
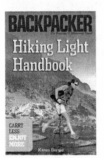
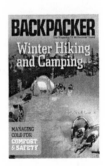

CPSIA information can be obtained
at www.ICGtesting.com
Printed in the USA
LVOW11s0432161116

513133LV00001BA/87/P